Fine Horses and
Fair-Minded Riders

NEW DIRECTIONS IN THE HUMAN-ANIMAL BOND

A dynamic relationship has always existed between people and animals. Each influences the psychological and physiological state of the other. Published in collaboration with Purdue University's College of Veterinary Medicine, New Directions in the Human-Animal Bond expands our knowledge of the interrelationships between people, animals, and their environment. Scholarly works, memoirs, practitioner guides, and books written for a general audience are welcomed on all aspects of human-animal interaction and welfare.

SERIES EDITOR

Alan M. Beck, Purdue University

OTHER TITLES IN THIS SERIES

My One-Eyed, Three-Legged Therapist: How My Cat Clio Saved Me
Kathy M. Finley

Identity, Gender, and Tracking: The Reality of Boundaries for Veterinary Students
Jenny R. Vermilya

Dogs and Cats in South Korea: Itinerant Commodities
Julien Dugnoille

Assessing Handlers for Competence in Animal-Assisted Interventions
Ann R. Howie

The Canine-Campus Connection: Roles for Dogs in the Lives of College Students
Mary Renck Jalongo (Ed.)

Pioneer Science and the Great Plagues:
How Microbes, War, and Public Health Shaped Animal Health
Norman F. Cheville

Cats and Conservationists: The Debate Over Who Owns the Outdoors
Dara M. Wald and Anna L. Peterson

That Sheep May Safely Graze: Rebuilding Animal Health Care in War-Torn Afghanistan
David M. Sherman

Transforming Trauma: Resilience and Healing Through Our Connections With Animals
Philip Tedeschi and Molly Anne Jenkins (Eds.)

A Reason to Live: HIV and Animal Companions
Vicki Hutton

Fine Horses and Fair-Minded Riders

Modern Vaquero Horsemanship

JuliAnna Ávila

Purdue University Press • West Lafayette, Indiana

Cataloging-in-Publication Data is available at the Library of Congress.
978-1-61249-950-5 (hardback)
978-1-61249-952-9 (epub)
978-1-61249-951-2 (paperback)
978-1-61249-953-6 (epdf)

Cover: *Partners*, Kathleen Kelley Fine Art.

*This book is dedicated to the generous horse,
who, to paraphrase Woody Guthrie,
never holds your hard traveling against you.*

In the stories of years ago it is brave horses that are the heroes in the memories of the old-time riders whose lives were just a series of different horses.

A. R. ROJAS, *THESE WERE THE VAQUEROS*

Your horse learns that he can do anything you want him to do and he's glad to do it; he's ready to do it. You have set it up for him. You've never discouraged him, you've never belittled him, you've really bragged on him and his good qualities. When he did something wrong you didn't make a big thing of it. You went along with him there, too, and showed him that wasn't too good a thing to do—yet you didn't criticize him or hammer on him. So, as time goes on from day to day, week to week, month to month, and year to year, I'll grant you that you can build a friendship and something that's unbelievable. Again, these horses are more sensitive than we can ever imagine. As we go along you'll see how sensitive they are. You develop this sensitivity.

Let them use their keenness to show you how sensitive they are—to teach us.

R. HUNT, *THINK HARMONY WITH HORSES*

CONTENTS

PREFACE

Humans were meant to live with the horse.
(Erdrich, 2012, p. 26)

BACKING INTO VAQUERO HORSEMANSHIP

Angel campaigned, from early on, to remain with us. A 12-year-old Appaloosa mare, who looked like a sturdy sorrel quarter horse, she had been purchased as what horse trainers call a "project." The plan was to train (I'll return to why this is a problematic word later in this volume), or retrain, her and then to sell her for a profit, with the work done by a horseman who was my boyfriend at the time. I had little idea then that this plan would turn into a life-changing stay, both for her and for me. I would subsequently shift my life around to keep her with me and, later, alive (once she was diagnosed with a life-threatening illness).

When I met Angel, I had not been around horses since I was in third grade. We had relocated from Los Angeles to Benson, Arizona, and my parents' friends, Tony and Milly, ranch and horse owners, had given me, homesick and lonely, a filly named Christmas for company. She was small enough to be approachable, and I felt wonder when around her. Since Christmas was so young, I was allowed to ride her mother. I remember my first ride vividly. Rather than being prefaced by anything as impractical as actual instruction, I was lifted onto a Western saddle and told by Tony, "If you fall off, you have to walk back. You better hold on." I recall looking warily at the rural Arizona landscape: All of the sagebrush and cacti and sky looked the same. And the mare's back seemed awfully far from the ground. I had too-long stirrups, no hold, and no fear—until she decided to bolt, and then I felt a new sort of fear, one shot through with exhilaration and possibility (perhaps this sort is a uniquely childlike and innocent fear, which Cixous [1998/2005] described as "extremely pure" since a child is able to "believe absolutely in the danger, and then at the same time not to believe in it" [p. 122]). When she'd had enough of our countryside tour, she headed back to the barn, with me still clutching on. "What were you thinking?" I would ask my mother as an adult, "Weren't you worried about my safety?" "You wanted to ride," she replied, "and you were fine. Mamas always return to their babies." My mother had ridden in her youth along the riverbeds in Los Angeles and seemed to possess some sort of sketchy and unscientific faith in horses, in me, or both.

CROSSING PATHS WITH
A SASSY ANGEL

Nearly thirty years later, I did not have horses on my mind and was instead busy being an academic in North Carolina. Work took up much of my energy and whatever was left went to the horse trainer/boyfriend, James (not his real name). We decided to look for a horse or two for him to work with, and so, using my research skills, I assisted. I was mostly motivated by wanting to help him, although surely my memories of a friendly filly and her fast mama influenced my willingness. Angel had been advertised online, but her ad had been pulled right after we saw it. The couple who owned her had lamented that those who were interested in buying her "did not understand her." They were afraid that she would fall into abusive hands. As those who have spent time around mares know, they can be what we might politely call "spirited," signifying that a mare might use her intelligence, her willfulness, and her physical strength to determine the course of things, which may or may not coincide with what you want to happen. When we first met her, she did indeed possess some sass. "But she's so damn sweet," James said.

Angel's owners knew James and his reputation as a fair and kind trainer, and so a deal to sell her to us was struck. She would live at the farm (which I would have called a ranch, betraying my Western roots) that James leased. Angel looked like an adult Christmas, and this no doubt ignited some sort of sentimental spark in my brain. I was also worried about her going to an unfit home, a worry that would reoccur a few months later. Perhaps because my first close-up encounters were with mares, I respect them and admire their will. But I know they can be dangerous, so I was a spectator at the beginning with Angel; I was also not yet formally learning to ride. When I stated that she campaigned to remain with us, what I mean is that she did her best to be agreeable and to do whatever James asked of her, sass be damned. When I was nearby, she would come to stand next to me, just to keep me company, in that calm and personable way that some horses have. You will read below about my having to find a new home for Angel, and when I went to visit, after not seeing her for several weeks, I walked into her stall; she looked surprised and immediately turned to me and planted her muzzle over my heart, not moving for as long as I stood there. This is purely anecdotal of course, but I believe that horses who are happy in their homes strategize how to stay in those homes and with those owners, especially horses who have been moved around as Angel had.

As an aside, this kind of campaigning is not unique to Angel. While writing this book, I met a ranch owner and riding instructor, Heather, who has been trying to sell a gelding, Romeo, who should have been easy to place. He is sound and well-built, friendly, registered, and a pleasure to ride, and he just happened to find himself, a young horse, at a retirement ranch while waiting for his next home. Whenever anyone arrived to try him out, sometimes driving for hours, he would lock himself down and refuse to move with the rider. He is rather polite about it and does not buck or rear, but he would prefer not to go to a new and unknown home; he is just fine where he is, among the retired and well-cared for. Heather said she stared in absolute disbelief the first time he did it, as did her husband, watching from the house. As of this writing, he still lives at her ranch.

Several months into owning Angel, the relationship with James wound down, and the question of what to do with her and the other mare we had purchased surfaced. I was not attached to the other mare, and we sold her without incident. Angel was intelligent and scrappy, albeit reasonable (and sweet), and never belligerent or aggressive, and I fretted over what would become of her. Without specific proof to explain it, I had become attached to her and wanted to protect her. Those who fell in love with horses as children will understand how binding and mysterious an attachment it is, not necessarily rooted in reason; for those who did not, I suggest that you imagine that your first love was a creature likely at least twenty times your weight with extra-large, innocent eyes and covered in fur that you are allowed to pet, who could injure or kill you but chooses not to. That love holds fast—often for the duration of your life.

The challenge that came with keeping Angel was that I knew nothing about, or no one in, horse boarding in the area. But my graduate school advisor, Glynda Hull, is a lifelong horsewoman, and a call to her yielded a lengthy list of what to look for, and what to avoid, in home-hunting for horses. I remember taking extensive notes, and when Glynda paused, I assumed she was done until she said in that blessedly straightforward way that some horsepeople have, "I'm not done yet. And you should look for . . ." Soon after, I found a new place to board Angel.

Finding a physical home for Angel was one task, and the next one was what to actually *do* with her as she was still young and healthy at the time. I decided to start taking riding lessons with other horses. She was not a beginner's horse, but she was my horse, and I was a beginner. Given that, I did not ride her until we were both ready, which was a couple of years later. Logic said to sell her, but I ignored it in favor of love, recognizable to the same horse-leaning heart I had when I was eight years old.

Angel and I remained together until a chronic illness, amyloidosis, took her after a five-year struggle against it; in the end, she died quickly and peacefully in my own pasture, having just been grazing, while I watched from the house, drinking my morning coffee. She had been present while I was learning to be an academic, a rough adjustment. Her presence and the world of horsemanship that she brought me into provided dependable and much-needed mental and emotional breaks; the ever-present honesty of horses can be a soul-saving antidote to thorny human interaction.

A CURIOUS SPECTATOR

The phrase "horse whisperer" has become part of our modern cultural lexicon, popularized through a movie, based on Nicholas Evans's (1995) book. Although, as Bennett (1998) asserted, the roots of the concept likely go back to the beginning of horse-human communication (p. 43). Even if a romantic story has helped to promote and commercialize the phrase, the concept behind it is tied to theories of animal behaviorism. Temple Grandin (2009) believes that

> the real secret of horse whisperers and expert horsemen is that they understand the behaviors associated with different emotional states and they have also figured out that a reward or cue has to be given within one second after a desired behavior occurs for the horse to make the association. Expert horse trainers understand the horses' emotions, instinctual natural behavior patterns, and the principles of behavioral training. (p. 124)

The most well-known horse whisperer (although it is more accurate to say that he trains people), as well as the inspiration and consultant for the film *The Horse Whisperer*, is Buck Brannaman, who himself, according to his website, practices a horsemanship based on "classical concepts from the California vaquero tradition."

Once I had Angel settled in, I heard about one of Buck's clinics happening in Clemson, South Carolina, and that the public could pay a spectator fee to listen and watch each of the three days. I drove back and forth each day from Charlotte and sat in the stands, taking notes as only a nerdy academic can (i.e., as if I were being judged on it). While observing those three days, I noticed what would become the motivation for this project. While Buck coached his riders, I observed that many of them looked to me like the Mexican and Mexican American cowboys of my youth, as the daughter of a Latinx mother growing up in Southern California. These participants were dressed and had gear that, to me, seemed out of geographical — and cultural — contexts, although I was admittedly ignorant about the horse world at that time. While there are, materially, items that cowboys and vaqueros might have in common, the distinctions in tack signify connections to certain styles of horsemanship; what these southeastern riders signified, to me at the time, has its roots across a significant distance. Therefore, this project began with wonderings (that later turned into research questions, which I share in the introduction): Is Vaquero horsemanship geographically and culturally specific? Does it, or can it, transcend both? What makes up this particular style of horsemanship, and how and why has it traveled? These musings themselves were a branch of a pragmatic need to find a language with which to communicate with

Angel. I had both an honest interest in, and a scholarly curiosity about, what I learned was called Vaquero horsemanship. In this volume, I aim to tell you some of the story of modern Vaquero horsemanship, which has become a hybridized form of itself now that it has left its historical, cultural, and geographical contexts.

INTRODUCTION

Studying Vaquero Horsemanship in the Southeastern United States and Beyond

These stories are not the science of animals; they are what we use to understand the importance of animals in our lives. (Rothfels, 2014, p. 11)

A S VAQUERO HORSEMANSHIP (VH) HAS BECOME HYBRIDIZED OVER TIME, this book is also a hybrid: My background in literacy and language education frames this study, but, mindful of the horses at the heart of this work, this is also very much about VH and the human-horse connection that it can encourage and nurture. Even though this project has from the beginning been an academic study combined with passionate personal interest, in the process of writing this, Vaquero horsemanship itself, as I learned more about it, enlarged my original ideas and intentions; one example of this is widening the interviewee pool to include mentors mentioned by southeastern participants.

My initial curiosity about this style of Western horsemanship (as I shared in the preface), which historically began in what is now California (before it was part of the United States) and has now spread worldwide, led to an inquiry into how technology and digital literacies affected the learning of Vaquero horsemanship. Although this would be one research question I had, the project itself then grew to be a collection of stories about learning VH more generally. As a literacy researcher, I have a persistent interest in expanded definitions of literacy beyond school-based reading and writing. In a sense, this project is also about literacy stories—if you take literacy to include learning how to read horses and how to author your own identity as a VH practitioner. Building upon my curiosity and interests, I describe, in this introduction, how I designed this project, bearing in mind that my audience may include fellow education and literacy scholars (including those who study adult learning in community contexts) as well as those with a more general interest in horsemanship and horse culture. My goal has been to make this volume accessible, language- and concept-wise, so that it might appeal to an audience beyond my own academic peers.

STUDY DESIGN
Theoretical Framework

The framework for this project is a sociocultural one (Vygotsky, 1978) guided by the assumption that learning is "conceived of as always being situated in participation" (Lewis et al., 2007, p. 16), a participation that "is a complex process that combines doing, talking, thinking, feeling, and belonging" (Wenger, 1998, p. 56). Relatedly, *practice is about meaning as an experience of everyday life*" (p. 52; italics in original). Barton and Hamilton's (1998) sketching out of vernacular literacy practices, which "are rooted in everyday experience and serve everyday purposes" (p. 251), is particularly helpful in understanding the learning of horsemanship within a sociocultural context. In this project, what is learned "in collaboration with more capable peers" (Vygotsky, 1978, p. 86) includes horses, although their experiences are interpreted by their human partners; this is an inclusion Vygotsky might have found suspicious, although participants very much feel that horses are their more knowledgeable teachers.

My own education and previous scholarship has been heavily influenced by New Literacy Studies (NLS), which Gee (2000) defined as "based on the view that reading and writing only make sense when studied in the context of social and cultural (and we can add historical, political and economic) practices of which they are but a part" (p. 180). NLS includes

> social practices in which literacy has a role; hence the basic unit of a social theory of literacy is that of *literacy practices.* . . . In the simplest sense literacy practices are what people do with literacy. . . . This includes people's awareness of literacy, constructions of literacy and discourses of literacy, how people talk about and make sense of literacy. These are processes internal to the individual; at the same time, practices are the social processes which connect people with one another, and they include shared cognition represented in ideologies and social identities. (Barton & Hamilton, 2000, pp. 7–8)

The NLS approach has lent a generosity of definition to subsequent literacy scholarship: My conception of literacy includes the learning of a socially situated sort of horsemanship and *some* of the accompanying social, cultural, historical, political, and economic influences on that learning; therefore, throughout this volume, I refer to horsemanship *practices*. In line with Barton and Hamilton's characterization, participants have narrated their personal journeys as well as depicted the social bonds and shared understandings that have been created as part of learning Vaquero horsemanship. They studied the Discourse (Gee, 1996) of Vaquero horsemanship, which then helped them to revise their own identities so that they would be recognized by fellow practitioners of the same style of horsemanship (Lewis et al., 2007, p. 20). In participants' lives, of course, labels that categorize different sorts of literacy, or horsemanship for that matter, do not necessarily matter much in the live messiness of existence.

In the "Vaquero Horse Gear" section of his *Vaquero Heritage*, when Ernest Morris (2014) described the making of a reata [a braided rawhide rope], he began by stating that "the rawhide is braided into a special weaving pattern, typically with four, six, or eight 'strands'" and that "rawhide braiding is both a skill and an art" (p. 85). I have done some theoretical braiding myself in this volume: In addition to the sociocultural foundations of this study, I have also turned to animal studies, cultural studies, and philosophy to illuminate the findings of each chapter (Barton and Hamilton [1998] noted that "literacy studies is essentially an interdisciplinary endeavour" [p.18]). While I have tried to be skillful, I ask for the reader's understanding that this is also an artistic endeavor, with human subjectivity woven in, and not an objective scientific report. I have turned to theoretical concepts and ideas that I felt would help tell the stories of this project and convey the braided realities of those living this kind of horsemanship.

Research Questions and Participants

My overarching research question was, how and why are horsepeople in the southeastern United States learning and practicing Vaquero horsemanship? My subquestions were: (1) Which significant learning experiences did participants identify as part of their development? (2) What motivated them to pursue this style of horsemanship? (3) How did participants conceive of expertise in VH? (4) How has consumer culture affected their practice of VH? (5) How do participants describe their horsemanship philosophy? (6) How would participants describe the cultural and historical roots of VH? and (7) What role did technology play in their learning journeys? Each chapter attempts to address these questions. In my own modest way, I add a response to Birke's (2014) call for "better ways in which relationships between humans and nonhumans, as processes of communication and interconnecting, might be studied" (p. 50).

My primary method in this qualitative project was ethnographic interviewing. There are two groups of interviewees in this project: the first group in the southeastern United States and the second group of mentors as well as two who provided historical context. In the first group, I interviewed 26 horse professionals (12 females and 12 males) and two amateur riders (both female) who resided in North and South Carolina, Georgia, Virginia, or Tennessee. This group consisted of those who self-identified as studying or having been influenced by Vaquero horsemanship. Because this was a convenience sample, these participants are not representative of those who study, or follow,

VH in the southeastern United States or elsewhere. Some in this group chose to use their real names and so are identified initially by their full names and generally thereafter by their first names and initials of last names (and if mentioned repeatedly in the same paragraph, sometimes just first names are used after initial identification). Pseudonyms consisting of first names only (no initials) are used for anonymous participants. I refer to southeastern participants in this way so that the reader can easily identify them. Appendix A contains the full names of participants who consented to using their real names.

The second group of participants included those who had been specifically mentioned by the first group as having been influential as they learned VH (all but one responded to my request for an interview); interviewees in this group are (in alphabetical order): Buck Brannaman, Mike Bridges, Tom Curtin, Cody Deering, Greg Eliel, Rodolfo Lara Sr., Bryan Neubert, Bruce Sandifer, Gwynn Turnbull, and Joe Wolter. Ricky Quinn and Jaton Lord also represent the next generation of this approach to horsemanship. Lastly, author and historian Bill Reynolds provided some California history about VH, and Melanie Smith Taylor (Olympic gold medalist in show jumping) spoke with me about being an early sponsor, along with her late husband, of Ray Hunt's clinics in the southeastern United States. Although this is obviously not a how-to book, I do include the full names of mentors so that the reader who desires to can further investigate this style of horsemanship. Some of the southeastern participants may also be available for lessons, workshops, and/or clinics so the interested reader is encouraged to reach out.

I tried to include as many women as men in this study, although in the second group of interviewees, I was limited to who the first group had cited. Sánchez (1995) noted that, "After secularization [in present-day California], certain women would take charge of a great deal of the production on the small ranches and become notable riders and farmers" (p. 211). However, their names may be lost to us; Rojas (2010) included the names of eight skilled "ladies-on-horseback" among a list of 382 male vaqueros (p. 244). No doubt there were more vaqueras then—and many now.

Throughout this volume, I refer to those included in this study as participants, interviewees, practitioners, and educators. Rather than use the word "trainer" (which many participants made a point of dismissing), I employ the word "educator." This came from some of the participants themselves as they feel that VH is "horse-centered," which makes "trainer," with its traditional connotations of harsher, human-centered methods, undesirable. Additionally, participants are schooling humans as much, if not more, than horses. As a veteran educator (of people) myself, I recognized in participants that earnest wish to make the lives of those you work with, human or not, fairer.

Data Collection and Analysis

Analysis requires that a knot be undone. (Serres, 2016, p. 79)

The first group of participants were interviewed in person with one exception during the pandemic (via Zoom). The second group of participants were interviewed either in person or over the phone. In both groups, I chose semistructured interviewing in an attempt to "make better use of the knowledge-producing potentials of dialogue by allowing much more leeway for following up on whatever angles are deemed important by the interviewee" (Brinkmann, 2015, p. 286). Participants were encouraged to speak freely in response to a given question and also to steer the conversation in a desired direction, which often resulted "in rambling, wily, everyday stories" (de Certeau, 1984, p. 89). Geertz (2000) stated that the methodology of anthropological fieldwork involves, not surprisingly, working from the inside out: "To discover who people think they are, what they think they are doing, and to what end they think they are doing it, it is necessary to gain a working familiarity with the frames of meaning within which they enact their lives" (p. 16); my goal was to explore these tenets in the context of participants as practitioners, to varying degrees, of VH. Once interviews were completed, they were then transcribed professionally. To supplement my interviews, I also took field notes immediately after conducting them and reviewed them while writing my findings.

To begin my analysis, I conducted an open coding (Corbin & Strauss, 2015) of all interviews to identify possible themes and patterns of response; these gave me initial insight into how participants conceive of VH and of its significance to them. Interviews were then placed into atlas.ti for descriptive coding (Saldaña & Omasta, 2018) as this can "lead to a well-indexed compendium of contents from multiple interviews" (p, 217). In order to focus on only "relevant text" (p. 215), all quotations relating to the most dominant themes were collected, along with interviewee identifiers, into a Word document for the second round of coding. I then identified the following subthemes within each topic (Saldaña & Omasta, 2018) and grouped quotations accordingly. This volume consists of the dominant themes, and subthemes, of this study, accompanied by descriptive narration to illustrate each aspect. But, as Serres (2016) noted, "[a]nalysis requires that a knot be undone" (p. 79). Even though I have unknotted the themes in order to present my findings (which is, in a sense, the opposite of the theoretical weaving that I have done), there are places of overlap throughout: Speaking about what motivates you to study VH might mean that you are also talking about a pivotal experience with a horse *and* also about the more philosophical aspects of your learning process; all of these elements might be present in a few sentences. So, even though this volume is about thematic analysis, I acknowledge that the boundaries of it are not neatly contained categories but, instead, overlap in the actual interviews.

Bruner (1994) maintained that "another property of Self as we encounter it in ourselves and in others" is that "[i]t is 'storied,' or narrative, in structure" (p. 43). Self as student or practitioner of VH primarily occurs between horse and human, but when the latter is asked to talk about this process, then it comes out, often, in stories. My goal was, and is, to synthesize their stories in order the share the larger narrative about learning and practicing Vaquero horsemanship in this specific context (which is distinct from its historical one). To that end, this volume is rich with participants' own words, rather than my paraphrasing. Even though academic writing often favors the latter, I found their exact words (often heartfelt, humorous, and compelling—sometimes poetic and uniquely eloquent) to be more effective at communicating the main ideas of this project. Therefore, you will hear from the "storytellers" of this project as much as you hear from me, for their words and experiences position this volume on stable ground, of the sort that horses might appreciate. Lastly, interviewees trusted me with their words and ideas, so when I thought that they might prefer it, I left selected quotes anonymous.

Researcher Positionality

As far as my own role, I write this not as a current practitioner of VH, but as an observer (although I do hope, one day, when I have the time and resources, to study it more formally). I approached participants as a university professor who studies literacy but, more importantly, as a horse owner and amateur rider who admires modern VH, so I occupied a place with some familiarity with, but not expertise in, their professional world. I also regularly shared my Buck Brannaman clinic story to explain my initial interest and curiosity, including that I had grown up in California and am a descendent of Spanish land-grant families on my maternal grandfather's side. The hesitation that participants might have felt about being interviewed by an academic was offset by my enthusiasm for horses and curiosity about VH. Before, during, and after interviews, participants and I would talk about horses, clinics, and people we knew in common, which functioned to establish rapport and a level of comfort. I truly valued their thoughts and views, and I think they, as people sensitive to what non-horsepeople might miss, appreciated that.

Anthropomorphism as a Research Feature in This Study

Just off the highway to Rochester, Minnesota,
Twilight bounds softly forth on the grass.
And the eyes of those two Indian ponies
Darken with kindness.
They have come gladly out of the willows

To welcome my friend and me.
We step over the barbed wire into the pasture
Where they have been grazing all day, alone.
They ripple tensely, they can hardly contain their happiness
That we have come.
They bow shyly as wet swans. They love each other.
There is no loneliness like theirs . . .
(Excerpted from Wright, "A Blessing," 1990, p. 143)

As part of the design of this study, I feel that I should outline my approach to anthropomorphism, both in participants' stories and in my own subsequent interpretations. Sober (2005) stated that, "Anthropomorphism is often defined as the error of attributing human mental characteristics to nonhuman organisms; people are said to fall into this error because they are sentimental and uncritical" (p. 85); Coetzee's (1999) "indignant reader" (p. 30) epitomizes those who find it offensive almost by default. I begin this section with a segment from Wright's poem to illustrate that anthropomorphism is also the domain of poetry, one of our more thoughtful arts. Furthermore, in this study, if it is expressed from participants' vantage points, then I do not feel it is my place to critique it. Instead, I accept it as a legitimate element of their narratives; however, I must also admit that I do not find it out of place in this project. When I examine my own beliefs about anthropomorphism in the context of VH, I find that I agree that one positive outcome of it is that it "ultimately enables people to benefit socially, emotionally, and physically from their relationships with companion animals" (Serpell, 2005, p. 127). Anthropomorphism brings a level of meaning to our interactions with animals that might not exist otherwise, and that meaning balances out the "sentimental" tone that some might find shallow. I understand the reputed "danger" of it, but I am unconvinced that the intelligent and thoughtful individuals I spoke with are simply foregoing criticality. Instead, I believe that they have made a conscious choice, based on their own experiences, to view horses as *sometimes* sharing emotional ground with humans; they do not view horses as identical to humans, and some, in fact, seem to see them as superior.

Associating anthropomorphism with an automatic lack of rigor seemed suspicious once I had insight into participants' thought processes as they learned a kind of horsemanship they chose for its emphasis on the horse *thinking*. Both Sober's and Serpell's chapters are part of a volume titled *Thinking with Animals: New Perspectives on Anthropomorphism* (Daston & Mitman, 2005), and "thinking with"—and not "thinking for"—is a motif of the modern version of Vaquero horsemanship. Daston and Mitman noted that, "In both scientific and popular contexts, thinking with animals is increasingly thinking with individual animals," and also includes "thinking about what it would be like to *be* that animal" (p. 10). Horsemanship includes a concentrated focus on an individual horse, and VH means that there is that same focus throughout years of development. Perhaps anthropomorphism is unavoidable (or at least nearly so) when you have a years- or decades-long relationship with another being you conceive of as capable of intelligent thought and action.

Anthropomorphism as an interpretive lens can provide clues as to whether horses are understanding what we are attempting to communicate. Bekoff (2002) argued that it

> can be useful if it serves to focus attention on questions about animal behavior that might otherwise be ignored.... Being anthropomorphic does not ignore the animals' perspectives. Rather, anthropomorphism can help to make accessible to us the behavior and thoughts and feelings of the animals with whom we are sharing a particular experience." (p. 50)

The thoughtful sort of horsemanship that I describe in this volume revolves around paying close attention to horses' "behavior and thoughts and feelings" as part of both horses and participants learning VH. If anthropomorphism can help those who seek not just a shared experience, but one that is mutually positive, then it should be respected instead of disparaged. Furthermore, anthropomorphism can aid those working with horses in understanding whether their approaches are successful; if they try something and the horse calmly "answers," then they can assume that it worked well.

Serpell (2005) contended that, "Anthropomorphism rules because, for most people, any other interpretation of the animals' behavior—any suggestion that it might be motivated by other than human feelings and desires—would instantly devalue those relationships and place them on a more superficial and less rewarding footing" (p. 128). Anthropomorphism can be viewed as a way of elevating horses to our level rather than easily simplifying their emotional lives. And if we are tempted to think that anthropomorphism is for those without the intellect or discipline to think beyond it, Bekoff (2002) reminded us that biologist and Nobel Prize winner Konrad Lorenz "freely used anecdote and anthropomorphism, [and] stressed that it was important to empathize with nonhumans, and believed that animals had the capacity to love, be jealous, experience envy, and be angry" (p. 36).

What Is Beyond the Scope of This Study

This volume is not a comprehensive survey of modern iterations of VH, since the focus is on two groups: those interested in, and influenced by, VH in the southeastern United States and their mentors, who are based throughout the United States and travel throughout it (and sometimes internationally). Because I limited myself to those

mentors who were cited by the southeastern participants, I did not include international practitioners of VH, nor did I include those who would describe themselves as
"purists." This is not to deny the presence of those groups but to affirm that they are outside of my unique orbit.

ORGANIZATION OF THIS VOLUME

Overall, I characterize the findings of this study about Vaquero horsemanship as a collapse of distance between geographical and cultural boundaries, digital and physical
spaces, and, most significantly, horses and humans. More specifically, I will explore
self-directed learning trajectories that included horses as equal educational partners;
the flexibility of apprentice and expert positions in relation to horses and other humans as participants learned VH; the influence of consumer culture; the philosophy
of modern VH; the ongoing significance of VH's cultural roots; the roles that technology played in the learning of VH, including a consideration of virtual community;
and, in the conclusion, what the future of VH might include. Throughout this volume, I utilize a few metaphors (sapphires and slow-craft creation; distance and travel,
including desire lines; and VH as circular) to help me explain the findings of this study.

In chapter 1, I assume that readers know little to nothing about Vaquero horsemanship, and so provide an overview of the landscape of it. I share some history of it but focus mostly upon modern VH, including its texts. Using these books as well as my interviews, and the metaphor of a Montana sapphire, I sketch out each facet of the modern
version, which has enrolled some horsemen (Bill and Tom Dorrance; Ray Hunt) who
would not have considered themselves vaqueros and has, in general, enlarged its territory. I also introduce readers to the gear of VH, which has traveled to us from the time
of historical vaqueros. Lastly, I consider the presence of romanticism and its influence
on historical and modern Vaquero horsemanship.

In chapter 2, I focus on how, and why, participants learned VH, drawing from the
many narrative instances in interviews where they described these experiences. I begin
by highlighting the influence of various inspirations, for example, early reading experiences, learning what they felt was the "better way" of horsemanship. I then turn to an
examination of significant elements of their experiences, including self-directed learning (which I explain with the metaphor of desire lines); the horse always accompanied
their studying and sometimes other humans did, too. Furthermore, this chapter allows
me to bring in Bruner's (1994) narrative "turning points" as well as educational philosophy (i.e., Dewey, 1938).

Chapter 3 is about the flexibility of apprenticeship and expertise in VH, and how
each affected participants' relationships with their horses. They see themselves as

continually growing and learning, with horses occupying the role of permanent—and humbling—teacher. Because of the necessity for humility, seeing oneself as knowledgeable was a tenuous and conditional position. Living and working with horses in this way could situate educators as "Pro-Ams" or professional amateurs; southeastern interviewees might be professionals when teaching less knowledgeable others but then occupy the role of learner when studying with mentors. To explore the ideas in this chapter, I draw upon local and vernacular literacies (Barton & Hamilton, 1998) and the concept of Pro-Ams (Leadbeater & Miller, 2004; Gee, 2010) as well as Lave and Wenger's (1991) work on apprenticeship and expertise.

In chapter 4, I explore the role of consumer culture in modern VH in both the southeastern United States and beyond. To do this, I consider the effects of consumer culture on the horses who live with humans and on the practice of modern Vaquero horsemanship itself by way of the distinctive gear as well as clinics. *Looking* like a modern vaquero has become mediated by consumerism in a way that can challenge the traditions of it, if they can, in fact, be bought—or if riders become caught up in "the costume" (as a few participants called it). While I highlight the negative sway of consumer culture, this issue is more nuanced than it might initially seem as the gear and clinics can transmit the traditions of it—and benefit both clinicians and artisans. I turn to cultural studies (Berger, 2010; Du Gay et al., 2013; Storey, 2021) and to Gee's (2015) ideas about Discourse to make sense of the negotiation with consumer culture that participants described.

Chapter 5 is about the philosophy underpinning modern VH, which, through the interviewing process itself, came to occupy a significant spot in this study. I look to the modern texts of VH as well as to my interviews to explain how this horsemanship applies to the whole of participants' lives. Even though VH has specific gear that carries on its traditions, its philosophy-in-action brings the horse-human bond to its full realization. I explore the soul-searching that participants described, including one of its results: generosity toward the horse. I also consider how mindfulness (maintaining moment-to-moment awareness and concentration) interacts with the physical work of horsemanship. Throughout, I analyze what the philosophical side of VH means to, and for, riders and their horses.

In chapter 6, I take a closer look at what southeastern participants said about the cultural roots of VH; I also share what the mentors reported regarding whether it is important to learn these roots. Additionally, I incorporate excerpts from academic texts that highlight the historical and cultural context(s) of VH. I consider whether we can, and should, collapse cultural distance in modern Vaquero horsemanship. The word *vaquero* itself is heteroglossic and layered with meaning from different cultural contexts (Bakhtin, 1982). It is also related to the words *buckaroo*, *Californio*, *caballero*, and *charro*, and so I briefly examine each one to try to determine, as I call it, the worth of the words we use, and could use, in representing the cultural traditions of VH.

Chapter 7 is about how technology helps and hinders the learning of VH, given that the Internet provides a unique opportunity for southeastern US participants to learn more about it. Additionally, what exactly technology means for the horse-human connection as they learn a particular style of horsemanship in our contemporary digital context is the focus of this chapter. I employ the lens of "vernacular digital literacies" (Barton & Lee, 2012) to explore this aspect by focusing on the themes of accessibility, virtual connection and community, flexibility, the need for "feel," and criticality. Although participants predictably turned to technology to further their own learning, this was complicated by how much digital information is available as well as the quality of it.

The conclusion is a substantial chapter in and of itself. It is also a variation of a traditional academic one: I reiterate the main themes of this volume, but also include the additional themes of the evolution of VH, blending disciplines, and participants' hopes for the future of it (including "pragmatist hope" and possibility [Stitzlein, 2020]). Furthermore, I explore the idea that VH has traveled a crooked circle (a different sort of evolution than the straight-line kind) through history to the modern version I partially document in this study. To bring these themes to life, I share three specific examples of how VH has evolved while simultaneously circling back.

Lastly, chapters 1 through 7 are followed by interludes: Seven participants recounted stories of horses and life experiences that have been particularly memorable and influential in their horsemanship careers. This is my way of bringing in the "voices" of horses who, even though they may seem silent in this volume, speak throughout it.

CHAPTER 1

An Overview of Historical and Modern Vaquero Horsemanship

VAQUERO HORSEMANSHIP (VH) WAS, AND IS, A SPECIALIZED FORM OF working, and living, with horses and other livestock. In our time, it also refers to a recreational form of riding that may or may not include handling cattle. What exactly VH means, as with many matters relating to horsemanship, depends upon who you ask when. Its historical meaning is more closely aligned to a working tradition of stockmanship: Arnold R. Rojas (2010), one of its major chroniclers, defined a vaquero as "the man who brought the cattle to the West and herded them for a hundred years or more before the United States took possession of half of Mexico's territory, and three quarters of a century afterwards" (p. 126); he credited Mission priests with having been "the most prominent in teaching the use of the horse in America" (p. 128), and so VH began after they arrived in the late 1700s. Vaquero horsemanship is associated with what would become California, and so another name for it is the California bridle horse tradition; however, it is not limited to that state and owes its ancestry in the Americas to Mexico: "The ranching tradition in Mexico evolved from a mix of Spanish and American Indian knowledge. This led to the emergence of the Mexican vaquero, who would develop the equipment and techniques needed for working the large haciendas" (Monday & Colley, 1997, p. 46). Monday and Colley (1997) also noted the vaquero's multicultural heritage, which "can be traced to expert horsemen who brought their knowledge to the Americas with the early Spanish settlers and passed it on to the American Indians" (p. ix). There would subsequently be variations in the western United States (i.e., Texas, the Great Basin), and other names (i.e., buckaroo, "a corruption of the Spanish vaquero" [Bennett, 1998, p. 363]). Lott and Hart (cited in Olmert, 2009), "note[d] that the social character of the American West is largely the result of the aggression that ranchers employed in the domination of their horses and cattle" (p. 178). This is not that.

In the United States, the vaquero had humble beginnings, according to Dary (1989, cited in Bennett, 1994): "The vaquero was, in the eyes of most sixteenth-century

Spaniards, nothing more than a poor laborer on horseback, as far down in the social order as you could get" (p. 311). Vaqueros might have been poor, but this did not prevent them from elevating horses to the status of "prince of animals" (Rojas, 2010, p. 11), and horses were the recipient of "a feeling of humanity" from their riders (Rojas, 2010, p. 141). Horses' skills could also surpass their riders': "But the *señor don* of the old-time [land] grants ... often remarked that the horse some vaquero was riding knew more about cattle than his rider and it would be less shameful to the horse if the man were to get off and let the animal work without the added burden" (Rojas, 2010, pp. 86–87). This same regard for the horse endures in modern Vaquero horsemanship.

However, as this chapter title hints at, historical Vaquero horsemanship is distinct, in some respects, from the modern version that is the subject of my study. One aim of this chapter is to explain how the two are similar and different, although I will spend more space on modern VH; accordingly, I provide an extensive definition of it, which comes from both practitioners' texts and participants' interviews. This leads into a preface about learning Vaquero horsemanship in the southeastern United States, and then a consideration of the romanticism that is to be found in vaquero (and cowboy) cultures. In sum, chapter one provides the groundwork (a term that applies in horsemanship and in scholarship) for this volume; as such, I focus on what is needed to understand this study in context.

HISTORICAL VAQUERO HORSEMANSHIP

In *Vaquero Heritage*, Ernest Morris (2014) provided history about "vaqueros that worked on the land from the 1700s to 1900s in California. They were of Spanish, Mexican, Indian and later of European blood" (p. xi). From the beginning, the vaquero was associated with a specific style of horse tack: "The Mexican vaquero migrated northward with the cattle industry into the ranches of 'Alta' California. This migration followed primarily along the trail of the California missions. The vaqueros took with them the art of rawhide braiding. Pride in the competitive nature of these 'rawhiders' elevated braiding into distinctive and beautiful classical styles. ... The vaquero took special pride in having good quality braided rawhide equipment and a well-trained horse" (p. 84).

Mike Bridges, who has dedicated his career to the preservation and continuation of Vaquero horsemanship and is still conducting his six-year Bridle Horse Projects where riders study with him to create one, added detail about how the "well-trained horse" of VH came to be. First, he defined his own take on it:

My particular style has evolved over the years leaning towards where the roots of the vaquero discipline came from, which is the classical side that you understand more about as time goes on. The more horses you ride, you find out it just really gets down to the horse's ability to balance and rebalance—and the rider's influence to be able to help him get in those configurations where he can be in balance for whatever you're asking him to do.

Even though his is a modern definition, I include it here because he is someone who has studied the history of VH closely, and, therefore, his view of it blends both traditional and contemporary elements. Second, he shared some of VH's history, which gives the reader a sense of how it developed in the United States:

> The California vaquero discipline originated from the Spanish Cavalry horse—the Conquistadors. When they arrived, they also came with priests and started a mission system, and in a relatively short period of time the missions had a tremendous amount of cattle. They had much more cattle than they had population, and so there was no market for the meat in the early days. All the market was for hides and tallow. The only people who were allowed to ride were military, and they finally had so many cattle that they couldn't handle them, so they had to start teaching the Indians that they had subjugated how to do that.

We also discussed how classical horsemanship traveled from European aristocracy to Native Americans in the "new world" (who had been enslaved by those who treated it as "new"). Native Americans were the ones who would develop Vaquero horsemanship in the United States; de Certeau (1994) discussed how "Spanish colonialization over the indigenous Indian cultures" entailed Native Americans "us[ing] the laws, practices, and representations that were imposed on them by force or by fascination to ends other than those of their conquerors"; this meant "ma[king] it [the dominant order] function in another register" (p. 32). I would argue that the historical practice of Vaquero horsemanship, bracketed by discriminatory laws, was part of this reordering; however, lacking firsthand, textual accounts, the horsemanship itself survives as the best record of their efforts.

Mike then elaborated on the European side of this horsemanship:

> The military training of the European horse came from the Iberian Peninsula and classical training from the royal courts. The French court was the primary one during the Renaissance where horsemanship was taken to a much higher level, and studied, and became part of the arts that a young royal male or female was exposed to in their development. So, all the royal houses of Europe were sending their young princes and princesses to Versailles to learn how to be ladies and gentlemen, and horsemanship was a big part of that.

He shared part of a talk that he had given at a museum in Santa Ynez about how VH began establishing its reputation beyond California's borders, which documented how the horses trusted their riders and vice versa.

> The California vaquero bridle horse was developed . . . into a cattle-working horse that was much admired around the world for its grace and beauty as well as its lightning responses to the rider's signal. So impressive were these horses that they have been written about in the history of the Republic of Texas—riders from Texas being the first outsiders to drive cattle to California and return with their glowing report about these horses that could do so many different things well while exhibiting such great bravery that the rider could get close enough to rope a bear or circle a cow to a standstill.

Lastly, we had the following exchange:

> JULIANNA: It was a perfect combination then. They needed a highly-skilled horse and they had the time—
> MIKE: To develop it. They just had the time to make it happen, and that's one of the main characteristics of the California discipline is that it was based on taking a lot of time to develop the horse—a number of years.

The late 1800s disrupted the vaqueros' existence. During our interview, author and historian Bill Reynolds described how the vaquero's lifestyle—and territory—was forever changed by environmental disasters: "California had this megadrought (in 1863–1864) preceded by incredible floods (1861–1862) and a million cattle were killed in these floods." Financial disaster was next, "and so land started getting sold off, and vaqueros started moving around to keep working. The cattle began migrating east, out into the Great Plains, and then farming came and pushed them up into Nevada, Oregon, Washington, and even into British Columbia" (see also Pitt, 1966/1994, p. 254). Vaqueros moved all around the western United States, and this meant that "their styles very much evolved because of the environment and the land that they were working in."

As mechanization took over, the vaqueros' way of life would be transformed again. Bennett (1998) stated that VH faded after World War I and "it is only the older generation [she cited Arnold Rojas, Ernest Morris, and Ed Connell and their respective texts] which remembers the great California ranches" (p. 381). That generation and its recorders are gone now. Rojas (2010) documented this decline:

> The vaquero as a unique individual with a unique culture was passing out of the picture in the twenties. The terrible depression of the thirties put an end to him forever.

The cattleman one after another went bankrupt. The vaquero was left to struggle to keep body and soul together. There was no money to buy the silver-mounted bits and spurs which were so much a part of his life. Another reason for the decline of the vaquero was that his sons did not want a life of hardship. Like most of the second or third generation of all peoples in the United States, the vaquero's son wanted a fuller, richer life than the one his father had had. Few sons of vaqueros took up their father's trade. (p. 512)

Some modern practitioners may yet resemble the "vaquero as a unique individual" of Rojas' time; within this study, participants are indeed unique individuals who study and practice a current iteration with historical overtones. Before I turn to a further exploration of this, I share a few cautions.

Three Caveats

The term "Californio," which some still use today to describe Vaquero horsemanship, has also become synonymous with highly skilled horsemanship (I will return to it in chapter six). Historian Prezelski (2015) stated that, "Outsiders writing of the Californios frequently described them as being among the best horsemen in the world" (p. 21); Monroy (1990) defined them as "among the best, or at least most practiced, horsemen in the world" (p. 179; see also Bennett, 1998, p. 375). Morris (2014) outlined who the label applied to:

The term "Californio" refers to the people who settled California prior to statehood. These people were a mixture of Spaniards, Native Americans, and Europeans. The Californio ranch horse is unique because historically its training was a combination of Spanish-style riding which is adapted to the California ranching lifestyle. The early California style of ranching evolved around the vast Spanish and Mexican Land Grants and the idyllic Mediterranean climate which closely resembled the climate in Spain. The primary business of the early ranchos was managing large herds of cattle that roam free in the hills and valleys of the sparsely populated paradise. (p. 45)

Morris' depiction includes the vaqueros' multicultural and multiethnic roots as well as the romantic tone that characterizes nonacademic accounts of Vaquero horsemanship. Even though his description does indeed sound "idyllic," it brings forth my first caveat.

Morris' tone can be contrasted with Sánchez's (1995) description of the power structure of the time: "Californio society was highly stratified from the arrival of the missionaries, military officers, and soldiers with their families; restructuring after secularization would merely bring a new ruling class, an oligarchy made up of several wealthy landowning clans related by blood and marriage" (p. 177). Even though this chapter is only summarizing historical Vaquero horsemanship, I include this quote to remind the reader that horsemanship, so often given a gloss of romanticism (a topic I will return to later in this chapter), still exists, in cultural and societal settings and so contains and reflects imbalances of power, then and now.

The second caveat has to do with an opposite of romanticism: "Remembering" historical vaqueros as using harsh and sometimes severe methods with their horses; this is an assertion that I heard from some participants. Because there are so few texts about historical VH, this is hard to support with any rigor. A few interviewees told me that Connell's (1952) book has some methods that would be considered unnecessarily harsh by today's standards, or at least human-centered in a negative way, like forcing the horse into a certain position and them "letting them figure it out." Connell's book aside, the impression that historical VH was sometimes severe has likely been passed along as part of the folklore of it.

When I asked Mike Bridges what he thought of the idea above, he said that he thinks that there was the same variation from gentle to harsh approaches in horsemanship that we have today. He shared an experience from the beginning of his career.

> When I started, which was 1950 for a living, I left the family ranch and went to Nevada. You could go through an outfit there. They might have really bad horses, and if you couldn't ride those horses, you couldn't work there. But that was their style—tough horses and rough on cattle. Or you could go to an outfit where they felt that stockmanship was an art form and how you handled the cattle was very important to them and how you handled their horses was important to them. So, what you would have is, if a guy was a rougher kind of guy or liked to ride broncs or just thought that was a normal part of life, he wouldn't last very long in an outfit like that. He would gravitate to the outfits that suited him the way he was. I was raised on an outfit that they thought it was an art form, and I thought that how you handled the cattle and how you handled your horses was really important. . . . From all the way back as far as you want to go—there were those that tried to do it in harmony with the horse and those that just tried to smother the horse to get it done and had no feeling or very little feeling—the horse was just a tool to use.

Mike's explanation makes sense to me, given human nature, which has surely been a constant from historical to modern VH. Overall, my academic take on the question of whether VH was harsher then than it is now is that while it may have been true of some vaqueros, we do not have the research and historical records available to know definitively one way or the other.

The third caveat is that referring to "historical vaqueros" or "traditional Vaquero horsemanship" is a shortcut; we can take it but need to recognize it for what it is. Bruce Sandifer described his approach as "a modern perspective on traditional Vaquero horsemanship," but also cautioned that using a phrase like "the California bridle horse tradition" leads to questions like: The 1940 tradition? Or is it the 1850 tradition, or the 1790 tradition? There is a range that we might take for granted, which does not factor into account that "traditional" VH has shifted dramatically over time.

MODERN VAQUERO HORSEMANSHIP

Bennett (1998), who used "cowboys" and "vaqueros" both in her book about "the horses of Spain in the New World" (p. 1), portrayed Vaquero horsemanship as having an enviable past: "In those days, California cowboys achieved a level of horsemanship which sounds fabulous to the modern ear, but only because there are so few people alive today who have ever actually seen it" (p. 381). She ended this section by mentioning that "the old ways are, however, alive and well on some private ranches and at horsemanship clinics led by Tom and Bill Dorrance, Ray Hunt, Buck Brannaman, Joe Wolter, Bryan Neubert, Harry Whitney, and others" (p. 382). Participants in this study are part of this ongoing effort, learning what they can from what has survived, filling in when they need to, and amending what they think needs updating.

Vaquero Horsemanship in Print

Part of the documentation of modern Vaquero horsemanship is, of course, in print. In this section, I will begin to explain how VH got from there (in history) to here, carried part of the way by books. Even though there is a relatively small number of books about Vaquero horsemanship, southeastern U.S. residents utilized what exists to learn about Vaquero horsemanship (since digital sources are more popular now, I devote chapter seven to that resource). In terms of traditional texts, there are two categories of books related to VH: (1) those written by, and for, practitioners and (2) academic and general interest books (which often include mention of vaqueros in a larger historical context). Books from practitioners' points of view include the mentors of it (Brannaman, 2012; Connell, 1962; Dorrance, 2010; Dorrance & Desmond, 2007; Hunt, 1978; Morris, 2014; Rojas, 2010, 2011, 2013a, 2013b, 2013c, 2014a, 2014b). The most popular of these among participants were (in alphabetical order) Brannaman's, Desmond and Dorrance's, Dorrance's, and Hunt's books. They often provided an accessible starting point, and participants mentioned returning to them as their learning progressed. Additionally, using primarily photographs, Stoecklein et al.'s (2010) book documented modern California vaquero life while providing some historical context (and includes photographs of the saddle Bill Dorrance won "in the Hackamore Class at the Salinas Rodeo in 1948" [p. 142]). There are also two out-of-print books that were not mentioned by participants in the southeast (i.e., Dobie, 1929; Mora, 1949).

The academic texts that contain a treatment of VH include accounts of California history including the vaquero (Pitts, 1966/1998; Sánchez, 1995); a history of two large and longstanding Texas ranches (Monday & Colley, 1997); the distinctions between vaqueros, cowboys, and buckaroos (Clayton, Hoy & Underwood, 2001); and the vaquero as a cultural icon (Figueredo, 2015). Three participants recommended Deb Bennett's (1998) *Conquerors*, a unique text written by someone who is both a practitioner and an academic. In a section titled "The Cowboy Loses His Voice," Bennett (1998) argued that historical vaqueros

> proved themselves well able to work with livestock, but because they could neither read nor write, their voice in the history and development of horsemanship has largely been lost and is only now beginning to be recovered. The error of European horsemen and historians—a very great and pervasive error—has been to equate illiteracy with ignorance. (p. 111)

While I rely more heavily on the first category of practitioners' books, I also draw from the academic texts for background and context.

Some gaps have had to be filled in since what we have to rely upon are a relatively few written accounts and what survives of an oral history. To that end, I suspect that one reason the word "vaquero" itself has persisted has been an attempt to recover what is fading. The foreword by the publisher of *Hackamore Reinsman* (1952) included a note that hackamore training had "been a trade secret with the descendants of the vaqueros for many years" and "[n]othing was ever written about the fine points of the art" (p. 1). (Connell himself does not use the word "vaquero"; instead, he used "the early Spanish Californians" [p. 11] although he did use it in the title of his 2004 book.) Bruce Sandifer noted that historical vaqueros kept their approach "a secret because it was competition for those jobs, especially after the Mission period." Rojas (2010) also lamented that "little has been written about the vaqueros" (p. 126) and that much of Western history during his time left out Mexican American perspectives (p. 459; see also Sánchez, 1995); incidentally, Rojas' works became hard to come by until Bill Reynolds republished them; Joseph Jacinto (Jo) Mora's *Californios* is currently out of print and used copies are prohibitively expensive. Clayton et al. (2001) stated, "The main literature of the life of the vaquero is found, according to Ramirez, in stories and *corridos*, the folk songs of the vaqueros" (p. 63).

Bruce Sandifer categorized modern VH as "interpretations of an undocumented system" because there are firsthand "accounts," like Rojas', rather than a collection of detailed, or objective, records like we have from other forms of horsemanship—for example, as he noted, from the Spanish Riding School. We discussed how this has opened VH to "interpretation" and "mysteriousness," which has more easily led to it being considered an art form (it has also opened VH up to the negative aspects of consumerism, which I explore in chapter four). Mike Bridges concurred that we do not have "how-to books" about historical VH and that Rojas, Connell, and Mora were, as he pointed out, "all from the Bakersfield area and worked on the same ranches." So, "that style where they talk about busting those horses . . . was more of a harsher type deal" and not representative of the *whole* of it. Therefore, if we now think of VH as more humane, that came, at least partially, from the modern texts about it—and that was when, and where, the tradition widened out. The written documentation from Tom and Bill Dorrance and Ray Hunt filled a void that has helped to keep modern VH alive, even though they would not have called themselves vaqueros.

Modern Horsemen Arrive and Alter Vaquero Horsemanship

Some current horsemen, like Buck Brannaman, *choose* to use "vaquero" (his website cites "the California vaquero tradition" as an influence). The choice of "vaquero" instead of its gringo offspring "buckaroo" (the latter is perhaps more widely used today in the United States) signifies an alliance with the Native American/Mexican/Spanish cultural roots of this style of horsemanship. During our interview, he explained this:

> JULIANNA: Why use the word *vaquero* instead of the other words that you could use?
> BUCK: Because there is a lineage that goes back to what were the original cowboys in North America. They were vaqueros, and they were documented to be around about 85 years prior to what we ever thought of as the first cowboy in America. There are people that maybe have only read white European history, and of course the vaqueros were Spanish and Mexicans and Indians, which really messes with the history of the whole cowboys and Indians thing because Indians were some of the first cowboys. . . . It's a rich history and that's where this style of horsemanship came from—yet through Tom Dorrance and Ray Hunt it has evolved into the way that we work with horses, but that's where it all started.

This association between historical vaqueros and modern horsemen like the Dorrances and Ray Hunt has been reinforced in both text and clinics. In Dorrance and Desmond's (2007) book, Bill Dorrance is described as having "adhered to the values and practices of the vaquero tradition and passed on his appreciation of this nearly lost lifestyle" (np). Ray Hunt's link to Vaquero horsemanship has been solidified by Buck Brannaman (who also uses the word in his annual Pro-Am Vaquero Roping event) and who speaks frequently about Hunt's life-changing impact. In our interview, he said, "I pretty much tell people anything I'm doing that looks pretty good to you, you could attribute to Ray Hunt . . . so I've just spent my life trying to the best of my ability to do what Ray tried to instill in me since I was a kid." His allegiance to both Ray Hunt's legacy and the word "vaquero" has likely caused some modern followers of his, who did not know Hunt personally, to link them together; others might disagree with that linkage, although I suspect all would agree with this: If one result of this association is to learn better, fairer treatment of the horse, then what harm does the label do? For now, I will say none, although I revisit, and further trouble, this question with respect to its cultural origins and significance in chapter four.

Jaton Lord, Ray Hunt's grandson, stated that he thought Hunt and the Dorrances "weren't your traditional vaqueros, but that's where their roots came from," and that they updated it. He also said, "I do think that if there wasn't a vaquero culture, there probably wouldn't have been a Tom and Ray and Bill." Similarly, Gwynn Turnbull shared a helpful narrative explaining VH's modern chain of correlation:

> There used to be a group of people that were into the vaquero thing, and they were peppered around at different ranches in California. Then when the cattle moved into the Great Basin of Nevada and southern Oregon, it took that kind of horsemanship with them. There were a couple of brothers, Tom and Bill Dorrance, who are very well-known, and they were very soft-spoken, kind of unassuming men. They started teaching people about considering how the horse thinks, and not just how to get the horse to do something, but how to get the horse to *want* to do something—to be motivated in a positive way and go towards what you're asking instead of going away from fear. So, their thoughts weren't specific to the California bridle horse but applied to all horses. They happened to be bridle horsemen, and so the two things got tied together. Then they had a protégé, Ray Hunt, who was a bigger personality, bolder, more outspoken, a decent-hearted guy. He really started doing clinics, and then that started this whole kind of horsemanship revolution, where you considered the horse and how they felt about things and tried to work within that framework . . . so, with all of that, the treating a horse this way was somehow tied to the California bridle horses. . . . It wasn't specific to that discipline. It was just that the men who started promoting a new way about thinking about horsemanship happened to be bridle horsemen.

Referring to VH, in Gwynn's first line, as "this vaquero thing" has a predecessor: Joe Wolter recounted that, "When I was with the Dorrances and Ray Hunt, they called it 'this thing'—'this thing with the horses.'" Perhaps they kept it general because the philosophy and approaches applied to life *in general*—and they were not overly concerned with labels. The more that I learn, and think, about the phrase Vaquero horsemanship, the more I appreciate "this thing with the horses" for its spaciousness.

My understanding from interviewees is that the Dorrances and Hunt had worked on ranches that had been influenced by vaquero traditions and that they utilized vaquero gear to create bridle horses but blended it with their own kind of horsemanship. There was consensus that they would not have called themselves vaqueros because they would have associated that term with the historical version sourced from cultures different than their own; there was disagreement about whether they would have called themselves buckaroos. The word "vaquero" is more restrictive than the phrase "Vaquero horsemanship" in our modern context, in that those who still place it primarily in its historical context are not apt to apply it to themselves or to the Dorrances, who grew up in Oregon, or to Ray Hunt, who was from Idaho. The further we have gotten from the historical vaquero, the blurrier the word has become.

Tom Curtin supports the idea that even though some of those currently interested in VH will cite the Dorrances and Hunt as influences, there is a distinction to be drawn:

> Tom and Ray spent their whole lives trying to teach horsemanship as coming from the horse's needs with some quality. I wouldn't necessarily say that they followed closely to a vaquero tradition. They understood and utilized that and tried to build on it because of the tradition and style behind it, but they brought it in a little bit different manner maybe than what the purist would do or even the traditionalist.

He also made the point that Hunt was more of a "realist" and "didn't care if you showed up riding in a dressage or a team roping or barrel racing saddle. . . . That kind of stuff meant absolutely nothing to him." Instead, he was focused on "your interest in getting better to be able to help your horse make things easier for you and him both. That was Ray's whole goal." Even though "he enjoy[ed] his bridle horses" and "was very versed and aware of what was going on in the vaquero tradition, he tried to teach this with a little more of an understanding coming from the horse's needs." Hunt was a highly influential founder of the evolution, and, arguably, improvement that continues today when it comes to VH, even if he did not set out to achieve this.

This is an apt point at which to briefly mention the distinction between Natural horsemanship and Vaquero horsemanship. The former is the term that has taken hold in popular culture, and there are some trainers who would be placed in both groups; however, there are some that would be in the former group but definitely not in the latter. One participant let me know that Natural horsemanship was created as "a marketing term" and that "most of the mechanics of a lot of Natural horsemanship is natural human-ship." Another wryly commented, "If they created it today it'd be 'Organic horsemanship.' It's not anything new. It doesn't really have anything to do with a particular discipline." Everyone that I interviewed did not like the term "Natural horsemanship" for various reasons. Bruce Sandifer contrasted the two: VH is "a working style that is derived from the instincts of the horse—that was developed through the natural tendencies of horses. So, I think it is so much truer a Natural horsemanship style than a lot of what is said to be Natural horsemanship." Vaquero horsemanship is a more specialized and specific term that only horsemanship insiders are likely to know—and to apply. But for those on the outside, they are often conflated. An example of this can be found in Olmert's (2009) book, which is aimed at a general readership. She included a highly favorable description of Ray Hunt, calling him the "high priest" of Natural horsemanship; she cited the "kindness" of his approach (p. 93) but did not get into a categorization beyond "natural." Now that I have dispensed with this label, we can consider the specifics of modern VH.

Facets of Modern Vaquero Horsemanship

Modern Vaquero horsemanship is as faceted as a cut Montana sapphire. I chose this metaphor because it is a durable stone, perceived to be beautiful, and sourced in the western United States, like VH itself. Not only has VH become more of a luxury and part of a marketing effort, but it also has been adopted recreationally by some who will never be working vaqueros and are simply *interested* in, rather than committed to, the bridle horse tradition. To some, it is just a pretty thing, and to others it is valuable and extraordinary. There is no one standard definition of modern VH, but the facets combine to reflect and refract its connected meanings, thus illuminating the whole.

Many study participants referred to VH as an art form (which, of course, is not a modern concept since Xenophon, over 2,300 years ago, referred to "the horseman's art" [1893/2006, p. 13]), and I will revisit this in the extended definition below. To return to the idea that VH is like a faceted sapphire, I borrow another descriptive term from modern jewelry design: slow-craft, which signifies a thoughtful, gradual, and deliberate approach (that might also be a luxury) and was created in response to disposable consumerism and junk production. VH is slow-craft horsemanship. In some of the modern texts about VH, there is support for this idea. Tom Dorrance (Dorrance & Desmond, 2007) reminded readers that the timeline we often subject horses to is not only unrealistic but contradicts how we treat young humans beginning their own learning journeys:

> It's really no different than being a kid in school. It took a year of kindergarten just to get you halter broke, and then there's eight more years you had to be there just to get out of the 8th grade. When they expected you to move ahead on new material and you didn't have a grasp on things that were spoken about earlier, why you are liable to not feel the best when pressure like that was any place around. What a kid in that situation needs is help. In one way it's not any different for a horse. In another way it's a lot worse. So many of these horses get all those lessons crammed in so fast and they have to sort things out in only a few months, when they aren't even three. (p. 170)

The unhurried and deliberate pace of slow-craft VH may well be a good match with the horse brain as it gives them time to build trust; Jones (2020) noted that "the horse's brain is still hardwired by evolution to fear us" (p. 26), and that "horse training is partly a process of teaching your mount to depend on you for prefrontal decisions" (p. 183). Tom Dorrance's student Ray Hunt (1978) extended this idea by cautioning against one likely outcome of a rushed progression: "This is where a lot of people get disappointed. They want instant results; then if it doesn't come through they think they have to get tougher or rougher. Then they get the horse bothered and upset, and they lose the softness we're looking for" (p. 62). We might sabotage ourselves and wreck our relationship with the horse if we become focused on the wrong notion of development and fail to "let the horse think a little bit" (p. 27). Understanding the philosophy of VH is slow-craft itself: "To digest these goals in the capsule form a person need only know 'feel, timing, and balance.' But the truth of the matter is that just those three small terms take a lifetime of chewing before they begin to digest" (p. 10). Capsules and facets are small but substantial; I next turn to the first one: relationships between horse and human.

MAKING SUSTAINED CONTACT WITH THE HORSE

The first facet that I focus on has to do with how VH followers initiate, and sustain, contact with the horse, including assumptions made about horses in general. One of Tom Dorrance's (2010) goals was "to help the person to be able to approach his or her horse with acceptance, assurance and understanding; to work towards *true unity*" (p. 7; italics in original). He advised readers, "The horse isn't trying to do the wrong thing. He is trying to do what he thinks he is supposed to do" (p. 129). This generosity toward the horse, which will become a recurring theme in this volume, was reinforced by Ray Hunt (1978), who advocated treating the horse with respect and consideration: "You can ask the horse to do your thing, but you *ask him*; you offer it to him in a good way. You fix it up and let him find it. You do not make anything happen, no more than you can make a friendship happen" (p. 1; italics in original). One of Hunt's goals was "to work these horses where there's no mental build up, no worries" (p. 27). Ed Connell (1952) also advised the rider to "keep [the horse] as quiet as possible" (p. 29), avoiding unnecessary upset, and "*when they are doing all right leave them alone*" (p. 44; emphasis in original). We know that horses are often subjected to humans *making* things happen, and that anxiety can result from that, so this is an alternative to horses as subordinates.

Bill Dorrance and Leslie Desmond (2007) depicted horses as possessing positive traits: "Horses have a lot more intelligence and emotions than most people would suppose. They enjoy being comfortable, and it's their natural curiosity and searching frame of mind that causes them to feel for meaning in what a person does" (p. 275). They promoted making "what the horse thinks and feels ... our greatest concern. *Or it should be anyway*" (p. 170; italics in original). Approaching a horse as you might a fellow sentient and smart human is bound to structure the interaction accordingly—meaning, if you assume that your partner is also trying to make the given situation calm and comprehensible, then you are less inclined to rely upon force or fear because you have the same goals.

Present-day clinicians and educators maintain the Dorrances' and Hunt's approaches. Jaton Lord summarized how he, applying what he learned from Hunt (his grandfather) makes contact by "getting a horse in a learning frame of mind" *before* work starts. He often sees situations "where the horse isn't wanting to be there or isn't in a learning frame of mind, and riders try to force stuff down." So, making contact begins with the effort and thought you put into the preparation. As an educator, this sounds to me like teaching a class effectively, where much of the work happens before the students arrive; working with all learners requires tapping into background knowledge to stimulate engagement. Another aspect that Jaton is focused upon applies to horse and human learners, as well:

> Every year, I have a theme, and this year it's how I can train a confident horse. To destroy confidence is telling them what they're doing wrong—riding them and telling them how awesome they can walk along versus picking apart how they stumble when they walk. I tell them, that was an awesome stumble, instead of, darn it, you stumbled there—because grandpa could get you set up so well that there was no failing, and he would get you so confident.

Notably, Hunt's way of setting Jaton up for success has continued with Jaton's own horses and the horses he educates. This is another collapse of distance: The same facets that sustain contact and build relationships apply to horse and human both—across time.

An additional example of how to make contact was articulated by Ricky Quinn, and there is some common ground with Jaton's thoughts.

> It's all about balancing the horse, getting to the feet, and one of the most important things is that before you ask for something, he's got to be ready to do it. If he's out of balance and out of whack, and you ask, you probably aren't going to get it, and he's going to be trouble when you do. So, the heart of it to me is getting that horse set up and balanced before you ask, and then he enjoys himself when I initiate him into something.

Note that he does *not* emphasize the mechanical action of getting something done but instead focuses on the horse's preparation and feeling about it so that when it does get done it is not an unhappy, tense exchange. Similarly, Reed Edwards outlined the goals of modern VH as including "to develop a very sensitive and willing horse that keeps their desire to do the work, that it's not a coercion thing—it's them looking forward to it . . . and they retain their self-respect and self-dignity." Overall, Rodolfo Lara Sr.'s statement that, "I'm not about imposing myself and forcing myself on a horse. I'm for acquiring their trust," is an appropriate summary of this section. This leads to the next facet: what this kind of contact can result in.

Tom Curtin and Ray. (PHOTO BY JULIANNA ÁVILA)

WHAT THIS CONTACT CAN LOOK, AND FEEL, LIKE

Pure touch gives access to information, a soft correlate to
what was once called the intellect. (Serres, 2016, p. 83)

There is intellectual work to be done in Vaquero horsemanship, but it is merged with physical and emotional work. Joe Wolter, who learned firsthand from Bill and Tom Dorrance as well as Ray Hunt, remembered

> that one of the reasons this [style of horsemanship] was so appealing to me was that it wasn't so much what they were doing—it's the feeling we had when we were around them and the horses. There was no drama. There was just joy. It was just joy. Sometimes things were hard, but they had a grin on their faces no matter what they were doing because I think they really liked it. They loved it probably.

A contemporary of Joe's is Bryan Neubert, who also worked closely with the Dorrances and Hunt. He recalled his impressions after seeing Tom work horses.

I said, you know, Ray Hunt told me, you just wait until you see Tom ride. You won't believe it. You know what? I've been riding with you for about a month, and to tell you the truth, you don't look any different than anybody else! And he laughed, but I said, your horses are nothing like anybody else's that I've seen. And he laughed again, and he says, you know why it is that way? I said, no. Because it's the little things that make the big difference, he said. It's so subtle that if you weren't practiced at seeing what you're looking at, you wouldn't even notice anything. It's not stirring up a bunch of dust and training like people think—the horse is learning these things and loving it. He's not there under a bunch of stress. It's probably differently subtle.

"Differently subtle" is an appropriate way to describe what modern VH looks like: There is still an exchange of communication and energy but not the comparatively "loud" cueing of some Western, or other horsemanship, traditions. When I observed both Tom Curtin and Jeff Derby riding after interviewing, I was struck by the quiet dialectic that occurred as well as a bond *not* contoured by force. Vaquero horsemanship does not automatically make an inherently dangerous activity less so, but dedicating years to establishing a relationship with a horse who is treated with fairness and respect can make riders who have had negative experiences feel, and be, safer. If you, and your horse, have suffered through contentious interactions, and have become tired of that (or hurt as a result of them), then why wouldn't you seek an alternative? Both horses and (some) humans seek peace.

One source of peace can be sharing ideas, or states of mind, with the horse. Linda Hoover portrayed this possibility as "[w]hen you understand each other so well the horse almost finishes your sentence." Emily Shields has been impressed with how, in VH, horses will "work with their people"; it has taught her "how to read them." For humans, this "reading" may require a different sort of learning than what we have been habituated to; Joe Wolter pointed out that "understanding how you could get your idea to become the horse's idea" can be "a whole different path than most people take. Most people go by steps and programs," and while we might "need that," we are also used to it since "that's how we're brought up in school. Our education system is set up that way." Several interviewees backed up the sentiment that in VH, even though there is, historically, a tack progression, the approach itself today is not comprised of a regimented set of steps or predetermined method. Instead, like the sociocultural school of literacy education, it varies according to the pairings of individual riders and horses.

WHAT IS REQUIRED OF HUMANS IN MODERN VAQUERO HORSEMANSHIP

A sociocultural approach to literacy education requires that the educator assumes responsibility for teaching in unique contexts that require flexibility and adjustment to diverse learners in real time. In modern Vaquero horsemanship, there are specific elements required of the human, and these are also connected by an acknowledgment of responsibility for our own role (which includes trying to understand the horse's point of view); VH texts support this. Tom Dorrance (2010) noted that, "When it comes to discussions about handling and riding difficult horses, I've noticed that people have a tendency to avoid taking responsibility for the horses' problems" (p. 10). Ed Connell (1952) reminded his readers, when dealing with a horse "with lots of life," that "it is up to the rider to see that this excess life is not misplaced" (p. 54). He also urged the rider to take responsibility when things do not go well: "Whenever he is doing nicely, and suddenly goes back in his work, the rider should never blame the horse; he should place the blame on himself, as he has overdone him. He should think back and try to find out just how it was done, then try to avoid doing it again" (p. 71). His direct and practical advice charges the rider with figuring out the cause of trouble that occurs, without falling into the easy trap of censuring the horse.

A more recent example of the human's responsibility can be found at the end of Buck Brannaman's (2012) *Groundwork* book; in it, he mentioned, when describing fence work, "your responsibility as [the horse's] teacher" (p. 90). Really, the whole volume is about that—the preparation that the human owes the horse without taking shortcuts that might cause confusion. In the "Changing Eyes" exercise, he highlighted that the "goal is to get him changing eyes from the ground first so he understands that when he's most vulnerable, you would not betray him" (p. 30). Brannaman advocated support and encouragement (and still does in his clinics): "Remember to pet him often so he doesn't get worried" (p. 18); "be considerate—he's just confused" (p. 21); "Keep offering this friendship and he will eventually take you up on it" (p. 26).

Because we have taken horses out of their natural environment, curbed their ability to roam (sometimes dramatically), and made them fit into *our* lifestyles, our responsibility has expanded. Greg Eliel reminded me that "horses never asked to be put in a pen ... when you start to increase their confinement, and you start putting them in stalls, you have to up your game. There's just no other way about it. If you're going to do that, you have an obligation." My impression is that those studying VH want their horses to have jobs, without question, but the designs of those jobs matter *and* whether they can be done without sacrificing the horse's welfare.

Bruce Sandifer believes that VH was "developed from the horse's standpoint because you can train a horse into anything but to have them just understand it right away without a lot of force being applied to them, without anything drastic happening" highlights the horse's well-being. Tom Curtin expanded upon this idea by sharing what he would like those who study with him to learn:

> The biggest thing that I'm trying to accomplish is for folks to understand that it's not about what we want our horses to do. It's what they need us to do to better educate

them to do what we would like them to because they want to—not because they
have to. That's my goal. And Ray [Hunt] helped me so much with that. It wasn't
about what we wanted. It was learning to better understand these animals and what
their needs from us are. They're easily taught. It's hard to change the human. We
get these preconceived ideas, or it's always the horse's fault—the human takes on
the blame and says, well, my feel's not the best. That's not what it's about. What it's
about is better understanding of what they need—being more aware of being aware.

For the human to try to be horse-centered is no small ask (or task), and may seem
impossible, except that we have accounts of those who have worked at exactly that.
Furthermore, Tom offered an example of horse-centeredness when we discussed the
idea of "untamable horses." His response to this was:

> I've had horses that I've had to really change what I was doing to be able to fit their
> needs more. They required a lot more attention. They required maybe a little differ-
> ent skill set. You take Buster [Welch] and Ray [Hunt], one thing they had in com-
> mon, very much so, was they were 100% positive about the horse. I've had some
> outstanding horses, and I've had some very, very interesting challenges... if you
> changed your train of thought, those horses weren't wild. They were just greatly mis-
> understood and extremely sensitive.

Being horse-centered can mean taking a concept like "untamable" or "wild" and turning
it around to understand that those concepts simply do not fit and should be replaced
by notions like sensitivity, which more accurately portray where the horse is coming
from and what they may need from us.

For Linda H., responsibility begins by asking:

> What are we willing to do for the horse? Because we invited him here, and it's our
> job to help that make sense—to help them become well-adjusted and to learn what
> I refer to as a functional braille alphabet—that they understand the individual aides,
> and then we put them together, and there are words and sentences and then a para-
> graph. Then we can have this story... when they misunderstand, it's our job to help
> them out, to stop and re-teach. If they get scared, it's to support. As a result of that
> the gifts, to me, are just huge. It's the essence of being human and having a connec-
> tion with another being—whether it's another human or another animal—to con-
> nect at that deep level. That gift is there, but it starts with us.

The connection, and the gift of it, can start by, in Joe Wolter's words, "look[ing] at the
horse through the horse's eyes—for everybody's sake." Looking through their eyes is

an imaginative act that might also require some research (e.g., Jones, 2020). Joe noticed that "if a horse has a pattern, usually you look at the person, she or he has a pattern—instead of trying to change the horse, they change their pattern and then see how the horse responds. That's getting the horse to be more of the teacher than us." Being humble enough to let the horse teach us is required in modern VH.

Furthermore, Joe Wolter and I discussed the need for humans to reset their minds to be able to recognize the incremental improvements that the horse might offer. Shelve your impatience and human-centered timelines, as Joe said, "for everybody's sake," and think about how you leave your horse *feeling*. Joe shared how he had learned to care about

> what's going on inside of horses—not what's going on outside of them, and that's what's important to the horse. I've experienced this so much. When I start thinking about the inside of him, and I'm not saying they don't get upset—that's life, but how it ends is what matters. When I was a kid, my dad had some good ideas. We had a rule in our family that you don't unsaddle until they're cooled off, and I thought about that a lot. It wasn't the cooling off—it was their insides that were settled. You can cool a horse off, but he's still troubled. That isn't going to do you a bit of good. But if he's settled inside when you put him away, that's what he's going to remember when you start again. So, that's what I'd like to get people to think about. Don't try to teach a horse something if he's upset. Just try to get him un-upset. Then you can try to teach him. It's like trying to reason with a crying baby. It's crazy, but we do it all the time to horses, and then people get upset.

This facet is clear: We have a responsibility to recognize that we have troubled a horse and to remedy it; this seems like common sense but, as Joe pointed out, we do not always think hard enough about how we treat horses and place unrealistic expectations on their powerful frames, taking for granted that they will bear them.

We might also question how we view the horse's general role in our world: Are they here just to be of use to us? Or does our responsibility include a more humane reciprocity? Jeff Derby explained his take on this idea:

> I dislike hearing in some cowboy cultures how a horse is just a tool. To me, that degrades us as cowboys. If he's just a tool, well, then we're just another tradesman.... There's more to it. There's more value to it—there's more that the horse is due. It's more that he's a partner and something that I need to be responsible for—not just keeping him alive so I can use him the next day as a tool, but his well-being—you could almost say his contentment—how he feels about things.

Cody Deering also mentioned this same distinction between those who view horses as a tool and those who see them as a partner; he feels that "If something is not working, the person must find a better way to communicate." When horses were used for every-day work and transportation (and this is the historical context in which VH was developed), it might have been easier to conceive of them as a mute, obedient tool, but modern iterations have brought new opportunities for horses and humans.

THE PRAGMATIC FACET

The next facet that I would like to explore is the pragmatic one and includes the utility of the physical work of modern VH as well as what it achieves in execution, including its philosophy. Mike Bridges defined modern VH as being

> about making a highly balanced horse who has the ability to really rebalance himself and can handle and do his work at speed. You try to do the work as slow and as methodical and correct as you can, but there's always times where you need explosive speed, and if you don't have high levels of balance, that doesn't happen very well.

While VH might be slow-craft horsemanship, there are times working livestock when speed is needed, as Mike pointed out, so it is also a highly athletic activity. It is this facet that was particularly attractive to Maggie: "What I liked about the vaquero tradition is that they brought those classical principles of the systematic advancement of the horse and his training and they said, we want him to be useful and be able to do a job and earn a wage. That really appealed to me." The idea that VH could be a marriage of classical training and demanding ranch work was mentioned by other interviewees as well, who saw it as a distinctive opportunity for the horse to do a job that matters outside of the ring, even if the rider is not earning a living this way.

Mentors' stockmanship backgrounds, not surprisingly, informed their definitions. Cody Deering characterized VH as "the art of working cattle in a graceful and sustainable way so as to also get your horse better." The last phrase, "get your horse better," has two meanings that both apply to this facet: to develop your horse's abilities and skills *and* to better understand your horse. Greg Eliel, who has a Montana ranching background, described his approach as being centered around "stewardship," and how they took care of "horses, cattle and our grass resources." The element of stewardship is one that has an historical counterpart, and although vaqueros would not have been landowners, they would have been charged with caring for horses and cattle ("Back in the hacienda, the vaqueros knew that he and his boss, the *hacendado*, did not hold the same social standing" [Figueredo, 2015, p. 86]). Otherwise, the definition of VH has shifted from applying primarily to those who worked livestock for a living to now include a whole class of recreational riders who own both horses and property.

That VH is now often passed on through clinics (a consumer-friendly "container" for horsemanship), is, undoubtedly, a transformation that educators/clinicians have mixed feelings about, although some clinics do include cattle work. Because many of those I interviewed started out as working cowboys, they surely always have the danger of the work in the backs of their minds. Bruce Sandifer described wanting a "workshop" (the term he prefers to "clinic") "to be as free as possible, but it also has to be disciplined because a lot of times there's not room for a lot of air in real cattle working because things happen quickly that can get you killed."

The pragmatics of modern VH include the additional challenge of working with participants who do not have an actual vaquero or cowboy background as well as with horses who may not have full-time jobs. Greg Eliel described it as having "to realize that there's an extra challenge to making a horse in a recreational capacity versus a work capacity. There are advantages to working on a ranch and making horses." With recreational horses, "you're talking about less hours, less miles, less intensity, softer consequences oftentimes." For him, this has led to a practical realization about riders:

> In spite of the fact that I talk about my primary focus as essentially stewardship of the horses, I think you have to be a good steward of the people and their relationships as well. And what you can't do is forget the days that you couldn't do this stuff because I certainly wasn't born with it. I'm certainly not one of the most naturally talented people you'll ever run across. I've just worked at it really hard, and I've learned how to become a teacher.

Modern VH is often highlighted with humility, as Greg's comments illustrate. Perhaps horses teach us humility that humans then extend not only to other horses, but to all beings they then encounter. I view the humility and empathy that so often came out in interviewees' narratives as a sort of pragmatism: Living the daily and demanding work of horsemanship has led to a realistic awareness of novices' motivations, which are often *not* rooted in the same work professionals do. Along those lines, I devote a whole chapter to the philosophy of modern VH that "equates to everything in life," including relationships with other people.

One last note about pragmatism: The fact that many practitioners come from ranching and/or working cattle backgrounds brings applied knowledge to their teaching. As Jeff Derby expressed, having "made your living doing this for a number of years" leads to "a better understanding of the functionality of this approach" and "an insight into what is needed and what the horsemanship has traditionally been after." He also noted that it leads to "a certain amount of pride," which is often expressed, I would argue, through loyalty to the tradition itself. Jeff also added that VH "has been about the functionality of getting the job done. Now, that's not all of it, and the more that goes with it, I would say, is, especially among the Californio-style vaqueros, that there is an aesthetic beauty to it. There is a culture where you're proud of your horses." That is where the art of Vaquero horsemanship comes in.

VAQUERO HORSEMANSHIP AS ART FORM

Vaqueros were men in love with their craft.
(Rojas, 2010, p. 263)

Bennett (1998) noted that working with livestock "is far more mundane than artistic, yet somehow, cowboys usually have higher ambitions. They are aware of higher possibilities" (and she then proceeded to quote Tom Dorrance and Ray Hunt; p. 103). These "higher possibilities" can include learning and honoring the artistic side of horsemanship, which, according to participants, certainly applies to VH. Linda H. described asking Tom Dorrance for advice: "If you were talking about a horse situation and you described it and asked, 'What would you do, Tom?' And he'd say, 'It all depends.' Like he needed to be there to see that horse.... That's what makes this an art more than it is a sport or just a certain doing-ness." There is much "doing-ness" in VH, but because it is artful, it is not standardized or predetermined.

Jeff Derby noted the "aesthetic beauty" of VH above, which applies to both the actual riding as well as the artisan gear. The combination of the two are the art of VH in action, which stands in comparison to other styles of horsemanship. Maggie explained why VH appeals to her: "There's so much out there that doesn't appeal to me. There's so much out there that offends me. There's so much out there that's so painful I can't watch it, and here are these guys riding, and it's so beautiful. It's so gorgeous." At its best, modern VH is poetic to watch, with its highly tuned sensitivity from both horse and rider and subsequent fluid and peaceful interchanges.

Bill Dorrance associated "feel" with "art," although he preferred the former term, at least in print (Dorrance & Desmond, 2007, p. 121). When discussing this facet, Greg Eliel echoed Dorrance's statement when he stated that "the feel is what makes it an art form," but "the human has an inclination to make it mechanical. So you have to fight your own human nature and you have to constantly strive to figure out what that feel is." Keep in mind that feel is not a once-and-for-all place that you arrive at, and some spend a lifetime pursuing it. As a follow-up to his comment, I asked Greg how the art of VH could be taught in a four-day clinic (his are four but many are three). He responded that, "You can't. Going back to the mechanics, what you can really do is give them a framework to be successful and then let them taste it.... And so it is absolutely an art form, and it is absolutely unteachable, but you can point people in the right direction and support them there." Perhaps this facet is the most resistant to the pushy influence of consumer culture; it is the least marketable because it might remain just a possibility, no matter how many clinics you attend.

Cody Deering also associated the art of VH with feel. He believes that feel does *not* include "a set-in-stone way to work with the horse." While in VH "there are principles to follow and specific gear to use, the well-being of the horse must come first." Just as "art can mean a lot of different things, and there are different kinds of art" so can there be various, valid ways to work with horses, selected "to fit the situation." The art form of VH therefore opens up *how* it is practiced; Cody equated it with being able to choose different paintbrushes, concluding that "what matters most is that you are open enough to follow your ideas, thoughts, emotions, and then place the brush to the canvas, having no doubts about your creative flow." That each horse is unique, and will need different methods, also adds to the fact that creativity is constantly required. Treating horsemanship as an art form, as Mike Bridges informed me, goes back at least as far as the Renaissance, "where everything that could be taken to an art form was," including riding. So, this facet of VH is a continuation, a sapphire (the second hardest stone in nature) from another era.

THE LAST FACET: VAQUERO HORSEMANSHIP IN THE SOUTHEAST

In this study, the last facet of modern Vaquero horsemanship concerns the territory where the first group of participants learned VH: the southeastern United States. As I have highlighted, VH was primarily an oral tradition with a limited number of printed texts about it—at least until technology came along. Now, knowledge about VH has been captured digitally and so is more easily disseminated across geographical borders, aided greatly by clinicians who have traveled to this area for decades and undoubtedly planted interest originally. Despite this, and digital documentation, VH is still not necessarily an easy thing to study in the other end of the country from where it was originally developed. Often, there are not close-by communities of practice, nor are there always frequent opportunities to work with likeminded others since a given clinician may only come through once a year. There is, however, a steady supply of both horses and cattle in this part of the country to learn VH with.

Both Tom Curtin and Jeff Derby mentioned southeastern beef production and that some use horses in this work; however, for those not working cattle, VH can be harder to source. As Emily S. stated, "You have to start changing the way you even think about your knowledge level because it's locally not very easy to find." Kathleen Kelley described it as "a little more stagnant out here, but it's growing." She also noted, "It didn't come from necessity as much on the East Coast" and contrasted being "born into the tradition" (or, at least, born adjacent to the tradition) with "seeking it out," as southeastern participants had. Amy Gaddis felt that VH in this area "is not well-known. Everyone I know has sort of stumbled upon it, especially in this area. Our ancestors didn't ride this way. We had nothing to do with it. So, it's like a secret club that you only become aware of if you're totally devoted to seeking out the softest horsemanship you can find." Tom Curtin's wife, Trina, who grew up in Florida and continued to live there as an adult, believes that it was "the art of Vaquero horsemanship that intrigued everybody about it, especially in the southeast"; she also thinks that those interested in it focused more on the evolution of the horsemanship rather than strict adherence to traditions, and that some of the harsher aspects would have not appealed to them (an example of this would be tying of the horse's head or leg that Ed Connell [1962] recommended). Those drawn to VH have to maintain a motivated interest to build knowledge over time, and while that may not be unique to the southeast, it certainly holds true there.

Melanie Smith Taylor (who wrote her own horsemanship book in 2015) and her late husband Lee Taylor were some of the first to sponsor Ray Hunt (and then Buck Brannaman) in the southeast (Tennessee) beginning when Lee invited Ray to conduct clinics in the early 1980s; she shared that her "interest was to spread this information to the hunter-jumper world." In the beginning, most attendees would travel from neighboring southern states, and she thought it "might be because some of the people teaching what they call 'Natural horsemanship' [were] not the real deal" and so that turned locals off from attending. Over time, even though "it's slow-going" because "you have to find people who are curious about developing their own horses," she has seen an increase in curiosity about VH.

Two bridle horses (Alicia Byberg-Landman and Buck Brannaman).
(PHOTO BY ALICIA BYBERG-LANDMAN)

THE GEAR OF VAQUERO HORSEMANSHIP

In the old days the vaquero took pride in his equipment and his saddle, bit and spurs gained merit with age. He believed that a mouthpiece could only be cured and tempered after years in a horse's mouth. He never failed to meet certain standards when selecting his gear. (Rojas, 2010, p. 213)

Traditionally, VH culminates in the creation of a bridle horse, who performs at a "re-fined" level and has earned elaborate and decorated tack through years of education. As Bruce Sandifer noted, it is critical to understand that VH "is a roping style" and so all of the gear "had a job." This tangible legacy of specific gear has influenced cow-boy gear more broadly: "The vaqueros of Mexico originally invented most modern 'cowboy' tools and techniques" (Bennett, 1998, p. 317; see also Pitt, 1966/1994, p. 291). Clayton et al. (2001) noted, "The unique skills, gear, tack, and character of the vaquero developed on the northern frontier of Mexico, its borderlands" (p. 2). In this section, I offer an introduction to the specific gear of VH, which was historically referred to as *"jáquima a freno"* (hackamore to bridle). In the box below, Tom Curtin narrated a summary of the tack involved in the refinement of a bridle horse; note that he is de-scribing the historically accurate progression, which did not include the now-popular snaffle bit. Interviewees reported that the snaffle bit was an import from the eastern United States and "the Anglo influence"; Bennett (1998) attributed the snaffle bit's popularity to Anglo-Americans being more interested in "practicality" and less will-ing to spend years developing a horse as well as a "move toward simpler designs which could be mass-produced" (p. 126). Historically, the gear also excludes the style of sad-dle we now associate with VH, the Wade saddle, which is a modern invention created by Cliff Wade and Tom Dorrance (for a description of vaquero saddles that preceded the Wade, see Rojas, 2010, p. 154).

Tack Involved in the Refinement of a Bridle Horse
by Tom Curtin

In traditional Vaquero horsemanship, you would start in a 7/8- or 1-inch braided rawhide hackamore (*jáquima*). (Remember that they were in the tallow and hide industry, so rawhide was what was available. The noseband itself is called the *bosal* and once attached to the headstall becomes the *hackamore*.) What you are doing while you are working in your hackamore process is building refinement. You are trying to keep scaling the bosal size down, so you would go from a 1-inch or a 7/8-inch bosal to a 5/8-inch as the horse continues his education. You keep graduating

Ray in the hackamore. (PHOTO BY JULIANNA ÁVILA)

him down until you get him down into a 1/2-inch bosal and then into a 3/8-inch. The 3/8-inch and 5/16 sizes are what you would use in the two-rein (when the horse is in both a hackamore and bridle bit). The hackamore is attached to horsehair reins, or *mecate*, which come in different sizes; you want to match this as closely as possible to the diameter of the bosal to keep things balanced.

How long each horse stays in each size of the bosal depends on the horse. Once I get my horse to where I can ride him anywhere that I need to off of my legs, seat, and feet, and I don't have to support him with my hands in his lateral movement or his vertical movement as much, then that is when I move onto the next piece of equipment.

Rawhide romal reins are used in the two-rein and bridle stages. One continuous rein is attached to a removable romal, which is a type of quirt. There are buttons that add weight and usually two buttons at the top—one you use to mark where you would hold your reins when you are riding him in a two-rein.

After graduating from the two-rein, the final stage would be the bridle (shank-type) bit alone, which are either leverage or signal bits. The signal bit is the more refined—once the horse learns how to carry himself in full collection without contact and with just a signal from the bit. How that bit is built, balanced, and placed in his mouth influences how he is going to carry his headset, which is very important for his performance. There are many different types of mouthpieces (for example, Salinas or frog mouthpieces, which are leverage bits or the Barqueño or full spoon spade, which are signal bits) and cheekpieces (for example, Nevada, Santa Susana, Las Cruces). Bits are often made of sweet iron steel with copper rollers and sterling embellishment. These different bits build a progression and refinement. You can have the control in a hackamore, so you don't need these bits for more control.

You are not even going to get to the first stage of the bridle bit until a horse is six because his mouth is not mature before that. One of the first things that I do when I start a horse in the bridle is feel and palpate the palette of the horse's mouth, and I also palpate the corners of the mouth. All of this—which equipment to use—needs to be understood through the conformation of your horses and his physical ability to carry the bridle.

I want people to understand that you do not just go and make a bridle horse quickly or easily. It takes a tremendous amount of time and experience with the steps before you understand what you are trying to achieve in your bridle.

For the uninitiated, bridle bits look medieval—like heavy metal torture devices (and if you are tempted to Google images of vaquero bridle bits, then you will likely share this impression). However, the critical thing to realize is that "[l]ight hands when handling the reins of a finished bridal horse is what the California vaquero is all about" (Morris, 2014, p. 68). Bruce Sandifer described the bridle as "a sophisticated system of balance" where "every piece of equipment has a purpose, and they would be adjusted for the horses" and centered around "light contact that was created through the hands of an expert rider." He pointed out, "A horse can totally control a spade bit. It's made to protect the horse." Despite the appearance of some of the gear, "these are the least intimidating tools because we're trying to push the energy to a spot, and if they're intimidated in that spot, it's hard to push energy to something they're scared of. So, every piece of equipment in this thing, from the hackamore on, is not scary." Furthermore, Bruce recounted how studying the mechanics of the gear led him to reflect upon his position as a rider and to place the gear in a modern context:

To figure it (VH) out, I'd just have to see how everything worked. How does the bit work? How does the hackamore work? Physically, mechanically—what are the parameters of it? It can work in this much of a turn, or this much of a bend, or this much application of pressure, and anything beyond that, it's outside of its working parameters. Then, from that, especially the spade bit, I changed everything I did, and it started with my seat and my body because that is the main tool—the main influence we have on a horse is how our body moves on them.... This system is really based upon control of the horse's body, but not putting it in a situation that is outside of its working parameters, too. This is more like classical dressage in that sense in that it uses very good biomechanics, where the horse's feet can move properly, for it not to create braces or counterbalances. What happens is, when we're off balance, the horse has to create a counterbalance.... I change my seat based on the way a spade bit balances. It returns to neutral every time you engage it; it has a very solid neutral system. There was an evolution of balance in the California system.

I include this excerpt because it not only provides insight into what the gear offers the horse, but it also illustrates the relationship between gear and the rider's position, and this may be hard to detect from observation alone. Fred Allen summarized it as, "When it comes to the bridle part of the horsemanship, it's making it look like, whatever you're doing, you're not really doing anything." He also recounted that Ray Hunt was asked, "If you claim that this can be done with a hay string, why in God's name would you put something like that in his mouth? And Ray's answer was, personal preference and tradition." The tradition includes learning to "read" when a horse is ready to progress to the next stage and so amounts to a different sort of literacy that takes years to cultivate. This literacy also extends to, as Rodolfo Lara Sr. specified, "understanding the tools" rather than automatically starting with one because you think you are supposed to. In this volume, there are some who are passionately dedicated to the bridle horse progression, and their voices are included alongside those who may "only" ride in a traditional hackamore (or a nontraditional snaffle) but are nonetheless committed to the philosophy.

THE ROMANTICISM OF VAQUERO HORSEMANSHIP

I am particularly interested in the bridle horses of California. Theirs is an ancient art conveyed from the time of Spanish rule and there is a solemn romance about these horses with their swan necks, their Santa Barbara Spanish bridles, their lightning quickness, and the steady whir of the rollers in their bits. (McGuane, 2013, p. 7)

Historical Vaquero horsemanship has metamorphosized while still retaining a tint of romanticism that has likely led to, as one interviewee mentioned, some "embellishment," or, as Bill Reynolds called it, an "amplification of facts." Filtering the history of California and the American West, especially its ranching past, through romanticism has been documented elsewhere (Bingmann, 2015; Clayton et al., 2001; Figueredo, 2015; Gutiérrez, 1998; Monroy, 1990; Prezelski, 2015; Sánchez, 1995). Monroy (1990) characterized it as "*California Pastoral*, or the fanciful re-creation of Spanish and Mexican Californian history" (p. 234). In an elaboration, Sánchez (1995) argued that "The often-repeated description of Spanish/Mexican California as a 'pastoral' golden period found in several historical accounts is of course a romantic, idealized, and highly complex construction of the conquered Californios that all but begs for disarticulation" (p. 165). This disarticulation is outside of the scope of my study, but I do want to acknowledge that even though my focus is to describe modern VH, I am aware that the romanticism still attached to Vaquero horsemanship has an uglier historical side of racism, prejudice, and inequality. By discussing this romanticism, I do not wish to present it as able to exist apart from that history, especially the "terrific social distinction" of historical California between "those who owned and did not own land" (Monroy, 1990, p. 162), of which vaqueros would have been the latter.

One danger to romanticism, even in horsemanship, is that it can tempt us to idealize the past and skip over injustice to focus on the prettier—and often more marketable—parts. If we preserve the romanticism, then we must also preserve knowledge of injustices done; picking and choosing resembles history-shopping and being a consumer rather than a critical thinker. Romanticism can eclipse *actual* fact and persuade us that maintaining a romantic tone is more important than learning the *actual* history.

We have inherited some romanticism from the author of one of VH's primary texts. Rojas (2010) defended his tone: "Those who read these pages may ask why the author always speaks tenderly of the men, horses and places of whom and of which he writes. He can answer that by simply stating that every one of the vaqueros and buckaroos with whom he worked was a better man than he was" (p. vii). His recounting is rooted in sentimentality and admiration (as is Morris' [2014]), but it is framed with humility, and because of that, it is hard to find fault with his tone. Still, we should remember that most of the primary texts about this style of horsemanship lamented what they saw as its decline. Romanticism has jobs, and in this case, one of them was to cast VH into an eye-catching light as that light faded (which is not to take away from the genuine emotion these writers felt). Given that VH has had to be reinvented to survive, we might, in our time, be tempted to romanticize it almost beyond recognition, and surely Western horsemanship more broadly is tied to a larger sentimentality that we have about the settling of the American West—all the more reason to take our romanticism with a grain of salt.

When Tom Curtin and I discussed romanticism in VH, he shared with me that he thinks that it has to be taken in context: If it was part of "the culture and the place that this style of horsemanship came from," and tied to "the ability to bring out the highest quality" in horses, then we should not try to extract it since it is connected to the skill and achievement of historical vaqueros. Rodolfo Lara Sr. reminded me that Mexican horse culture also has a healthy dose of romanticism, and he "think[s] there is romanticism in every horsemanship in the world," even in literature: "Don Quixote is riding a skinny horse, and Sancho Panza is riding that other one, and tell me they were not proud of their horses." He feels that if romanticism helps "you to feel proud on your horse" and is used "to promote horsemanship and get people onboard for the horse, have at it." Fair enough.

As Tom Curtin also pointed out, there is a mystique to VH that appeals to us in our heavily mechanized and modernized world. VH's gear (save the saddles) comes to us from a time long ago when we can imagine life with horses was simpler; this is tied to a broader cultural romanticism about horses, who "symbolized American nostalgia for a rural past before cars, telephones, and electricity" (Tompkins, 1992, as cited in Bingmann, 2015, p. 99). Imagine how that might be amplified now given our dance with constantly advancing technology.

CONCLUSION

In this chapter, I have attempted to give readers the background knowledge needed to understand this volume in context. After providing a brief sketch of historical Vaquero horsemanship, I utilized the metaphor of a faceted Montana sapphire to share the collection of characteristics that make up modern VH; I also depict VH as slow-craft horsemanship, in contrast with our immediate-gratification society. VH has taken a social turn as a geographically bound, often guarded, form of horsemanship to one that has been disseminated and transformed by modern practitioners (who would not all call themselves vaqueros). Perhaps inevitably, as horses have become more recreational in our world, so has Vaquero horsemanship, although some practitioners are still fiercely loyal to the traditions of it, including the gear. So, the renaissance (as one interviewee described it) of interest in this style means that modern VH has unfurled beyond its original territory—and has been altered as a result.

Tom Curtin and Mike, one of his bridle horses.
(PHOTO BY JULIANNA ÁVILA)

INTERLUDE 1

Joe Wolter and Curly

THERE WAS A HORSE I HAD IN NEVADA THAT WAS THE FIRST HORSE THAT Ray Hunt ever coached me on. Ray was the cow boss on this ranch I was at, and that horse made such a change in such a short period of time that I couldn't believe it. I knew Ray was a good hand. I saw the look on his horses' faces versus most other peoples', and there was definitely a difference. But that day that he helped me with that one horse, I think that was a turning point in my life right there.

Now, I had quite a few horses before that set me up for him. My dad used to rope years ago. When we were little, when he quit roping—he used to team rope some—I rode his rope horse. Anywhere you went, this sucker, he would just jig and jog, and go sideways. Now, in hindsight, when my dad rode him, he would just put his head down and walk. But when any of us kids rode him, and it was just jigging, and he looked like those horses going to the starting gate at the Kentucky Derby—just sideways like that. He couldn't tell me what he was doing different, and I didn't know what to do. All I knew was that it wasn't fun. Then later on, I rode other horses that were troubled, and they didn't know they could walk with a rider.

That one particular day, I had a horse like that. My friend Bryan Neubert was there, and I asked him what he thought. He said, "Well, we're going to meet Ray down at this place in a little while with his cattle, and after we eat lunch, we're going to trail these cattle out of there. Why don't you ask Ray what he would do?" And that was another thing that was different in those times—you could ask an older guy something on those ranches, and I think they didn't know what to say. Their saying was, "Just pay attention. Watch what we do." Because I don't think they had the words; people weren't used to talking about that stuff or any kind of problem. It was just, "Keep your eyes open and your mouth shut." It wasn't easy to ask a question—not for a guy like me either.

I told him, "Ray, this horse, I can't get this horse to walk." I mean, we've gone probably 10 miles that morning, and then we had another five to trail these cows. He said, "I'll tell you what. When we leave with these cows, we're going down this gravel road. You make sure you're in the drag. I'm coming with a pickup and I'll watch you." Okay, good. So, sure enough, these cows are lined out—300 or 400 cows, and there was a whole crew of guys there. I made sure I was in the drag. Ray called me over—and the horse was jigging and jogging—and he said, "Okay, I want you to turn the horse loose." "What do you mean turn him loose?" I said. "Give him slack. Give him slack on the reins. And when he breaks into a trot, just take one rein and just hold him until he stops. Just before he stops, turn him loose," he said. "Okay—when he breaks into a trot. I got it." So, I turned the horse loose, and he went about three strides, and then he's off to the races. So, I double him and turn him around, round, round, and pretty soon, he stopped, and I turned him loose. We went a little farther, maybe three steps, and then he broke into a trot, and I double him the other way around. Pretty soon, he'd stopped. I turned him loose. Then Ray hollered at me, "Don't doubt him!" Those were his words. "Don't doubt him!" I thought, "Okay. All right." When I pitched the slack to him, I pitched it all to him. He went about three strides, and I reached for one rein and went the other way. Pretty soon, he went four strides before he broke into a trot. Then he went six strides before he broke into a trot. Then he went ten strides before he broke into a trot. By the time we got those cattle at our destination, Ray said, "Put the reins over the saddle horn!" I just draped the reins like this, and this horse was just walking. I mean, it was a shocking turn of events for me. I was sold. I thought, I want what this guy's got.

CHAPTER 2

Learning Vaquero Horsemanship: Motivations, Desire Lines, and Turning Points

ACH PARTICIPANT TRAVELED THEIR OWN TRAIL IN LEARNING VAQUERO horsemanship as they taught themselves (using books, videos, and the Internet), learned from other humans (in clinics and through in-person lessons), and, of course, from—and with—horses. Throughout our interviews, they shared learning experiences that were pivotal and significant, which are the focus of this chapter. In particular, I concentrate on what motivated them to learn VH, the unique routes, or desire lines, they created along the way, as well as positive and negative learning turning points. Learning horsemanship inhabits a unique place in adult learning because the horse is an assessor without equal—by that I mean a horse can rapidly, usually instantly, judge how effective a particular approach or method is, providing immediate feedback. To begin, I explain what motivated southeastern participants to seek out an initially distant form of horsemanship.

MOTIVATION TO LEARN VAQUERO HORSEMANSHIP IN THE SOUTHEASTERN UNITED STATES

What might motivate a horseperson to study a form of horsemanship that originated on the other side of the United States and only infrequently traveled to the southeast? In this section, I share participants' thoughts about what motivated them to learn VH, as well as what they perceived to be its ultimate goals (the more philosophical aspects of their motivations are discussed in chapter five). In this first part, I share some thoughts from participants who had found motivation through reading about Vaquero horsemanship.

Reading as Early Motivation

Even though VH has to be learned with a horse in hand, motivation to learn it could come from the quiet pages of a book or magazine. Five participants reported that they had first become interested in VH after reading about it. For one interviewee, reading was a substitute for taking much more expensive riding lessons: "I bought every book I could get my hands on, and I couldn't really afford to take lessons for a long time." Reading provided access to VH when otherwise she would not have had it. Melanie Allen reported that because she had already done some reading about this style of horsemanship before learning to ride, she "knew that there was a way of working with a horse's mind." Like Melanie, Fred A. also realized, through reading, that there might be a better way than the "just a good ol' boy, redneck way of beating your horse into submission" that he "couldn't stand." When he then went to see a local practitioner of VH at a clinic, he proceeded to ask him questions about his approach, and this practitioner remarked, "I knew you had known something, did something, had seen it, done it, or read it ... you had legitimate questions and comments." As I discuss in chapter seven, reading about horsemanship has its obvious limits but still served as early motivation for some interviewees.

Literacy could also lay a foundation for future action, as Fred A. described it: "I would read about this, and I couldn't get it from here to there. I didn't know how. I had knowledge in my head, but I didn't know what to do with it." For him, it took crossing paths with a practitioner, mentioned above, who then motivated him to begin learning how to apply it. Alex was already working with horses when he read about it, and this was enough for him to change his approach:

> I read an article about Ray [Hunt]. It may have been in *Western Horseman*, and it was so different I thought. They were talking about the results, and that will kind of light a fire in you—and I'm riding colts. I found out Ray had his book, and I read it and started trying things on my own. Well, everything I tried worked so much better than what I'd been doing that it really, really, really helped.

Once Fred A. and Alex had this knowledge-in-mind, they then pursued knowledge-in-action, either firsthand or by observing others on a similar path. One theme from this subset of the interviews is that participants were influenced by what they read and their horsemanship underwent significant change as a result; they did not simply read and subsequently forget about it as we frequently do when we read for school. This type of reading had a three-dimensional purpose, lifted off the page by live learning with horses.

Motivation Meets Economics

Money is not a major motivation to learn VH in the southeastern United States (or likely anywhere in the world, for that matter). As Jeff Derby described it, "Some of us have found ways to make a living at it. I think it can be beneficial to raising cattle, to raising horses, to stewarding your land. There are versions of it that can be financially beneficial. But it's not plain and simple along those lines, and it's not an easy way to make a buck. It's quite the opposite." The gear, lessons, and clinics are costly, and the main way that expense might be offset (unless you have a separate career) would be to offer training and lessons yourself. Therein lies a hitch because even though practitioners are spread out geographically in the southeast, the teaching market, which includes well-known clinicians who travel through on a circuit, can still be competitive. Teaching a less well-known form of horsemanship does have the advantage of appealing to those who wish to be unique, but that means educators still must vie for business within what may be a relatively small pool—and that pool would need to be patient with the process that is VH education.

Across horsemanship disciplines, one negative consequence of training as a consumer transaction is the owner wanting fast results regardless of what is best for the horse. This time factor makes VH less consumer-friendly, as it is not the method to study if you want your horse to be "trained" in thirty days. Jeff Derby extended his thoughts above by adding that VH, which can "make huge changes in a short amount of time," is still "not about quick fixes or about how fast you can get something done. This is about the sustainability of how well it works both for you and for the horse over the horse's lifetime, over a career." Often, horse owners expect—and want—to see results on human timelines, governed by, in their view, getting their money's worth. Learning VH, with its horse-centered timelines, involves economic risk—to go against what the paying public demands. This is putting what you believe are the horses' best interests above your own economic gain (as it might well cost you business). Although, as Marilyn Obie remarked, "This is a faster approach to get a soft, trusting, willing horse . . . and I think the foundation of this is teaching the horse to seek peace." So "fast" is a relative term in VH—and peace, which might take more time to achieve, is often more important to practitioners than economic gain is.

When we talk about the time that VH can take, that often refers to the creation of a bridle horse, which I discussed in chapter one; however, not all pursue this goal, or they do so for themselves but not for clients' horses who will return to owners not prepared to ride a bridle horse. Instead, some choose to practice VH with a snaffle bit (or stop in the progression with a hackamore). For Maggie, this is simply a more relevant goal for her and those she teaches:

What I really wanted to do was to focus on snaffle bit horses because I'm realistic about how far I'm going to get in this progression of the snaffle to the hackamore to the bridle horse. I don't have delusions of grandeur that way. I thought a lot of horses you get from the general public, the horse is never really going to be good in a snaffle because they've already ruined him. They've ruined his mouth. They've ruined his mind through his mouth.

What she spoke about is the reality of working with horses who have already been "trained" wherein some "ruin" has occurred (as someone who has owned horses in this category, I can relate to this, having tried to remediate the effects of it). Maggie has focused her efforts on creating her own snaffle bit horses from youngsters and not having to do this remediation, so she has amended the traditional trajectory of VH, and the accompanying motivation, to suit her own needs. She was not alone in that amendment as riding in a snaffle bit is often more practical when teaching the public and training horses they will then ride. Additionally, some choose to use a snaffle bit even when they are creating bridle horses, and they know this was not how historical vaqueros did it, but believe it is nonetheless a beneficial tool. As Tom Curtin noted, the snaffle bit is particularly effective at "providing the most lateral support." Rodolfo Lara Sr. agreed with this and said, "I say use the tool that helps you communicate better with your horse, and then grow from that." Selecting what they think is the best tool, which changes according to what each horse, rider, and situation requires, provides a segue into the next section.

"A Better Way"

I think VH is made for people who will not put their horse second. They won't put the relationship with their horse second to win a ribbon. It really has to be about having something to offer him that he can understand. That takes a lot of time. You just have to be dedicated to being fair. I think when you're that dedicated, you don't accept anything less. . . . You have to really want an equal partnership to stumble upon this Vaquero horsemanship. . . . This horsemanship is special. I want people to use these methods, and I want them to be just as common as all the other less humane methods. I want those to be extinct. I don't want to see chains and whips and using things like sedatives and tie downs and side reins. Those don't have to exist anymore. There's another way. (Amy Gaddis)

What devotees of Vaquero horsemanship might sacrifice financially they gain back in "passion" (this is a term used in a variety of responses about the appeal of VH). Some participants had passionate views about VH being, in Alicia Byberg-Landman's words, "a better way" to work with horses; as Amy Gaddis's quote illustrates, they felt strongly that it could exist as a fairer alternative to the other disciplines that they had previously observed and worked in. Admittedly, many forms of horsemanship can be gentle depending upon the hands and aids of the human using it, but the point for participants is that VH is *comparatively* kinder to horses. Even though modern VH might be milder than the historic version (and, again, it is difficult to know this definitively), current practitioners understand it to be gentle, and so they practice it as such. Furthermore, passion is strong enough to fuel "the hustle" that Marilyn O. mentioned when describing adopting an "attitude of just like, there is no other option—not having a plan B. This is what's going to be in my life."

This same passion energized, for some, a desire to learn the practice of VH in order to preserve it; they noted that they were afraid that VH, "such an honorable tradition for the horse and for the person" might be "dying" (Elijah). Linda H. elaborated on why this would be negative—not as much for the human as for the horse:

> You want to see [Vaquero horsemanship] kept alive because the horse will suffer when it dies out—when it is no longer a benchmark of what's fitting to the horse, not what's of interest to the human. That's always the struggle—of what's important to the horse and what's of interest to the human. The two aren't always hand in hand.

Part of the appeal of VH to participants was, and is, feeling like they had found a form of horsemanship where the two could be hand in hand, and it is fair to say that if there is conflict between what is important to the horse and of interest to the human, the latter usually wins out. Another aspect that marks VH as "a better way" is that it is perceived to be a safer approach to working with horses, aided by the fact that, as I noted in chapter one, it is also relatively slow-craft horsemanship. Working with horses has risk enough, but if pressure and stress are added in, then that risk only multiplies. Emily S. noted that for some of her students, a willingness to learn VH was "usually from a series of incidents, such as falling off when you're middle-aged, that gets people interested." When asked about the appeal of learning VH, Amy Skinner said, "I think people get excited by the fact that they don't have to fight with their horses . . . they start to think they can teach their horse to do something without being upset or scared, and I think a lot of people like the safety aspect of it." Likewise, Alicia B. believes that

> most of the people that seek this way of riding have done so many other ways of riding that didn't feel good or they got hurt . . . their confidence is completely shot and they're like, there's got to be a better way . . . so, I think a lot of the people that seek it out, it's because they are so interested in the art and the craft of making a wonderful, safe horse.

Seeking safety after trouble applies to both horse and human, but Joe Wolter made the point that horses might not need as much as people do before looking for a safer way:

> It seems like people have to go through so much first to find this. Thinking about my students, it seems like I have more success with people if they've already had a little bit of trouble, and so, then they're hunting this—they're searching for it. . . . Now, horses don't need as much trouble as people need to change because I think they're searching all of the time.

Hunting for "a better way" motivated those learning with Joe and the other mentors in this study, and many participants came to VH after having trouble themselves. Maybe we would be wise to let the horse also teach us how *not* to need so much difficulty before changing course.

Linda H. remarked that VH is attractive "if for no other reason than riders are going to be safer because the horse is less troubled." She added, "Then you have the intimacy that comes from connecting with an animal when it feels understood. It's like a drug." Having a personal relationship with your horse lessens the likelihood that you will place unnecessary pressure on them; the pressure you apply becomes the pressure they feel, which then becomes the pressure you feel.

Some interviewees had migrated over to VH after showing horses in other disciplines, where the agenda can be centered around competition and "accomplishment" and "people showing in spite of their horse" (Amy S.). Maggie contrasted VH with what she had practiced as part of the culture of competition: "I had been used to being able to fight with a horse and win—intimidate, dominate, and all those kind of tactics that we did with the show horses because you're not really concerned about his mind. You're just concerned about getting his body going the right way so he can win because that's how you get paid." She also reported studying VH despite the lack of money in it, so this fits with her move away from the emphasis on "get[ting] paid" that she described above. Alicia B. outlined a similar dissatisfaction with competition-centered approaches:

> I love dressage, but I also don't want to be labeled a dressage rider because I feel like there's more dressage riders out there that I don't enjoy watching because it's way too pressured, and you can tell the horse doesn't have joy in it anymore . . . and I want it to be more about an easy relationship where I'm not a trainer, where I used to—that's all I wanted to be was a trainer, and now I think horses don't really like that. They want you to have relationships with them, and they want you to understand them, but they don't want to be forced into anything, and old training techniques—that's how it was. You just drilled on them.

Her comments, and her shift from training to relationship, reflected the reality that many participants work and ride at the edges of several disciplines, most often dressage and VH (although they were not overly concerned with labeling their horsemanship). They are committed to "a better way," and for those in this study, that includes VH, or the elements of it that they choose to learn.

Emily S. embedded her critique of competition into her thoughts on the overall appeal of VH:

> I think for a long time, really high-quality horsemanship's been around, but that is not what you see in most of the show ring stuff. You see the horses that are stuffed into their frames, and forced, and unless you're real educated, you can't see the expression difference—the confidence of a horse that truly knows what their job is because somebody's taken the time. That's why I'm so dedicated to Vaquero horsemanship as a style because you don't go, oh, I'm going to make a vaquero horse to show. You say, it's an art. It's a true art form.

Participants like Emily S. had chosen this "slower" art form, with its inherent need for patience, over the rushed and unfair treatment of horses that they had seen in other disciplines; their participation in VH was itself a rebellious act against the "forcing" they had seen.

TEACHING THIS BETTER WAY

Part of learning this better way was the wish "to break it down for the human" (Amy S.); Daniel described it as "a big piece of the motivation behind [learning] it." Once they knew about it, they wanted to spread this knowledge for the sake of horses and humans although, as Alex said, "the really hard part [of VH] is trying to communicate it to other people." Here again, passion comes in handy. Bryan Neubert has spent his life helping riders search for a connection with their horses: "I like to help people that are interested and want help, and that's fun because a lot of the things that I have I wouldn't have if people hadn't made a passion out of my progress. And I've got a passion for helping people that are interested as well." He has helped to create the next generation of (passionate) seekers. The way Linda H. described teaching VH captured the ambitious nature of this goal. She stated that "I want to be that individual to my horses and the people that I work with where I can help them understand more and give them that taste of what I saw Buck [Brannaman] offer me back in 1991, where I said, wow, it's magical."

Even though it might be (or at least seem) magical, this better way is a practical sort of magic that comes about, for example, by teaching horsemanship lessons to children, which several participants did. Natalie wanted her students to be able to work with horses "and do it properly and respectfully and be respected." Her fear was that "in the future horses might not be a huge thing" due to the expense and availability of acre-age; she sees horses as "very important to our community" and wants "to keep them [around] for as long as possible." Working with children, who are particularly recep-tive to a unique form of horsemanship, was seen by some participants as a key way to recruit others to what they feel is a pragmatically magical horsemanship.

To conclude this section, once participants started learning VH, the challenge of this better way motivated them to keep improving. Tony stated that "The ultimate goal [of VH] would be to have a horse that would have no weak links no matter what I would ask of him. It may be like striving for perfection. We may never reach it, but why settle for anything less?" Emily S. also mentioned that she appreciated, along with "the quality and the history" of VH, that she had "to work at" learning it. Reed E. remem-bered learning about the pedigree of a horse he owned early on and finding out that due to his bloodlines, he "could be tough to ride" so he thought, "I need to get better at what I'm doing here to have a hope of having this thing work. So that's what got my ball kicked into motion, rolling to really try to pursue improving my horsemanship skills." Whether it was an internal motivation to learn, like Tony's and Emily S.'s, or a specific horse, as in Reed E.'s case, the result was similar: They wanted to find a better, if tougher, way.

THE EXPERIENCE OF LEARNING VAQUERO HORSEMANSHIP

In this section, I focus on participants' explanations of their experiences learning Va-quero horsemanship. In *Beyond Learning by Doing* (2012), Roberts cited Martin Jays's definition of experience, which is also relevant here:

> In it [*Songs of Experience*], he [Jay] explains how "the English word is understood to be derived most directly from the Latin *experientia*, which denoted 'trial, proof, or experiment' (2005, p. 10). Curiously, he goes on to note how the verb 'to try' in Italian (*expereri*) shares a root with the word for 'peril' or 'danger' (*periculum*) which suggests a 'covert association between experience and peril (and that expe-rience comes) from having survived risk and learned something from the encoun-ter.'" (p. 13)

These origins of the word "experience" hold an unmistakable overlap with the practice of horsemanship: With its inherent danger, and the experiential nature of learning a style like VH, it is often about "having survived risk and learn[ing] something from the encounter." Earlier in this chapter, I discussed how trying to make horsemanship safer was one motivation for learning VH, and I am reminded of someone who sustained a concussion after her horse broke out of his crossties and knocked her down; even *standing* alongside horses can be risky. That risk multiplies dramatically once you climb onto a horse's back; educating and riding horses brings a wide world of possible peril, as those who work with them well know.

Roberts (2012) also highlighted, in his discussion of pragmatism, that "experience, as constructed in pragmatist theory, can be framed as decidedly *social* and *transactional* in orientation" (p. 48; italics in original); correspondingly, Dewey (1938) stated that "all human experience is ultimately social" (p. 38). These two statements correspond well to Lave and Wenger's (1991) contextualization of situated learning "in the trajectories of participation in which it takes on meaning. These trajectories must themselves be situated in the social world" (p. 121). Learning VH involves social experiences between humans, but, even more significantly, includes horses as social beings and equal partners in the process.

Self-Study and Desire Lines in Learning Vaquero Horsemanship

I begin this section with an obvious point: Self-study and individual initiative played crucial parts in southeastern participants' learning experiences. Since they often learned with little to no nearby community, this was a practical option, and they seemed to accept it as a matter of course. Simply put, if they wanted to learn about VH, they had to walk their own roads, accompanied by their horses. "Learning by doing" and "hands on" were phrases that several of them employed to describe these experiences.

A helpful metaphor to explain the significance of this section is that of desire lines—one I have used before (Ávila, 2008; 2015). In 2008, I utilized the Wikipedia definition (which gets hassled as an academic source but is nonetheless useful [Jenkins et al., 2015]): A *desire line*, or *desire path*, "usually represents the shortest or most easily navigated route between an origin and destination." Desire lines, as I wrote previously, are about arriving in your own time and on your own terms; they might well be, for those traveling them, the shortest routes, even if that is not obvious to outside observers. A more recent, detailed definition comes from an article in *The New Yorker* (Moor, 2017):

> Desire lines, also known as cow paths, pirate paths, social trails, *kemonomichi* (beast trails), *chemins de l'âne* (donkey paths), and *Olifantenpad* (elephant trails), can be found all over the city and all over the world, scarring pristine lawns and worming through forest undergrowth. They appear anywhere people want to walk, where no formal paths have been provided. (p. 2)

Additionally, "they also fascinate scholars, inspire artists, and enchant poets" (p. 2). The other labels for desire lines, many of them animal-based, lend an informal and common-place connotation to the concept, akin to the vernacular literacies I discuss elsewhere in this volume. Having the freedom to create a desire line can speed up the pace of learning, and, perhaps most importantly, remove obstacles that might slow that learning down.

While not a particularly complex metaphor, desire lines share conceptual ground with Dewey's (1938) statement about implementing change in education: "After the artificial and complex is once institutionally established and ingrained in custom and routine, it is easier to walk in the paths that have been beaten than it is, after taking a new point of view, to work out what is practically involved in a new point of view" (p. 30). Participants did not learn VH from close-by customs and routines so they had the benefit of choosing "a new point of view" from which to study it. They did, however, all have years of formal schooling under their belts, and many had learned other kinds of horsemanship so studying VH necessitated a new point of view (and desire line). New points of view, and new desire lines, require work, but *all* thoughtful horsemanship is work, and so it is just a question of degree.

A desire line can be a somewhat isolated place since it may lack others learning along with you. Jeff Derby talked about "an advantage and a disadvantage of being self-taught for a while. The advantage was I was an open slate. I didn't have a lot of pre-conceived ideas, and I think that's important. The disadvantage is I didn't have access to much knowledge. It was all trial and error." Participants who started out with self-study, which was a majority, needed to be comfortable with trial and error and with feedback from horses rather than humans; this was sturdy preparation for their future lives in horsemanship since that experimental attitude would serve them well. Those learning VH in the southeast would continue to study on their own as they progressed, even if their desire lines included human company at times.

Desire lines might contain early self-study (including the reading I highlighted at the beginning of this chapter) and can also be pathways where educators had to recon-cile the conflicting views of horsemanship that they experienced. Alicia B. described being in her "own little bubble" at her first professional barn and then realizing, after branching out, that her reality with horses was not necessarily a general one:

> Then you go to other boarding facilities, and there's all these different ways. People haven't been exposed to what feels good to a horse, and you see all this other stuff, and it's like, whoa, I had no idea that there was that much combative nature between human and horse. That was mind-blowing to me. But that's why today I look at it and if somebody can't get a tube of Bute in their horse's mouth, why wouldn't they research ways to do it better, to make it where you're not having to twitch the horse and turn it into a big fight? And it still goes on all the time.

Alicia's home barn was where she had started to learn about VH, since her boss there had recruited Buck Brannaman to give a clinic; Alicia would subsequently ride in his clinics for many years and create her own bridle horses. What she experienced early on was then tested by seeing so "much combative nature between human and horse," but this solidified her commitment to VH—and caused her to wonder why others were *not* taking initiative to learn more peaceful alternatives. She feels like it is part of her "job to research horsemanship and be skeptical and to really find what works and what doesn't." Learning VH might be a slow process, but it is an active one.

Ideally, self-study would result in an experience that matches Dewey's (1938) description of a valuable one: "If an experience arouses curiosity, strengthens initiative, and sets up desire and purposes that are sufficiently intense to carry a person over dead places in the future, continuity works in a very different way. Every experience is a moving force" (p. 38). Even though Dewey had humans in mind, it is reasonable to state that participants wanted their horses to be curious, to have initiative and a desire to continue learning, and to be part of the moving force of the process of learning VH. They wanted willing cooperation, present and future, from their horses so that they could continue to progress in their learning. Having educational experiences form a continuum, a moving force that gains its own momentum, is perhaps the most desirable outcome of working with horses. Successful education cannot consist of fragmented or disconnected sessions with horses as having to start over each time you approach them will get you nowhere.

Desire Lines and Observation

The company of horses aside, participants generally did not move along desire lines in social vacuums, even if those lines were sometimes lonely; instead, there was consistent observation of mentors and peers. Observation provided motivation to continue on, moments of realization, and just plain idea-giving. Being able to watch widens the learning opportunities as you can study, and therefore learn, every time you are in the company of another horseperson, even if they know less than you do. Observation was a significant learning method for those who considered themselves visual learners, as Natalie described herself; she contrasted reading about horsemanship and being able to "understand a little bit" from it but needing to observe it in real time to be able to fully experience it.

Linda H. spoke about observation in the most detail. She described it as the primary way she had learned VH over the years. Like Natalie, she needed the visual component since "what one word might mean to me, it's going to have a different meaning to you. If we can apply that to something visually, we can at least for a moment agree, that word meant that." Also, her observational method required learning what to pay attention to "because there's not anybody pointing out what you should be looking at." You must be comfortable with a lot of unguided looking around, sort of like wandering around your desire line, until your gaze becomes more educated, as Linda H.'s did. Johnny Crooks outlined how he made what he observed his own: "I'll take an idea, something I see somebody doing, and then I'll work and get that, and then I'll sort of modify that a little bit."

Lastly, observation included learning how to mix approaches and disciplines when it came to, returning to Dewey (1938), "set[ting] up desire and purposes" (p. 38). For example, Linda H. expressed that she appreciated blending VH with a growing awareness of biomechanics:

> [After observing a clinic] I'd come home and start to apply—a piece of that works but some of it isn't working. Then, I'd go learn about biomechanics [how the horse's body should function] and then I'd adjust something that I might have heard from Buck and go, okay, but now I've heard from Gerd [Heuschmann]—so I'm going to adjust my approach to this to be able to incorporate both aspects. That's going to fit the horse in a better way.

Therefore, she traveled a little further down her desire line, bringing in what she felt were the best elements of what she observed—whatever would "make sure that the horse's body is going to be comfortable." She was consistently thinking about what her horse needed so that her learning experiences were, and are, inherently social and shared.

Eclecticism and Desire Lines

In the last section, I highlighted Linda H.'s blending of what she observed; in this section, I extend that idea to describe an eclectic approach to experiencing VH—or pulling horsemanship approaches and training ideas from a variety of traditions. Borrowing the concept from a magazine that is popular in modern VH, *Eclectic Horseman* (www .eclectic-horseman.com) features many of the mentors and techniques that participants studied; its videos and online community forums also provide access to further learning.

One advantage to following your own desire line is that you can pick and choose whatever moves you further along without worrying about whether the experts in the field would agree or would even use the same label. As an example in VH, my sense was that none of the southeastern participants were worried about being "purists," as Maggie called them; she stated that, instead, there are those who "are very accepting of experimentation and individuality, and it's those people who keep [her] attracted to the tradition." When I asked Mike Bridges about "purists," he replied that one would have to be working livestock full-time, using traditional gear, to come close to what historical vaqueros were doing. The relative rarity of that, especially in the southeast, makes eclecticism understandable. We also live in a more diverse and connected world than historical vaqueros did. Mike, who has a particular interest in the history of the vaqueros, mentioned

> the isolation of California for 270 years—they had no outside influence to its horsemanship other than the Iberian Peninsula. Then the Spanish leave California in the late 1700s, and the Mexican government takes over, and they really expanded the land grant program for those that stayed, and that's when the cattle industry really starts growing considerably. So, now you have a closed society.

If their society was closed, ours is anything but as we are now exposed to what feels like *everyone's* opinions and views on horsemanship, carried forth by books, the Internet, videos, and clinics, as well as those in our immediate circles. Once you sort through all of this, eclecticism allows you "to find what fits the horse as individuals the best . . . to change it up a little bit for each horse" (Emma). Individuals can blend what they have experienced and then apply this individualized approach to their horses.

What were the sources of this eclecticism for participants? The searching that leads to "collecting" different approaches was not random or haphazard. Instead, participants reported serious seeking out depending upon what they were interested in as individuals, or needed to learn, at the time. Several studied dressage along with VH, believing that they share common roots and complementary ground. Some had started by studying a particular expert who was not following VH, and then had moved into studying Vaquero horsemanship and settled there but had brought forth what they felt was valuable from their pre-VH experiences. As I discuss in chapter seven, the Internet has been a game-changer when it comes to exploring one's curiosity, and Johnny C. used it while "looking for anything that [he] could find that would give [him] an edge, some more understanding"—so this is not aimless scrolling but actively searching with an agenda in mind. This exploration was, unsurprisingly, not limited to virtual sources. Amy G. had worked with different mentors over the years as part of "trying to come more into [her] own." Even though she had years of horsemanship to her credit, she stated, "I'm still trying to figure out, what are my beliefs surrounding horsemanship? What am I going to promote? What am I going to teach? It's kind of a collection of what I've learned from everyone." This eclecticism was rather labor-intensive, taking years of effort, resulting in a collection wherein her horsemanship would reflect her beliefs.

I would argue that the ability to be eclectic is a luxury of our modern relationship to horses in that we, if we have the (usually financial) means, are able to access different traditions relatively easily. Even if eclecticism is a luxury, it might yet have a pragmatic aspect in that it motivates further learning since you can search and then blend as you see fit; this calls to mind Dewey's (1938) statement that "the most important attitude that can be formed is that of desire to go on learning" (p. 48). If an individual's desire line includes, and leads to, eclectic sources of learning that extend further, both in theory and practice, than a traditional path might, then they are worthwhile.

Differentiation and Desire Lines

Differentiation, or adjusting methods according to learners' needs and strengths, can be critical when working with a wide variety of both horses and humans, and it has become a prevalent and popular idea in (human) education. To return to Dewey (1938), he offered a more comprehensive definition although he did not call it differentiation:

> [The educator] must survey the capacities and needs of the particular set of individuals with whom he is dealing and must at the same time arrange the conditions which provide the subject-matter or content for experiences that satisfy these needs and develop these capacities. The planning must be flexible enough to permit free play for individuality of experience and yet firm enough to give direction towards continuous development of power. (p. 58)

He also categorized it as "a much more intelligent, and consequently more difficult, kind of planning" (p. 58). According to Dewey's definition, a horse educator judges where the horse is currently at, and also where the horse might get to with development, and then implements the best learning experience for that individual horse. Intrinsic to the concept of differentiation is setting up learners to succeed, and this is an idea that is also very much present in Tom Dorrance's (2010) and Ray Hunt's (1978) writings as well as the stories that still circulate about them. As an example of the latter, Jaton Lord recalled that Hunt, who was mentored by Dorrance, "could get you set up so well that there was no failing."

In Dorrance's and Hunt's books, they included statements that summarize differentiation. Dorrance (2010) specified, "That's another thing I think is important to emphasize—*this is an individual process*" (p. 30; italics in original). Later in his volume he made sure that the reader understands that this applies to horses, as well: "It is so ever-varying, what you're doing, depending on one horse or the other" (p. 110). Ray Hunt affirmed, "A good teacher is able to encourage all students to develop their abilities" (p. 42). Between the two of them, we have a clear directive to understand that their approach is the horsemanship equivalent of "survey[ing] the capacities and needs of the particular set of individuals with whom he is dealing" and "arrang[ing] the conditions which provide . . . content for experiences that satisfy these needs and develop these capacities" (Dewey, 1938, p. 58).

It did not seem that anyone had specifically told participants to differentiate, or called it that, but, instead, they had identified a need for it as part of what they observed by paying close attention, including to their own learning experiences. Greg Eliel talked about how he created his own desire line when he faced failure as an undergraduate in Montana:

> At the university, I did a grand wipeout, and it wasn't that I wasn't studying. I was in agriculture and the dean sent me a letter three different times that said, Greg, if your GPA stays this low, you're going to go home and irrigate for a living because we don't want you here anymore. I was overwhelmed by the visual aspects of a university environment, and my brain would get overloaded. I couldn't keep up with it. My auditory skills weren't strong enough. So when all my friends left campus, I went to the library and I re-wrote my entire day's notes, both organized and clearly written. Then the process of moving my hands to re-write the notes, and observing it with my eyes, started to engage my brain, and that's when I realized that that's how I needed to learn. So not only was I able to go ahead and complete my degree, but I finished my last year on full academic scholarship—completely turned my world around. What also happened at the time, when I was really struggling with school, is I had a real dip in my self-confidence, and that was about the time I ran into some of my mentors whom I needed badly, and what I recognized in them is that they had what I so desperately wanted in my life. So it was a combination of learning how to learn and then surrounding myself with the right people that put me on this pathway.

Surely because Greg had to create his own desire line while learning, he is now more sensitive to, and incorporates, different learning styles while teaching horses and humans. Usually, differentiation is a social process between teacher and learner, but he basically differentiated for himself—and then generalized what he learned from this to help his future students. When Susan Hopkins first told me about him, she emphasized how helpful his individualized approach to teaching in clinics is. I have also included his comments about finding badly needed mentors to emphasize how crucial they can be, even when you first have to establish your path alone.

Sometimes, desire lines, and the differentiation that can accompany them, reverse more traditional routes of knowledge and acknowledgement. Moor (2017) noted that "The more democratic approach to managing desire lines is to listen to and learn from them" (p. 4); they then might lead to realizations that come from unexpected sources. Even though Greg's experience began at a university, formal education was not necessarily needed by some participants to realize that differentiation might be helpful. While working with teachers who wanted to learn how to rope as part of a project on Western horse culture, one complimented Fred A. by saying that he had "hit every learning style" after commenting, in what sounds like a backhanded compliment, "I bet you don't even have a college degree." He did not, but he did know that "if you're not getting it this way, I need to find another way to present it to you, so you do get it. That's my job, and a gift that I did have is that I could take this same thing and re-word it, rearrange it a little bit, to where that person could make it work for them." Fred took it upon himself to reword and rearrange rather than leaving the learner to struggle if the information was not accessible to them, which works with both humans and horses. Differentiation can be marked by a generosity on the teacher's part as they extend themselves to try to meet students over halfway (rather than waiting for the student to "arrive" at the material). Traditional schooling where everyone is moved along on a predetermined and often standardized path can exclude anyone who wanders from it.

Amy S. shared that she was one such wanderer: "I really struggled in school because I don't think my brain is wired in the way that our schools are. So, when I started learning about horses and how they learn, I was like, oh, they are not stupid. This one just needs to be taught this way—they all need to be addressed in a different way." In her case, similar to Greg Eliel's, this heightened sensitivity caused her to create an approach to horsemanship that respects the complex interplay of minds who learn differently. She elaborated the realization that she had after connecting her own school experiences to horsemanship.

> So I started really thinking about how to teach people, and I realized that people, though they have the ability to tell you, they don't always know how, and they sometimes can't or feel like they can't, so you have to teach a person from their personal experience, not from yours, and you might not know that they're scared to death on their horse because they had an accident six years ago, or they're triggered by certain words, or they're intimidated by you and they're not going to say anything, or you can't criticize them or they'll cry—you know, you're dealing with the horse's mind, your mind, and a person's mind, and you've got to figure out how to address—get all of those three things connected and on the same page in real time while stuff's happening.

These comments captured her trajectory of awareness, beginning with her own experiences in school, then leading to a reflection on horse intelligence, and *then* to a realization that even though people can communicate, they do not always—and so she has to bring that same sensitivity to humans that she brings to horses. Getting those three things connected, as she phrased it, in the moment of interaction is tenuous indeed. It is perhaps too obvious to state that communication between horses and humans is fragile, too; the thoughtful and reflective methods of VH, which participants had adopted, aided the circuit of communication that Amy described.

"Your Brain's Your Best Horsemanship Tool":
Reflection in Learning Vaquero Horsemanship

Creating your own desire line is a conscious and often thoughtful task; it might come after reflecting upon your choices and wanting to create an alternative. Relatedly, eclecticism and differentiation require you to assess what is happening in your own learning and with the learners, both horse and human, that you are working with. Reed E. described the brain as "your best horsemanship tool," and, after reflecting on his own learning journey, realized that "the biggest thing is using your head and questioning everything." When I asked him what he meant by questioning everything, he elaborated: "It's not just that something works, but *why* does it work with the horse?" In his case, reflective questioning led to an understanding that (circling back briefly to differentiation) "you're going to need multiple ways to do the same thing because one horse will respond to one way and another horse is going to respond to something else better."

The significance of thoughtfulness was highlighted by other interviewees as well. Fred A. quoted Ray Hunt, who "said this method of working with a horse is a thinking man's way of riding." Linda H. described the essence of VH as "doing something and noting your result. Tom Dorrance would say observe, remember, and compare. You can't beat the thinking aspect of this. Ray Hunt would rarely sign an autograph, but if he did, he'd put 'Think—Ray Hunt.'" In his book, Hunt (1978) encouraged readers to "[g]et in the habit of thinking" (p. 19). In VH, the human brain is actively engaged with the horse brain; this is not mindlessly moving the horse in circles or the human issuing auto-pilot commands. A different sort of engagement is required—one that means remaining in the moment the entire time and then reflecting on how things went before the next session. Mental activity is as vital as the physical action involved in learning VH.

For some participants, part of using your brain to learn VH involved a willingness to be wrong and make mistakes, and you could not get very far down your desire line without this. Elijah commented on what he saw as the inevitable role of error: "Anybody who's making a bridle horse is going to go, hey, I made that mistake on that horse. If you're not willing to say, 'I made mistakes,' you're not going to get very far." Marilyn O. described needing "a degree of grittiness toward just going out and doing it—not being scared to make mistakes." We might be tempted to think of making mistakes as the mark of someone who is not yet knowledgeable enough, but, in learning VH, it can signal a sort of license—an ability to think your way through to more expansive possibilities of learning and doing.

As Dewey (1938) argued, "The only freedom that is of enduring importance is freedom of intelligence, that is to say, freedom of observation and of judgment exercised on behalf of purposes that are intrinsically worth while [*sic*]" (p. 61). There is an undeniable freedom in being able to choose a desire line of learning, but making mistakes also can be a component of freedom of intelligence, especially when mistakes positively affect future judgment and action. Participants have already decided that learning VH brings purpose to their horsemanship; they are trying to communicate to their horses that it is worthwhile in horse terms, which, with an animal who would likely rather be grazing with friends, is no small task.

To reflect a bit more on Dewey's assertions, what does it mean to be free as a learner of horsemanship? It can include being able to follow your own interests and to work at your own pace; not having to answer to an external expert or justify the choices you make (except to the horse); and deciding how fast or slow you work and with whom you choose to work. Unless you choose them, there are no tests or external measures of achievement. This freedom is mediated by the presence of the horse, who is not free in the way that you are. The human is still at the helm, although one thing that I heard throughout these interviews was that participants chose VH because there is room in it for the horse to be a learning partner and not just a passive recipient.

LEARNING TURNING POINTS

In the remainder of this chapter, I turn to autobiographical turning points (Bruner, 1994), which, in this study, are times when participants turned a corner of sorts in their own learning because they had a realization with—or because of—a horse. Due to this experience, their learning of VH either began or changed course. Bruner (1994) defined turning points, recalled in autobiographical retellings, as "vividly particular, even though they carry some affective or moral message with them" (p. 49). He observed that "though they may be linked to things happening 'outside,' [they] are finally attributed to a happening 'inside'—a new belief, new courage, moral disgust, 'having had enough'" (p. 50). They "ride into the story on a wave of episodic memory retrieval, rich in detail and color" (p. 50) and "usher in a new and intense line of activity" (p. 50). The last characteristic of turning points that Bruner included is that they "are drenched in affect—certainly in the telling and presumably in the living" (p. 50). In this chapter, these turning points include personal, firsthand experiences, both positive and negative, and receiving early inspiration from seeing mentors in action.

Positive Personal Experiences as Turning Points

In this section, I include positive experiences of two kinds: times when participants felt the trust and cooperation of the horse they were riding, and times when they, early in their horsemanship careers, rode in clinics, both of which then spurred their VH education. Positive personal experiences with horses were of the "vividly particular" sort that Bruner (1994) wrote of, and, in Emily S.'s case, this turning point included both types and subsequently brought "new courage" (p. 49). She shared that, during one of Buck Brannaman's clinics, she rode an ex-racehorse who "was flying around 100 miles an hour" (the horse was used to that speed rather than the slower pace of clinics). Buck worked with both Emily and the horse, and the result was that by the end of the clinic, in her words, "I rode her with the reins draped over the saddle horn, holding the rope around the base of her neck, and she did flying lead changes and cantered like slow motion slow. It was so cool because she was a crazy steeplechaser." [We talked briefly about how it is we humans can make horses crazy by training them to perform in a certain way for certain sports.] She described that this was an experience that solidified her commitment to VH because she had *felt* the transformation of this high-strung horse. Emily would go on to be self-employed as a horse educator and riding instructor so this very positive feedback from the horse gave her confidence to pursue that path.

Next, I turn to a story that Fred A. recounted, which was full of "affect—certainly in the telling and presumably in the living" (Bruner, 1994, p. 50). He shared it as an example of learning how to communicate with a horse using persuasion, often a time-consuming practice, rather than force. He was working with "a horse that refused to give in to any pressure—would not give his head, one way or the other; he just locked up." So he just "sat, and waited on him. This is something that I learned over the years, from Ray [Hunt] and Buck [Brannaman]—trying to have patience, and we sat like that for almost an hour." He was "waiting for the least amount that the horse could offer. And, that horse's head went like that [gestures indicating a slight bit of movement], and I let go, and I got off of him and unsaddled him right then. And I went and put him up. The next day was different. I got on him, and I reached up, and he just brought his head on up. It was awesome." He noted that he "could have forced it and made him go around and around the pen, but that wouldn't have helped him." Fred's approach was akin to taking the long view in education (Dewey, 1938; Frank, 2019), reaching for a way of communicating with the horse that will not only take years to accomplish, but the effects of which will reverberate far into the future, a reach that is at odds with the rapid results we so often seek in our society—and in our horsemanship.

When participants described turning points that occurred while riding in clinics, near the beginning of their learning VH, they were often the most detailed stories of the interviews, containing dramatic curves, even if the stories themselves were delivered rather matter-of-factly, as in Ben's case. He described, when he first became interested in VH, going on a Buck Brannaman clinic binge and riding in all of the available classes at that particular event; he had audited before and was ready to take his learning to another level on the advice of a mentor (although he mentioned that at the end of it he "was glad to come home just so [he] could rest"). He was impressed that Buck "was real handy with a rope" even though he had not yet started working with cows, which would become his future career. He stated that "I learned—I was so hooked, and I was like, I'm going to learn how to rope too. So, after that we ended up buying this place [his own farm] in 2008 after that clinic." Deciding to buy a farm after choosing a particular lifestyle is a consequential choice indeed, although horsepeople will understand the passion and commitment horses inspire. Clinics, even though they only took up a matter of days, were fertile ground for intense learning experiences that could greatly influence participants' futures.

Susan Hopkins' learning turning point took a longer span of time than a single clinic. Her participation made her distinct in the dressage community in which she worked and also made her a target of envy because she was game to try these "new" methods—and she was successful at them.

> I think when Buck Brannaman showed up here, people were ready to figure out a better way to do things, and he was pretty hard on a lot of dressage riders at first. Some of them got mad and left. He's not a big fan of lunging in mindless circles. He's not a big fan of tying their heads down, but I didn't really care because what he had to say fit with what I thought was right. So we went right on with it [starting colts], and it was about three clinics before I got one where I had it right. I hadn't done a lot with the colt because I didn't want to mess it up. It's not like I was afraid to try. But at the same time, it was like, I know I'm not really getting it yet, and I was like, by God, I'm going to get Buck one that is going to be good. And I did it. He'd have somebody else's horse, and it wouldn't be doing as well, and it wouldn't be as soft, and he would say well, you pulled on that one harder than Susan. They actually thought that he was trying to make their horse look bad. I mean, some people were that resistant to what he had to say instead of figuring, well, I've been to a few clinics, and I've been working at it. That's what Buck said. He said, 'Susan has been working at this. And this horse is really soft.' I'd actually worked at it. I actually finally figured it out—how to get it going.

The phrase "to get it going" is telling as it communicates an ongoing process, as opposed to getting it done once and for all. Furthermore, this captures the fact that it took Susan a series of clinics to "actually finally" learn how to start a colt so that she felt that she "had it right." Her positive experiences with these colts had a profound influence on her horsemanship, although it took time to accomplish and was the result of much effort in the context of some envy. (I am confident that the positive feedback from Buck Brannaman offset this envy.) Being the subject of jealously exemplifies the often solitary process that learning VH can be, especially if riders migrated over from other disciplines, as Susan did (although she remained a dressage rider). Even though she was annoyed by the comments from other envious riders, the learning turning point happened between her and her colt, aided by the education she received over a period of years. Notably, Susan was an early sponsor of VH clinicians in the southeast, so she had the additional task of being an ambassador of it.

I include Susan H.'s story so the reader will recognize that a turning point in VH is not necessarily a single event or clustered together in a matter of days. Even though "point" sounds like a neatly contained incident, it might well spread itself out in an untidy way over time. To return to Bruner (1994) again, turning points can "usher in a new and intense line of activity" (p. 50), some of which happens internally. In horsemanship, learning a new discipline takes time, especially in an area without ready access to it, or where there might be resistance, so by necessity, these shifts in activity took months and even years to play out.

Negative Personal Experiences as Turning Points

Even though Susan H.'s story had elements of negativity, her overall result was a positive one. In this section, the experiences that interviewees had were more straightforwardly negative and can be defined, overall, as realizing, in Riley's words, that "there was a big hole in [their] horsemanship," and this often involved injury. An approach that might be reasonable when one is young and flexible can wear out fast, in Amy S.'s words:

> I just rode them until they stopped bucking because they were tired. I didn't have a clue what I was doing. And looking back on 18-year-old me, I'd like to kick my own butt. But eventually, I started getting tossed enough and starting having problems that I couldn't fix from just sticking on long enough—then I started going to clinics and taking lessons.

Realizations like Amy's did not always occur at the beginning of interviewees' time with horses: Noah mentioned being twenty years in and realizing that "after a couple of broken bones and some stitches, you start to realize that there is a better way of doing things." For Riley, studying VH was about becoming "safer" as she jokingly remembered that she kept "getting thrown off by centrifugal force or something." To return to Bruner's definition, the "things happening 'outside'" that can spur a turning point were falling off and/or getting injured, the most physical of the learning turning points; it took numerous occurrences to have a full effect and then to lead "to a happening 'inside'"—a seeking out of a different form of horsemanship.

Outside of injury, there were also negative experiences with horses that motivated participants to take a different route. Alex recounted that, while working as a full-time vaquero, he "was doing way too much," although he wasn't "doing anything mean but just by dragging on the reins a little bit when [he] shouldn't have been it was keeping those horses dull." This might seem like a small thing to focus on, but it matters in VH, which is generally a nuanced form of horsemanship; a rider ideally is providing unobtrusive cues and paying attention to the smallest of responses. To a non-horseperson, Alex would not likely have seemed to be "doing way too much," but in his estimation he was.

In a similar vein, although a more dramatic example, Daniel remembered seeing a family member use a metal chain to try to halter-break a young horse, which made her panic. He felt that "nobody was trying to be mean to her in any way—they were just doing the best that they could. That made a pretty big impression on me. I thought, there's got to be—we can do something else, surely." As someone who was told that "spirited" horses *needed* to be walked with metal lead chains in order to control them, I shared Daniel's dismay; this is one of several "horsemanship" practices that I have observed for which there is not enough silver in Santa Fe to convince me to use. I am also disheartened that a practice like lead chains often seems accepted without question by mainstream horse culture. It is easy to read about Daniel's memory and think, why would they do that? However, I would argue that there are many things happening in horsemanship more broadly that if we stepped back and critically examined them, we would ask, why are we doing this? Isn't there a better way? Dewey (1902/1990) reminded us that it would be wise to scrutinize our habits, lest they control us and contradict our intentions. Furthermore, the affective message (Bruner, 1994) that was conveyed in these retellings is that what participants saw and subsequently felt was *not* an acceptable way to work with horses, and so they (and I) sought out a better way. What may seem acceptable to some horsepeople might be too heavy-handed to VH practitioners; they are continually trying to learn to get *quieter* in their horsemanship.

Early Inspiration as Learning Turning Point

Lastly, I would like to expand upon the early inspiration that several interviewees received from seeing VH mentors in action (although some had already been riding in other disciplines for years, they were not yet studying VH). In chapter three, I will discuss how riding in these clinics was a significant learning experience for some; what I summarize here are the effects of seeing mentors ride (but not riding themselves). These learning turning points influenced participants to begin pursuing VH as a "new and intense line of activity" (Bruner, 1994, p. 50).

Because Buck Brannaman has traveled widely for decades (at the time of our interview, he said it had been 40 years since his first clinic) and has been commercially successful and popular, for many participants this experience came during one of his clinics. Emily S. had a strong and immediate positive reaction during her first clinic: "I knew the minute I saw how he worked with this horse, I wanted to do what he did." Fred A. described it as "watching some kind of magic show" the first time he saw him.

Figuring out that particular magic would occupy Fred for decades. Maggie remembered her first clinic as powerfully moving: "This would have been about 22 years ago in Eagle, Colorado. There was a buckskin horse that was really, really scared. The work he did with that horse—I had just never seen anything like it before. It made you cry" (she also called it "magical"). The novelty of what they saw, combined with the emotional responses they felt, propelled their learning in a new direction. Amy S. said that observing one of Buck's clinics made her realize that she had not been questioning why horses behave the way they do; instead, "it was all behaviors you had to fix—it wasn't an approach to the entire horse's education and experience." She "hadn't ever thought about that. So, that opened everything up, and that was when [she] was hooked." For Alicia B., this experience of observation was life-altering (which I think many of her peers in this study would agree with): "It changed my life because I was like, that's what I want."

We can see from participants' comments that deciding to begin the journey of learning VH was a life-changing decision for them that would forever alter how they relate to horses. Bruner (1994) identified turning points as "thickly agentive" (p. 50). It certainly takes agency and initiative to decide that you should be going, or learning, a different way, and you may have to lead that way yourself. The concepts of desire lines and turning points, which I have applied to memories of how participants learned VH, both include agentive acts in response to what were judged to be better, and worse, forms of horsemanship. It is arguably easier to be agentive when you have the freedom of determining your own desire line based upon personal motivations.

CONCLUSION

In this chapter, I have shared what participants said about their experiences learning Vaquero horsemanship, focusing on motivation, self-directed learning including the creation of desire lines, and significant turning points. Throughout all of these experiences, they were accompanied by their horses and other humans in their social orbits. Vaquero horsemanship is built upon an exchange of what the human offers and how the horse subsequently responds in a continual loop of communication; this is a delicate transaction. Interestingly, the Latin origin of "transaction" is *transigere*, or to "drive through" (www.lexico.com), and we can imagine that both horses and humans are driving through many obstacles on the way to understanding each other. To amend the desire line metaphor a bit, the path to VH was wide enough to accommodate the aspects that I have discussed in this chapter: individual motivations; self-directed learning; eclecticism; differentiation; thoughtful, reflective, and responsive practice; and turning points. In sum, participants conceived of modern Vaquero horsemanship as having freedom enough to allow the learning of it in distinctive and personal ways.

INTERLUDE 2

Alicia Byberg-Landman and Marlin

WHEN I GOT MARLIN, HE WAS TWO YEARS OLD. I DID NOT PLAN ON buying him, but I had gone to help friends start some colts in Indiana, and I didn't have a colt to bring with me, so they said, "Well, just come down and we'll match you up with one." So, that's the weekend that I met Marlin. He could untie any knot as a two-year-old, so we also called him Houdini because he was the master of working his lips to do anything. I started him that weekend, and I just loved the feel of him. The guy who bred him called him "real catty," and at that time, I didn't know what "catty" meant. I was like, "I guess that's cool," and when I got on him, I started feeling what he was talking about. He watched everything, he was so responsive, and that first ride was the best ride I ever had on a horse. During the second ride, we were moving cattle around, and he just naturally wanted to do it, and that was my first time really feeling a horse want to help you do a job.

I have always worked him bright and early. He was usually the first horse I rode every day before I rode everybody else's at work, and then, as time went on, I was using him at work to help with some of the other horses. So, I was a teacher to him early on, but then, honestly, I think it started to flip, where I was like, oh, I'm not the teacher to this horse—this horse is teaching me. Over the years, it took me a lot of focus to intentionally think every ride about what I was doing, and how I was going to help him get better and myself get better. He just kept me thinking a lot all the time, and he helped me with all the other horses because he was so quick to think, he was so sensitive, and he still is, to this day.

He's almost 20 years old, and so, it's been a really fun journey to have a horse for that length of time and see how, at first, I was taking care of him and trying to get him with me, and now, I get on him, and we just go together. He's the first bridle horse I ever made. It took me quite a while. I think he was about nine years old when I finally put him in the bridle, but from then on, he stayed in it. Somebody made this comment a couple years ago, "Gosh, I just don't know if my horse is ever going to feel or look the way your horse does when you ride him," and I said, "Do you know how old this horse is and do you know how long I've been working at this?" I knew what my ultimate goal was, and I didn't really set a time limit on it because I didn't want to feel like I had to pressure it down his throat, but it takes the time that it takes. It's more about enjoying the process than anything, I think, and if you like the process, then if it takes you your lifetime to do it, who cares? As long as you like it.

We've traveled so many places together, and he's helped me start so many young horses. I took him to the "Legacy of Legends" in Las Vegas. He's the horse I took to Buck's Pro-Am Vaquero Roping and roped off of him — that was a bucket-list item for me. I told him, "We're going to go and do this, and then I promise I'm not going to haul you across the country ever again." It's fun to have a horse where they've been with you that entire time, and he just never says, "No, I don't want to do something." He's always game. I'm like, dude, you are a saint, and I tell him that all the time.

I rode him while I was pregnant, and he took care of me then. The most rewarding part of all of this has been when I turned the reins over to Riv [her daughter] two years ago, and she does everything with him. Now that she's starting to think about the next horse, she said, "This next one, I might want it to be a bit younger so I can learn how to get one to feel like him." She started showing him, and they were reserve champions in the 13 and under age division. She also placed 14th at the AQHA World Show in Ranch Riding, so they have done great in the competition world. It's so awesome to watch a horse take care of a little person — and the confidence that he has given her. That's pretty special.

CHAPTER 3

The Flexibility of Expertise and Apprenticeship in Vaquero Horsemanship

Pragmatically, it is always best to start smack in the middle of the glorious mess that is the actual world, where lived abstraction is always already spiked with lived importance, giving thinking-doing real stakes. (Massumi, 2014, p. 52)

THE "LIVED ABSTRACTION" OF EXPERTISE IN HORSEMANSHIP HITS THE hard ground of live work with horses, where the "real stakes" that Massumi referenced include the safety and well-being of both horse and rider. Knowing the how's and why's of various horsemanship approaches is but one part of the equation: How well those how's and why's work with large live animals is always yet to be determined in the moment. As Menary and Kirchhoff (2016) stated, "Expertise is usually thought of as an individual achievement. The expert is a receptacle for knowledge and skills" (p. 47). Expert horsemanship is a deviation from this as it is a shared achievement between human and horse, and each needs the other to achieve it (although the horse could live happily without our notions of performance or expertise); expertise lives in the space between the two, where partnership occurs. Practitioners of Vaquero horsemanship can believe themselves to be experts and can even present themselves as such to other people, but the stakes that count the most are whether horses will accept expertise in the complex dance between horse and human. While expertise and apprenticeship are human constructs with little to no relevance to horses, both are very much features of our larger world. In this chapter, I will share participants' views on expertise (a concept they were reluctant to accept) and apprenticeship.

EXPERTISE: "TOO MUCH TO LEARN YET"

Expertise Without Arrival

The more people I meet that, in my eyes, are experts—I realize that
they would never consider themselves experts because the more they've
learned and the more they know, the more they realize they don't know.
It's never-ending. And of course, when we create a website or we put
our names out there to teach other people, we suddenly then become the
expert. I don't feel good saying that I'm an expert at it. Every time I get
my hands on a new colt that is just a little more challenging, then they
humble you instantly, and you're like, I don't know anything. Maybe I
should just start knitting or something. (Alicia Byberg-Landman)

Alicia B.'s comments summarize two entwined main ideas that all participants expressed about expertise in VH: It is a destination that you never arrive at, *and* it must also be tempered with humility, as horses require it with their unpredictable reactions. Bryan Neubert described it in a similar way: "It's hard because by the time you think you know something, then God steers the horse in your path that makes you think that you're not quite as smart as you think you are." Expertise without arrival signals a process without end, or, as Susan H., who is in her 60s at the time of this writing, stated, "I've just always been learning from somebody." However, educators know that they must assume the label of expert to be able to advertise themselves as knowledgeable, even as their own feelings about it were less straightforward.

Barton and Hamilton's (1998) groundbreaking study of vernacular literacies provides a helpful filter through which to view the local expertise of this project. They defined these literacies as encompassing "what people do with literacy," including "the social activities . . . the thoughts and meanings behind the activities" (p. 3); they also described these literacies as "rooted in everyday experience and serv[ing] everyday purposes" (p. 251). Local literacies, and how we use them in everyday and immediate ways, can be contrasted with more formal school literacies (where there is an abundance of expertise). Barton and Hamilton (1998) reminded us, "What counts as useful and valid knowledge and expertise in the local area may be subject to different criteria from what counts in the professional or academic realm" (p. 244). I conceive of the professional or academic realm of VH as being the clinics that participants might attend, taught periodically by their respective mentors. So, most of the time, local knowledge and expertise were more accessible. Furthermore, what participants expressed about their own levels of expertise supports Barton and Hamilton's (1998) statement that, in local literacies, "Expertise is uneven and it is developed in relation to real-life contingencies"

(p. 243). In VH, the most significant real-life contingency is obviously the horse, who determines depth of knowledge and expertise and is always the *local* in local expertise. Four participants, in addition to Bryan Neubert, specifically mentioned encountering a new horse that would then test expertise. Amy S. described it as: "Each time I think I know what I'm doing, I get one that doesn't make any sense to me." If they were ever tempted to feel like experts, a local horse would curb that temptation.

Studying VH "in the professional or academic realm" (Barton & Hamilton, 1998) would be with one or several mentors, who each had been influenced by their own mentors. In this project, the mentors conceptualized of expertise in similarly tenuous and personal terms, and there was humility across the board as well as an acknowledgment that they did not feel, not one of them, that they measured up to the expertise of the Dorrances or Ray Hunt (or their other mentors, for that matter). And a lifetime of experience did not make the difference, either: Even Mike Bridges, at the age of 83, stated that he wished he had known at 70 what he knows now, and at 60 what he knew at 70, and so on; expertise is "just an ongoing process that never ends—you just recognize another part of it, a nuance to it that was always there" but that you did not appreciate at the time, according to Mike.

As I have stated, most of the mentors were heavily influenced by Bill and Tom Dorrance and Ray Hunt. Ray Hunt's grandson, Jaton Lord, recounted a story that captured the Dorrance brothers' humility.

> The philosophy back then was, if you can't get a horse to do something, just get a bigger stick or a bigger bit, and so, Ray met Bill in Salinas because he was living in Hollister. And Ray admired how Bill was getting things done without getting that bigger bit or bigger stick. So he asked Bill some questions, and Bill said, Well, I'm not too good, but I've got a brother that's really good, and he'll be here. So, Ray met Tom, and Tom comes up to the ranch, and he said when Tom would come, the horses were just like lions, but by the time Tom left, they were like lambs running around.

One inheritance we have from the Dorrances and Hunt is a disposition of being highly successful but *not* bragging about, or indulging, it. Because these men would not have called themselves experts, those who apprenticed to them feel it would be inappropriate and disrespectful for them to do so. They do not see themselves as arriving at the same place of expertise that their mentors occupied, powerful models that still live on in the memories of those who knew them. Joe Wolter, when complimented for his kindness with learners, stated that:

> That's what I got from Tom Dorrance. He taught me that. He wouldn't tear anybody up. Nobody. He'd head things off. He was a total genius. He knew what was going to happen way before it was going to happen. If he thought it was going to be a wreck,

he'd change riders before it happened and then come back to that rider. . . . You ask me why I'm not an expert? That's why. We saw the expert. We lived it.

Greg Eliel also used the word "genius" when describing Bill Dorrance's way of giving guidance "in a way that allowed you to think your way through it and come to the conclusion on your own, and that was part of his genius." This kindness and consideration for learners shows regard for the emotional responses they might have as part of the learning process, an aspect that I will return to later in this chapter. Joe's longtime friend, Bryan Neubert, who also "lived it," is now one of the elder statesmen of horsemanship and so has earned the right to brag (which he does not do); his disposition can be summed up by his statement: "I learned the more I learn, the more I find out there is to learn."

As I have mentioned, horses themselves offer a source of perpetual learning and are also the compassionate judges of both expertise and failure. In VH, they are the experts that matter to those I interviewed. Joe Wolter remembered "looking for praise from Ray Hunt" and realizing that he "need[ed] to get praise from the horse" instead. Tom Curtin stated that "I could never be as good as the horse. All I can do is work at having more to offer the horse." (He was also the one to contribute the subtitle of "too much to learn yet" when explaining why he does not see himself as an expert.) To "work at having more to offer" aligns with interviewees' conception of an expert as one who has "arrived" and is no longer searching as earnestly; there was something static about the word that they did not like.

Tom Dorrance, in his book (2010), hinted that this search for connection with the horse will likely be a long-term, and possibly elusive, project: "You think, and that horse feels something going on in your body and he is ready to go. It may not be that way for quite a while and it may never get to be, but that is what you have in mind" (p. 128). Being willing to search is an aspect of this horsemanship that has survived and has been passed along. Kathleen K., who is helping to educate the next generation of riders, summed it up: "Stay humble and keep learning."

EXPERT-LEARNERS

I think that anybody who's on this path wouldn't say they're
an expert. They will die saying that they're a student and
just wish they had more time. (Linda Hoover)

Characteristic of never arriving at expertise includes a disposition as an expert-learner (rather than a "learning-expert" since participants placed more importance on remaining a learner): Professional horsepeople actively practice their craft and so are necessarily more knowledgeable than novices, but they are also continually learning more about a craft that itself evolves with each new horse. (Their situation calls to mind Mishler's [1999] statement that "[his] respondents claim a dual identity as craftartists" as a way to negotiate the "distinction between the crafts and the fine arts" [p. 6]). Avoiding thinking of yourself as an expert yields the benefit of continuing to become more skillful at horsemanship without having to bother about what to call yourself: expert or novice or something in between; this is also an advantage of working outside of close communities of practice as there are relatively few people to judge one's advancement. The work these educators do is often on their own timelines (although they do have to negotiate horses' owners and students' expectations of progress), and I would wager that some amount of freedom within this lifestyle is part of its appeal.

Expert-learners are able to seek out their own opportunities for growth, which come from both horses and other teachers. The same ribbon of humility runs through this set of responses—as Susan H.'s answer to the expertise question below illustrates:

> You just never will be an expert. I mean, I'm the last person who will tell you how well I can do this. I ride every day, and the horses tell me I can do better. I ride with people who tell me and show me that I can be better, and that's the fun of it. If I thought I had it all, I wouldn't bother, ... But that's why I still go to clinics and why I ride with other people.... There's just a lot out there to learn.

So, the mentors still mentor each other, both in clinics and more informally. Bryan Neubert mentioned that sometimes he will share a horsemanship challenge with Joe Wolter and, after thinking about it, Joe will suggest something to try that he had not thought of. Bryan observed that "a lot of people don't want to share with other people because they're afraid it will put them equal with them. I hope that people I work with will get equal with me" so that "they can just take it and go with it," creating a new chain of knowledge.

Overall, participants counted on experience and "miles" to improve, which corresponds with Ray Hunt's (1978) portrayal of the horsemanship process: "Pretty soon it's just feel following a feel, whether it comes today, tomorrow, or next year. You'll never quit learning and I don't believe the horse will either" (p. 5). Never becoming an expert brings to mind the concept of the Pro-Am (a contraction of "professional–amateur"). Most of the participants had been influenced directly by Buck Brannaman, who created the annual Pro-Am Vaquero Roping and Team Branding, so *Pro-Am* is a term that is in circulation in horsemanship, even though it was not mentioned specifically in interviews. Pro-Am matches well with what these educators expressed about expertise, since the "pro" part conveys an element of expertise, while the "am" part captures the willingness to keep learning; although, I should note that I do not think that the participants in this study would have characterized themselves as "amateurs" given that it connotes a lack of professionalization and know-how. In this case, it is simply a linguistic substitute for the idea that they were willing to continue learning in significant ways.

Leadbeater and Miller (2004) characterized Pro-Ams as "innovative, committed and networked amateurs working to professional standards" (p. 9) and stated that "being a hard-core Pro-Am takes dedication, passion and perseverance" (p. 39); they "are often practitioners and teachers" (p. 46). They outlined in more detail what constitutes a Pro-Am:

> Many of the defining features of professionalism also apply to Pro-Ams: they have a strong sense of vocation; they use recognized public standards to assess performance and formally validate skills; they form self-regulating communities, which provide people with a sense of community and belonging; they produce non-commodity products and services; they are well versed in a body of knowledge and skill, which carries with it a sense of tradition and identity. (p. 22)

The above characteristics would apply to VH practitioners, but there are parts of Leadbeater and Miller's description that would not. For example, they argued that Pro-Ams "would not be regarded as full professionals" (p. 22), nor do they see themselves that way (the main marker of this being how much income they derive from their activities); however, they also believe that "Pro-Ams demand that we see professionals and amateurs along a continuum" (p. 23), although Pro-Ams would stop short of arriving at the full professional end of it. Some participants would see themselves as full professionals, so this is where the overlap stops.

The following exchange with Maggie illustrates how she balances being a Pro-Am:

MAGGIE: I'm in an elite group because I'm pursuing this at an academic and practical technique-based level that a lot of people aren't pursuing it at. So, it is very isolating.

JULIANNA: Do you feel like an expert?

MAGGIE: I don't feel like an expert because I know there's people that can ride rings around me and academically know way more than me. . . . Now, there are a whole lot of people out there that I can ride rings around. . . . I have a bunch of experience, and I have a lot of knowledge, and I store stuff really well, and I'm very discriminating about where I get that knowledge from—that it's good quality knowledge, and it's academically sound and experientially sound. A lot of people don't do that, but I don't feel like an expert. I feel like a learner.

As her comments indicated, being a Pro-Am can be "isolating" because one is dwelling in between learner and expert and not fully belonging in either community. As she and I discussed, there were few to no other experts in her physical community (and that was the case for the other participants as well), and so students of this style of horsemanship were challenged to cultivate expert-learning without the resources that might normally accompany apprenticeship. The word "elite" is notable because it can recast the word "amateur" in a more positive light if the two words are combined; we might think of amateurs as inferior in terms of knowledge (Leadbeater & Miller, 2004) but being a Pro-Am allows trainers to keep learning, which was, as they described it, an essential part of their progress. Although, again, I do not know if anyone would actually want to use the term "elite amateur" since the latter word is so stubbornly attached to a negative connotation.

If the label of expert is too human-centered to apply to modern VH and "Pro-Am" is helpful in a limited way but still not quite the right fit, then which word might work? For this, I turn to the mentors. Tom Curtin described Ray Hunt and his other mentor, Buster Welch, as having "had enough confidence in themselves to know what they knew and that's all they needed." Tom sees himself as "a student of a tradition and lifestyle of these animals in stewardship." Similarly, Bryan Neubert stated that he would refer to himself "as a student of horsemanship." He thought Tom Dorrance would also have been comfortable with that descriptor. After saying this, he remembered "Tom explaining something at a clinic. Then, when he was done, he would say, 'at least that's the way it seems to me.'" There again is that trademark humility, and it also runs through acceptable alternatives to expert: student, experienced learner, and steward.

Even if there is "too much to learn yet," participants, especially the mentors, know that riders are coming to them for "expertise," so presenting themselves as *a* source of horsemanship knowledge (but not *the* source) is a tactic they can live with. When I asked Joe Wolter if he had always had this humility, he responded that "No, I think I've developed it more as I've gotten older. When I first started, I thought, Joe, you've got to produce." He felt that he had to give students answers but has, over the years, puzzled out a way to facilitate learning without promoting himself as an expert. He keeps in mind Tom Dorrance's method: When "you'd ask him a question, he'd say, 'well, I'll ask you a question back.' . . . And we were all wanting him to give us the answer. I think he was trying to get us to find the answer." As a teacher, asking questions is an invaluable strategy; we have the more formal Socratic method to stimulate critical thinking but also modern versions of questioning (some of which are still similar to the Socratic method) to encourage dialogue and investment in the lesson; questioning is one of my favorite pedagogical activities because it is a nearly no-fail way to bring students into a learning mindset and get them to think (recall that Linda H. mentioned that Ray Hunt would sign an autograph with "Think").

VAQUERO HORSEMANSHIP APPRENTICESHIP

You should be leaving people behind you that, in time,
know more than you know. (Mike Bridges)

I always felt like the best place you could work was where you were the greenest
hand because if you knew the least, then you could learn the most. (Alex)

Just as expertise assumes a nontraditional role in VH in the southeastern United States, so does apprenticeship. While for some participants, it did mean close and individualized work with a mentor over a period of time, apprenticeship also included less personal and less frequent forms. Across these forms, the common element is that participants positioned themselves as actively seeking knowledge, like "the greenest hand" of Alex's comment, just as a traditional apprentice would.

Traditional Apprenticeship

In this project, there were 11 in the southeastern group who had experienced traditional apprenticeship (Wenger, 1998); by that I mean they had had opportunities to work closely with an expert of their choosing (albeit usually a geographically convenient one) over the course of many months or even years; however, the concept of apprenticeship is doubled in horsemanship: You need both time with a mentor and time to practice on your own with horses. So, the mentor does not determine access to horses but should be the one who facilitates quality work with them. Some of these mentor/apprentice relationships had begun when participants were young or just starting out while some had occurred further into their careers. They described these experiences in generally positive terms (and I suspect that negative experiences were not highlighted due to an awareness that they were speaking not only to me but to a digital recorder). They also noted that these mentorships usually came to a natural end after they had served their purpose of initial learning and development, and they had, in a sense, outgrown the apprentice role.

When describing the evolution of these mentor/apprentice relationships, there was also a component of seeing what they did *not* want to replicate in their own approaches, or, as Alicia B. described it, "I had to go there to figure out that that wasn't what I wanted." Overall, despite outgrowing, and disagreeing with some of what they saw and experienced, they echoed the positive tone that Maggie described as "really, really key in getting me started with that foundational stuff that everybody should have access to" (although she noted that, in her case, this came not from a big-name mentor but from someone less well-known who was, nonetheless, knowledgeable, and, crucially, more accessible); however, since everyone did not have access to long-term and concentrated apprenticeship, other forms had to do.

Other Forms of Apprenticeship

Learning from books and videos was significant for participants and helped to fill a mentorship void in the absence of personal and individualized learning. This sort of learning, while not uncommon, crossed over into mentorship because of how carefully and seriously participants took it as part of their professional development. Rather than casual spectatorship, these resources created by VH mentors might be much of what could be accessed in the absence of local sources. Along with this general form of mentorship, the most common form was personal but infrequent: clinics.

Clinics where mentors could tutor participants and where riders can observe and learn from peers were a highly popular option. Although clinics often cost hundreds of dollars (not including travel and lodging), with an occurrence of once or twice per year per mentor, they are still a more manageable option than full-time traditional apprenticeship, which may pay little or not at all. Emily S. mentioned that she was "sure if you actually got to go and work with a person it would be way more than that, but a clinic does function well enough." That is not to say that clinics still do not economically stratify opportunity as there are some who simply cannot afford to attend—or can rarely do so. Undoubtedly, some, including those in this study, have had to sacrifice to participate. The reward is that it gives you the chance to see mentors in action, even if only for a few days. If you are willing, and able, to travel, then you might follow your favorite clinician around, as Ben described doing with Peter Campbell: "It was always two to three clinics each year. That was my vacation and where I spent every extra dollar I had. I went everywhere." Clinics are a necessary substitute for traditional apprenticeship.

It might be tempting to view such short bursts of apprenticeship that happen in clinics as inferior to longer, more traditional forms; however, as Marilyn O. noted, even though she wished clinics happened more frequently, "in those three or four days that you ride with the clinicians they give you a year's worth of stuff to work on anyway." Clinics could also be concentrated learning experiences that influenced them forever after. Susan H. mentioned, after attending one of Buck Brannaman's clinics early in her career, "that's why I liked Buck so much the first time I saw him...he could back up everything he said. By the end of five days, I was ready to follow him anywhere to see what he had to say." Reed E. also described a similar intensity present when the clinician makes themselves available after working hours; he cited Mike Bridges' clinics where participants signed up to prepare and share meals, resulting in many informal chances to ask questions after processing what happened during riding. These clinics were necessarily smaller, which made it possible to provide individual feedback.

These initial clinic experiences often generated intense loyalty as participants would then follow their selected mentors for years and even decades; they spoke of these mentors in sometimes emotional tones, remembering words of praise received over the years. For example, Alicia B. recalled receiving advice from Buck Brannaman that was especially helpful for someone studying a less common form of horsemanship: "Just ride like you have blinders on. Do your thing, and stay committed, and don't let other opinions sway you from what you know is the path that you're on." This advice became a guiding light for her, even when she felt alone on her path.

Dynamic Mentorship and Curricula

Interviewees discussed how apprenticeship, like expertise, could be dynamic—much like horses themselves. Being dynamic meant that knowledge could pass back and forth between peers and that the curriculum itself was not set or static. Concerning the former, Alex described mentoring a younger horseman: "I passed along what I'd picked up, which he has since done such a great job. He used to call me and ask a lot of questions, and I find myself calling him and asking him questions now, and he's done the same thing for others." He said that this was a natural result of working with horses together and sharing knowledge in the moment as part of the process. Even though these interactions do not formally follow an apprenticeship model, they are still significant for both the teacher (who then might become the learner) and the student.

Three other participants, Linda H., Charlotte, and Reed E., detailed learning without a predetermined curriculum in both camps and clinics. For Linda H., studying at Tom Curtin's ranch suited her learning style, given that she was willing to be curious and self-motivated:

> The best way to go to Tom's camp is, for me, not a hard thing at all—I was coming with specific things I wanted to work on, which I knew would then lead to many other things that I needed to work on. Tom just lets me ask a million questions. He's great with that. To think that he's going to have a format and say, this is what we're going to do, and this is what you need to work on—no. He expects that you're going to have a little fire in the belly—that you're coming hungry and want to know something. If you're coming to be entertained or have the format given to you, you're probably going to struggle a little bit. If you didn't ask a question the entire time, he's probably only going to intervene if he thought you were going to die. It's a little bit of the cowboy culture—that they don't go where they're not asked.

The sentiments above were supported by Charlotte, who described her experiences at one of Joe Wolter's clinics: "Whatever's going on he'll work with you at that moment. In other words, it's not a structured, everybody-do-this approach." Crucial to this learning situation is positioning oneself as a questioner; if you are not asking questions, then you are not likely learning. Being responsible for your own learning also prepares you for expertise, even if you do not want the label, since you are then constantly acquiring knowledge and experience. We might think of experts as "knowing it all," but that disposition does not really bear out with horses and their thought-provoking and sometimes perplexing natures. Just as cowboys might not go where they are not asked, learning might not go where it has not been invited in, as some participants highlighted.

The way that some clinics are structured also lends itself to this sort of invitation. As mentioned above, Reed E. attended Mike Bridges' clinics for many years and noted that there was not a "a curriculum that Mike had to stick to"—instead, learning was driven by "whatever we wanted to work on." A critical element of this approach is trusting learners to set a relevant pace by essentially taking over the curriculum. Spreading expertise around, and foregrounding participation, makes the clinic a more engaging process for all rather than focusing on one expert leader.

Flexible and Approximate Apprenticeship

A sort of flexible apprenticeship can be cultivated that benefits both human and horse. This apprenticeship is not about learning to have *the* answer, or knowing it unequivocally, but being willing to experiment, drawing upon the full range of what you know and what you have experienced. Reed E. described it as having to adapt knowledge to the demands of the moment, a necessity of working with horses:

> It's one thing to be working with somebody, lessons or clinics or videos or whatever, but when you're out in the middle of the field there on your horse and something happens, what do you do to deal with it? There's not somebody there today to tell you, more leg, more rein, less, more, now, stop it, whatever. So you kind of just have to try it, and then pay attention to what happens, and does that get you a little closer to where you're going, or does it make you a little bit further away?

Horsemanship is practiced more often with just the horse and not one's mentors observing, so for these participants, being an apprentice with, and to, the horse had to be flexible and dynamic.

The other apprenticeship category that I identified in participants' responses was what I am calling "approximate"; like the label of expert, approximate apprenticeship is also flexible and context-dependent. This included seeking out more accessible and local mentors as well as taking advantage of spontaneous opportunities to learn from more knowledgeable others. Maggie shared that one strategy she had adopted came about after hearing a story on National Public Radio aimed at "businesspeople and entrepreneurs" about finding "somebody who is incrementally ahead of you on the same path—not the guru," because the guru would not have time to work with you individually (the role of the guru is "mostly about inspiration" and less about actual tutelage). She had chosen Alicia B., in a neighboring state, for this purpose. As Leadbeater and Miller (2004) noted, "[P]rofessionals [or gurus] create a distribution bottleneck" (p. 11) and so "near-peers in the circulation of knowledgeable skill" (Lave & Wenger, 1991, p. 57) can serve a vital function in terms of distributing knowledge.

In a similar move, Susan H. had found another local horseman earlyish in her career to work with, who was also a Pro-Am following Buck Brannaman; she would visit him for instruction in order to feel like she was making progress until Buck made the rounds again. This helped her "to keep putting it together and figuring it out." This strategy echoes Gee's (2010) assertion that Pro-Ams "know how to collaborate with other Pro-Ams to put knowledge to work to fulfill their intellectual and social passions" (p. 14). Both Maggie and Susan H. sought out near-experts to be able to continue their journeys when they might have been stalled otherwise.

Emotional Aspects of Expertise and Apprenticeship

The last aspect of expertise and apprenticeship that I would like to discuss in this chapter concerns the emotions felt while in these roles (even given that being called an "expert" was undesirable). Below, I share a story from Susan H. because it effectively epitomizes both the informal mentoring that can occur during clinics as well as the feelings that can fuel learning horsemanship.

> I watched Joe Wolter teach this woman in a big group. They were cantering one at a time, and she was going around on the wrong lead. I'm thinking, for God's sake, Joe, tell her she's on the wrong lead. Tell her she's on the wrong lead. When she finally quit, he said, "That was really good. Next time, you might want to try to be on the inside lead instead of the outside, but it's good you kept him cantering that long." And I thought, I'm so stupid. I'm never going to get it because he got that for her to be out there cantering in front of everybody by herself and keeping that horse cantering was a big deal, and if he had yelled at her and said, "You're on the wrong lead," and said it in that tone of voice that sounds like, you're a damn idiot—do you not

know you're on the wrong lead, it would have completely devastated her probably. So yeah, I'm no expert at all.

Notably, Susan H. *is* considered an expert and is both highly accomplished and has a lifetime of learning horsemanship behind her, but she did not feel like one in that situation. When I shared her story with Joe Wolter, he responded that

> I was that lady at the thoroughbred farm [where he started out]. I worked for a trainer, and he coached me on riding those horses over jumps and on dressage. I tried so hard to do what the guy told me to do, but my focus was totally on him. If I didn't get it right, he'd get louder and louder and louder. For some reason, I didn't want to quit. I quit him, but I didn't quit horses. I was that lady. I know what it's like. She was doing the best she could, and that horse was doing the best that he could. Sometimes you got to get with them like letting that lady lope around there on the wrong lead. I'm going to get with her, and then maybe she can get with me. You got to get with these people. Don't tell them they're doing everything wrong.

Susan H.'s story reveals the sensitivity that is ideally involved in effective teaching, both with horses and beyond. Joe's response revealed that he had learned firsthand how negative feedback can squash a burgeoning apprenticeship. He would come to be known for his kindness in working with riders, and, whether he realized it or not, he mentored others in how to steward a rider's emotions.

Other participants also highlighted the role of emotion in learning horsemanship (and I am using a more general term here instead of VH because I think this applies to all disciplines). Johnny C. described "want[ing] to be more like him [one of his mentors] because he is the kindest, gentlest person that I've ever seen," and Maggie stated that one of her mentors "listened to me, and he never made me feel like a dingbat, even though I really was at that time. I look back at it now, and I'm like, thanks, man." Being on the receiving end of kind and considerate behavior positively impacted participants both at the time and in their future work with their own students and horses.

Another feature of vernacular literacies is that "they are entwined in people's emotional lives" (Barton & Hamilton, 1998, p. 255). "Experts" and mentors are also modeling the emotional literacy of effective horsemanship in addition to the more visible moves of training. In Greg Eliel's case, his own emotional reactions to a certain teaching approach, similar to what Joe Wolter described, motivated him to adopt a different tack:

> I don't do well when people are yelling at me and getting gruff with me. It makes my brain shut down, and I can't think, and so it gives me empathy. Why am I teaching

you any different than the horse? I wouldn't tolerate you thumping and bumping your horse around. Why would the teacher do the same thing to you verbally? It doesn't do the horse any good—doesn't do you any good. And what I learned a long time ago is that essentially horses just want to be comfortable, and they want to do their job, but they want to be comfortable. That's the greatest overriding thing, and people are the same way, and they'll migrate to comfort. So then you've got to kind of push them because it's not an easy journey—when you start to look inside your-self like that, it's not always very comfortable.

The vernacular literacy of VH, including its emotional side, involves learning how to interact with both horses and humans in a way that gives them a comfortable place from which to learn while also recognizing that the work itself might push them out of their comfort zone.

Even though this learning process is emotionally challenging and can be uncomfortable, this does not mean participants want to escape it. Linda H. and I had the following exchange about the road to expertise and the emotion involved:

LINDA: Because you realize it's a journey—it's not a destination. Every horse is different—every moment's different. I guess you realize you want it to be a journey.
JULIANNA: Because?
LINDA: You're glad that it's a journey and not a destination because then it never ends.
JULIANNA: Because you love it so much.
LINDA: Yeah, and what you learn—sorry—(tears up).

For participants, working with horses is emotionally involved work, just as working with people would be, and perhaps even more so. The road to expertise, even without arrival, again, overlaps with Barton and Hamilton's (1998) categorization of local literacies and vernacular practices as "entwined in people's emotional lives in very obvious ways" (p. 255). The work of apprenticeship, and reluctant expertise, that participants described doing was work close to the heart. That VH is "entwined in [their] emotional lives" is part of what made their relationships to the concepts of expertise and apprenticeship personal, even though we are talking about their professional careers and work lives.

Obviously horses themselves fuel an emotional motivation to increase knowledge. Amy G. described this as a worthy fixation:

I think you have to be obsessed. I mean I think that's step one—just like Bill [Dorrance] and all the old timers say, you have to be determined, and you have to really want it. I feel like I'm obsessed—who knows if I'll ever be considered a master, but

I'm going to keep trying for that, and it's not to impress people or anything but just to have that level of connection with a horse.

Amy's remarks about this topic are in line with one component of expertise that Dreyfus (2002) described: "After one becomes an expert one can rest on one's laurels and stop this kind of obsessing (reviewing one's performance in a methodical way), but if one is to be the kind of expert that goes on learning, one has to go on dwelling emotionally on what one has done" (p. 423). According to Dreyfus' characterization, Amy's "obsession" with creating "that level of connection with a horse" is necessary to becoming the sort of expert that is valued in VH. There was evidence throughout the interviews of dwelling emotionally on how well particular interactions with horses had gone and how they might be improved in addition to reflecting upon what they learned from working with those they felt were experts.

Being perceived as an expert by others did not matter, but being able to get along with a variety of horses, each with their own personalities, did (and does). Furthermore, these emotional elements of expertise can then influence interactions with other people. Kathleen K.'s musings echo Amy G.'s above: "Who knows if I'll ever master this. It's different with every horse I meet. Then you start to transfer it (VH) into your life, and it's the same with humans. I think there's an element of what we're learning that makes us better people. So, yeah, clearly I'm passionate about it." To return to the concept of Pro-Ams, they "have passion and go deep rather than wide" (Gee, 2010, p. 14). While a hallmark of VH is often the calm demeanor that educators have while working with horses, stronger emotions play a part in the cultivation of knowledge and also motivate commitment to the practice and lifestyle.

SITUATED APPRENTICESHIP AND MASTERY

Lave and Wenger (1991) recast the expert and apprentice roles in the learning process in *Situated Learning: Legitimate Peripheral Participation*. One of their focal ideas was "that learners inevitably participate in communities of practitioners and that the mastery of knowledge and skill requires newcomers to move toward full participation in the sociocultural practices of a community" (p. 29). They utilized the terms "peripheral" and "full" to describe participation but not in the dichotomous way that we might expect; instead, "[p]eripherally suggests that there are multiple, varied, more- or less-engaged and -inclusive ways of being located in the fields of participation defined by a community" (pp. 35–36). Peripheral participation leads to full participation, a term that "is intended to do justice to the diversity of relations involved in varying forms of community membership" (p. 37). Therefore, it is not that, while learning, you are in the

borderlands until one day you suddenly arrive at the center of expertise. Rather, learning means that you are consistently participating in (a variety of) ways that are recognized by your particular community; acquisition of knowledge is situated in specific
communities. According to this view, learning is not confined to a brain working on
its own, but involves a brain working with other brains (including equine ones) in social transactions that result in new knowledge.

For our purposes in this volume, Lave and Wenger (1991) also had some intriguing
things to say specifically about the roles of experts (whom they call "masters"), which
"are surprisingly variable across time and place" (p. 91). As we can see from participants'
comments, mentorship took different forms in their lives, and no one form was considered superior. Additionally, Lave and Wenger (1991) put forth the idea "that mastery resides not in the master but in the organization of the community of practice of
which the master is a part" (p. 94). This makes mastery a sort of free agent among practitioners and means that more people might be able to access it than would otherwise
be able to since it resides in the community itself and not just in select individuals; this
is particularly useful for those learning VH since the experts/mentors are relatively few
and often working at a great distance.

What about the horse as both apprentice and expert? The horses that worked with
participants were learning VH alongside them, but, of course, they are already experts at being horses (and will remind you of that if your ego gets bigger than an actual horse). Horses have the last word on whether what you learned about horsemanship from the human expert will actually work. Lave and Wenger (1991) stated that
"in shaping the relation of masters to apprentices, the issue of conferring legitimacy is
more important than the issue of providing teaching" (p. 92). While masters might
decide whether you are a fellow expert, your fellow learners are instrumental as well
since, generally, "apprentices learn mostly in relation with other apprentices" (p. 93).
Horses, as both experts and fellow learners, ultimately decide whether you are a legitimate horseperson while you are teaching them *and* while they are teaching you. They
both simplify the teaching and learning process with their immediate feedback and
complicate it, as they may reveal that you are, in fact, more of an apprentice than you
thought you were.

Lastly, there is one component of apprenticeship that Lave and Wenger (1991) described that does not fit with this study: They stated that for apprentices there are "less
demands on time, effort, and responsibility for work than for full participants" (p. 110).
This is not the case with horsemanship. Both masters and novices can experience the
same demands on time, effort, and responsibility when working with horses, and the
horse does not necessarily recognize a distinction between expert and apprentice, as
the latter might have natural talent and inclination to make up the difference. Because
so much of horsemanship takes place between one human and one horse, there can be

no withholding of effort. Showing up for a horse requires all that you have at that particular moment.

CONCLUSION

Since there are only two subjects they [vaqueros/buckaroos] can talk
on intelligently, one of them being about horses and cattle, it generally
gets priority on such [social] occasions. (Morris, 2010, p. 202)

The humorous tone of Morris' statement in *Vaquero Heritage* applies to expertise, as well: The label of expert is simply not taken too seriously in modern VH. What *is* taken seriously is that expertise is calibrated differently, according to how horses respond, which is ever-changing, and *not* to how humans conceive of success or even achievement. Participants' views on expertise remind me of Rorty's (2007) description of aspects of Dewey's philosophy: "All our judgments are experimental and fallible. Unconditionality and absolutes are not things we should strive for" (p. 188). Judgments in the company of horses can be especially experimental and fallible. Overall, what participants communicated about becoming an expert at VH was that being one was not as desirable or realistic as making progress toward a continually shifting goal of becoming better for, and with, the horse. This is expertise by perhaps another name (e.g., expert-learners, Pro-Ams) and certainly another notion (a conditional and tenuous one).

Rather than thinking about expertise and apprenticeship in dichotomous terms (i.e., I either am or am not one), it is more useful in this context to think of both as existing on a continuum. Interviewees saw themselves as continually growing and learning, with horses occupying the role of permanent, and humbling, teacher and mediating the entire process of apprenticeship and expertise. Because the *work* and the *life* of VH are, to a large degree if not entirely, one and the same, expertise is not confined to a career; this "personal journey" of "just trying to get better . . . so it's a better deal for the horse" (Buck Brannaman; personal interview) has no arrival point. For those teaching horses and humans, there is, in addition to the personal work done with their own horses, always another individual to try to reach, thus edging out expertise ever further. And these educators seem to be fine with that.

Furthermore, in this study, the cultivation of expertise, including apprenticeship, did not follow a standardized or predetermined path. Instead, it took many forms, including spontaneous and abbreviated ones, which were more widely available than working closely with one individual over time and, moreover, resembled a live music performance, with improvisation and changeability. Geeves et al. (2016) depicted playing live music as follows:

Live performance requires an expert musician to recall a thoroughly learned piece of music with a high amount of accuracy in the charged setting of a performance venue. . . . Yet not only must an expert musician recall encoded material accurately, it must be done in such a way as to allow for the unknown and unpredictable variables that inevitably arise during performance to be handled effectively. (p. 112)

Of course, work with horses is itself a live performance and sounds identical to how Geeves et al. characterized the work of an expert musician. Your prior knowledge of horses joins, like stringing musical notes together, to experience-in-action. Performance in horsemanship results in new and revised knowledge, but humans have to leave room for the "unknown and unpredictable" reactions of horses (our co-musicians). Then, innovation, which is helpful when working with dynamic partners, can occur—a new song between horse and human.

Even if the label of *expert* does not necessarily apply, it certainly does not mean that its absence leads to some sort of learning utopia. Undoubtedly, participants would have preferred to have more access to their preferred mentors, but they had made do with what they did have, and this did not slow down their pursuit of more knowledge; more experience could always be found in the company of horses and that would then lead to even more knowledge. That an animal is more significant than a fellow human is part of what makes horsemanship unique as a site of learning. It is possible to romanticize the lifestyle, or horses themselves, but it is harder to be romantic about the determining influence the horse has on the human in terms of teaching us how expert we are *not*. Make no mistake: Acquiring knowledge in this context can be tough, intellectually and emotionally.

What purposes might be served by shying away from not only the label of "expert" but the concept of expertise? Being an expert-learner can become a "disposition" (Holland et al., 1998, p. 136) that acknowledges, and even honors, the challenging, fragile, and sometimes tense nature of understanding and educating horses. Being wary of being an "expert" also helps keep the horse at the center of your work instead of worrying about the self-promotion that often accompanies this designation. Joe Wolter shared that, "Millie [Hunt, Ray's first wife] told me the last time I saw her, when we started, we were just trying to make things better for horses and cattle and dogs and kids. That's what we were trying to do on those ranches out there. We weren't seeking to be somebody's idol." Participants knew that you could have significant knowledge, and perhaps even expertise, but accepting that you have arrived where experts reside is dangerous territory indeed; rather than dwelling there, they preferred to travel on ahead to more experience and further understanding.

INTERLUDE 3

Bruce Sandifer and Mooney

I HAVE A HORSE, MOONEY, THAT I ACQUIRED WHEN I MET MY WIFE; SHE HAD him when he was a colt. He was a stud horse and unstarted. I started him when he was three and a half, I think. He was a little obnoxious, but he fit my personality. I got to working with him, and he taught me so much. He was just such a nice cow horse that we ended up doing a lot of things together. As time went on, he was one I developed a lot of stuff on as I was coming up with this system—and started to work on myself more than fixing the horses. So, it was that transition from working in the horse trainer world to becoming a people trainer, I guess you'd say.

The best story about him was when we were showing at the Vaquero Fiesta, which used to be a big event Richard Caldwell put on. I'd just had this amazing ride where he was sitting down and stopping beautifully, and we went and called our other cow and a bunch of really wild, big heifers. We started down the fence out of that, and the cow kind of stuttered, and Mooney hit the breaks for a second and then kept going, but I popped my pelvis, and my pelvis broke and split four inches. So, when that happens, every muscle in your back just starts spasming out. We're running, and I'm pushing on my horn, and I've got my mecate in my belt. And I'm thinking, the only time I'm really going to able to get off is when he turns that cow, and I've got both hands pushing down on him because I'm just trying not to fall off. He goes down—he turns that cow, and okay, boom. He turns the cow, and I just roll off over the left side, and I think, man, it's really going to hurt when he hits this mecate because he doesn't stop on cows when he gets going on them. But he felt that and stopped instantly. He's a rope horse, so he's been backed off the rope a few times. I've got this mecate in my belt, and I'm in excruciating pain. These people start running up to help me, and I'm like, oh, easy, easy—because I know he's going to start running backward and pull this mecate on my belt. But he never moved a muscle all the time. It was amazing. They flew me to Reno, where I had surgery, and he didn't see me for like two weeks; some friends of mine hauled him home. So, my wife brings him out when I'm home. I'm in a wheelchair, and she wheels me out on the porch, and she leads him up. About halfway down the driveway, he starts whinnying. I knew, at that point, that I must be doing something different—something better than I'd ever done before, because I'd never had one be so concerned about me. When you submit a horse into doing what you want, they look for any opportunity where you're out of control to leave you—when you're not in dominant command. So, the fact that that just came together like in that way, with that particular horse—that was a very meaningful thing for me.

CHAPTER 4

The Crossroads of Vaquero Horsemanship and Consumer Culture

The bit he silvered for me [Bill Dorrance] is one that I designed from an old Santa Barbara style bit that dated from the days of the early California vaquero. Most people don't know anything about these bits. And they know even less about the fella who's knowledgeable enough to use one properly, or the preparation that goes into a horse that qualifies him to wear one. I'm in hopes that this will change. (Dorrance & Desmond, 2007, np)

IN THIS CHAPTER, I ASK TWO QUESTIONS: (1) WHAT ARE THE EFFECTS OF CON-sumer culture on the horses who live with humans? and (2) how does consumer culture affect the practice of modern Vaquero horsemanship? While consumer culture may not matter to horses, it *does* matter to humans, so, considering that, what I focus on are the consumer choices we make that do affect, positively and negatively (and sometimes both), the lives of horses by way of the gear we buy and horsemanship clinics we pay to attend. The field of cultural studies, to which I turn in this chapter for some introductory concepts, illuminates the consumer influence as it relates to VH. If you are tempted to think that an academic discipline like cultural studies has little to do with horsemanship, consider this analysis of the word "culture":

> In *Keywords* (1976) the cultural theorist and critic, Raymond Williams, defined *culture* as one of the four or five key concepts in modern social knowledge. He re-minded us that the term was originally associated with the idea of the tending or cultivation of crops and animals—as, for example in *agri-culture*—from which we derive one of its central modern meanings: culture as the process of human devel-opment. (Du Gay et al., 2013, p. 5)

So, horsemanship is historically, and still, a cultural activity—and caring for horses was associated with culture from the beginning. The "refinement" that we might connect

with the arts of "high" culture has a correlation with the progression of the tack resulting in a Vaquero horsemanship bridle horse. The material choices that VH followers make perpetuate the tradition (as Dorrance's quote illustrated), on one hand, but
also serve to distract from it. Participants had thoughts about negotiating this tension.

THE TENSE INTERSECTION OF CONSUMER CULTURE AND VAQUERO HORSEMANSHIP

All types of animal-human interaction are shaped
by distinctive constellations of artifacts, from horse
tack to milking machines. (Grier, 2014, p. 125)

The "distinctive constellation" of Vaquero horsemanship tack makes it stand out and
marks the wearer as following a particular horsemanship philosophy (at least in theory). Grier (2014) also outlined how consumer culture and animal ownership inter-
sect: "The material culture of pet keeping in America is part of a larger system of text,
talk, and objects through which the attitudes of Americans toward the animals they
care for as companions, ornaments, sources of leisure, or emblems of social status are
articulated and performed" (p. 137). (Note that I am including horses in this category
since they are often cared for in similar ways). "Text, talk, and objects" may seem like
suspiciously abstract stuff from which to draw conclusions about horsemanship, but
they provide the inspiration for this chapter; I look to the talk and text of participants'
interviews and also to the objects that make up the material world in this tradition.

Before progressing further with the idea that horsemanship transmits portions of
consumer culture, it is helpful to back up a step and discuss the horse as a cultural ob-
ject. Storey's (2021) depiction of the moon as such can help us imagine the horse in a
similar cultural position:

> The materiality of the moon can exist just fine without human culture. To describe
> the moon as a cultural construct is not to claim that it is culture that brought it into
> being. Rather it is the claim that what the moon signifies and how the signification
> helps organize our relations with the moon is always a matter of culture. The moon
> is real enough but for us its reality is entangled with signification and this significa-
> tion frames our interactions with the moon. Once it is caught in the human gaze it
> becomes a cultural object—a significant object in popular culture. (p. 239)

Again, substituting the horse for the moon gives us insight into the position the former
occupies in this chapter: The horse is still always itself but is *also* a cultural construction
that is part of the larger subculture of VH. Horses "can exist just fine without human

culture," but horsemanship holds them "in the human gaze." Once there, they become entangled with consumer culture.

Clearly, one assumption of this chapter is that people practice VH in the context of consumer culture. As Sandlin and McLaren (2009) noted, "The ideology of consumerism is currently one of the most dominant forces in society; we undoubtedly live in a consumer world, and we enact processes of consumption in almost every aspect of our lives" (p. 2). Specifically in horsemanship, one manifestation of this is treating horses as a disposable commodity. Linda H. described it as horsemanship "that's a pursuit of an award and whatever it takes to get there and if this animal won't do it, then get another one." This "ideology of consumerism" shapes the practice of horsemanship in obvious ways (e.g., what Linda described and by influencing our identities as riders) and in sneakier ways (influencing which identities we can afford regardless of skill with horses).

To continue with a relatively straightforward point from cultural studies about what our possessions represent, Berger (2010) asserted that in "consumer-crazed societies ... the things we purchase are no longer evaluated in terms of their use or functionality but rather in terms of what they signify about us—what they reveal about us, such as our taste, our style, our socioeconomic level, and our attitudes toward authority" (p. 50). Horsemanship provides an exception to the dichotomy of use versus signification: While VH gear has a tangible, practical utility, it also communicates messages about those who choose this "style" among the other kinds of horsemanship ("style" carries this double meaning since it also marks the material features of dressing oneself and one's horse in a particular way). Additionally, "objects, artifacts, things, 'stuff,' ... are very complex and can reveal a great deal to us, if we know what questions to ask of them" (Berger, 2010, p. 177). As I mentioned at the beginning of this chapter, I ask what VH "stuff" means *for* (not *to*) horses and for its practitioners; it plays a distinctive role that distinguishes riders from other, usually more popular—at least in the southeast—disciplines.

Horses certainly know which gear used by their riders is more or less functional and comfortable, but the gear itself uses horses, in a way. Daston and Mitman (2005) stated, "Striking images of animals are in great demand by global advertisers because—in contrast to equally striking images of humans—age, race, class, and culture do not interfere with identification and the desire to acquire" (p. 6). Animals, innocent though they are, transmit our consumer culture; horses are particularly striking, even without effort, and so they are unsuspecting advertisements for VH gear. Rather than being chosen by clever advertisers, they are enrolled by their owners who have chosen this style with its distinctive gear. While it would be too cynical to state that riders are using tack to advertise in a conventional sense (to encourage others to buy it), I would argue that they are advertising their identities as VH practitioners, which, of course, is what the tack of all of the different disciplines does.

Modern VH, or horsemanship for that matter, is not the first time that horses have collided with consumerism. Bingmann (2015) described the private Western ranch schools that, one hundred years ago, "promised the elite that through 'simplicity of living,' ranch life would develop 'self-reliance' and courage in boys" (xiii); horses played a significant role in these schools (p. 99), and the word "vaquero" was used in their "public displays of horsemanship" (p. 101). Based on "an American concept of a mythic West of the past" (xiii), they were partially conceived of as an antidote to the creep of consumerism affecting youth (xiv). However, they contained their own "paradoxes and ironies," one of which was that, despite their "aim" to counter consumerism, they actually encouraged it "[B]y creating an image of the West as devoid of consumerism, the region itself became a consumable experience, available only to the very wealthy who could afford tuition fees, a horse, and the plethora of western accouterments needed to truly remake oneself" (p. 20). The intersection of horses and consumerism still provides tensions, paradoxes, and ironies, and there is a real sense in which VH is more readily available to those who can afford it.

THE "STUFF" OF VAQUERO HORSEMANSHIP

A new mecate is pretty, but an old mecate is beautiful. (Morris, 2014, p. 98)

There was general agreement among participants that the "good, true horsemanship" at the core of VH could exist and "be just as valuable" without the specific gear that might accompany it; I use "might" because you could certainly practice elements of VH without all of the tack, and, as I have mentioned, many were practicing it without working toward the traditional goal of creating a bridle horse; however, the gear is still a thing—by that I mean, it is still a consideration and an influence on the practice of VH, even if some ignored it. The gear is what makes VH visually recognizable to other humans, but how much does it matter to the horse? This distinction might be the consumer litmus test: If your tack matters to the horse, then it can be called essential, but if it does not, and especially if it only matters to other people, then it is a consumer luxury or material indulgence. Back to the word "might" again because we also need to consider that modern VH is a continuation of historical traditions in horsemanship, and the gear itself carries a good bit of that history. It does not *just* exist in our modern consumer society; it also carries a story forward, one framed by traditions that practitioners find valuable and honorable for both human and horse.

In a story of a different sort, Storey's (2021) introductory ideas about materialism and popular culture also provide a constructive way to think about the gear of VH beyond its obvious utility as "stuff" needed to ride a horse. Storey stated that "the material objects that surround us do not issue their own meaning; they have to be made to mean and how they're made to signify informs how we think about them, value them and use them" (p. 237). Our purchases are more than just innocent consumer choices of innocent objects (although they might be until we assign meaning); instead, they are a substantial way that we make sense of our world and simultaneously place ourselves in it. The distinctions between vaquero and Wade saddles are an example of this.

Historical vaqueros rode in a different saddle than most modern followers of VH do. The saddle that is now associated with VH is the Wade saddle, an invention by Tom Dorrance (whose humility caused him to decline being its namesake) and Clifford Wade, as many interviewees made sure to tell me (a few noted its resemblance to a *charro* saddle, and the following backstory mentioned the influence of the "old Spanish Vaquero saddles": https://freckerssaddlery.com/about/wade-saddle-tree-history/ ; see also Reynolds [2004] for a history of the Western saddle). A Wade saddle, from the time it is made by someone who deliberately chooses this style to craft, until it is sold to someone who selects it from the wide variety available, signifies that the owner values a certain kind of horsemanship, even if they are not skilled at practicing it. This saddle can also make you stand out in a cluster of English riders, if uniqueness is part of what you are after; as one participant noted, in the southeast, if "you show up in a Wade saddle, they're like, what kind of saddle is that?"

One obvious influence of consumer culture on VH is that a Wade saddle, made for long days of working cattle, is not necessarily needed by some, especially recreational riders, who use them. Feeling like a Wade saddle *is* needed is due to the consumer culture in which modern VH is practiced. The gear has become synonymous with the label itself because using it is akin to saying, "I follow Vaquero horsemanship; I am placing myself in this tradition," and others will accept you faster as a devotee if you have all of the "stuff." Another example would be amateur riders who have ropes on their saddles that they do not use, or do so infrequently, and so are privileging signification and value over actual necessity.

One irony in this gear-as-identification is, as Tom Curtin observed, that *what* exactly people are identifying themselves with is somewhat muddled since historical VH developed into a buckaroo-influenced (i.e., the Wade saddle and snaffle bit) style: "You've got to have a certain saddle, and you've got to have this and that, and it's not even what you would call traditional vaquero equipment. A lot of this is coming from what it has evolved into with this style of horsemanship. I'm not saying it's right or it's wrong. It's different than what it was." Some riders believe the equipment (like the Wade saddle) "signifies" VH, that they value it, and are continuing the traditions (Storey, 2021, p. 237), but they are actually promoting a relatively recent variation of it. Knowing whether riders care about this, or are even aware of it, is beyond the scope of this study, but the point I wish to make is that even when using the stuff of VH, what it means is more complicated than it seems. While you need "basic" tack to ride other than bareback, investing in more than that, if you can afford to, is a choice with effects on both riders' identities and on the practice of VH; I will deal with each of these in turn below.

Identity Markers

Even when certain gear is not a necessity, it can serve as a way "to be able to identify our tribe" (Maggie) and as part of "do[ing] things to fit in" (Marilyn O.). As I mentioned earlier in this chapter, tack communicates to the other humans around you that you ride in a certain style and ascribe to a particular brand of horsemanship. Featherstone (1991, as cited in Berger, 2010) included as one of the aspects of consumer culture "the different ways in which people use goods in order to create social bonds or distinctions" (p. 35). This is not an entirely modern conception: Rojas (2010) mentioned that, when it came to historical vaqueros, "It was a poor vaquero indeed, and one entirely without pride who did not have some things made of silver about him or his horse" (p. 52)—although he noted that gear was prized and used as long as it lasted.

Gee's (2015) definition of "big D Discourse" also applies here as "[c]ombinations of ways with words and ways with 'other stuff' (bodies, clothes, objects, tools, actions, interactions, values, and beliefs) that can get people recognized as having certain socially significant identities" (np). If "small d" discourse covers the actual language used in communication, then Discourse includes the whole identity kit that some wear to be recognized—in this case, as VH practitioners. Participants mentioned that some riders made sure to buy all of the stuff of VH Discourse in an attempt to be recognized quickly within the community (although that does not always work, as I will discuss below), whereas others only adopt parts of the Discourse and forego others. Those who follow the philosophy of VH, for example, but ride with English tack would not be recognized as vaqueros.

The crossroads of Vaquero horsemanship and consumer culture can make it seem that some are simply spending at the mercy of outside influences and attempting to just purchase the Discourse. But Du Gay et al. (2013) asserted that "[c]onsumption is becoming more of a personal act of 'production' in its own right" (p. 15). We are not without agency in this process as we can produce our desired identities by using our style to associate ourselves with VH mentors. Marilyn O. commented that "You are who you hang out with" and that she chose to use the same gear as her mentors, and she noticed that the students she worked with at her barn would then emulate what she wore and used. This is materialism as membership, or, using stuff to visually identify with those you admire. Again, this is part of Discourse, or "hav[ing] to 'pull off' a complex performance, where 'pull off'—to be 'right'—here means getting others to recognize and accept you" (Gee, 2015, np). To this end, mentors function as "cultural intermediaries"

(Bourdieu, 1984, as cited in Du Gay et al., 2013) "who play an active role in promoting consumption through attaching to products and services particular meanings and life-styles with which consumers will identify" (p. 56). While mentors may not set out to encourage consumption, it becomes a by-product of emulation, even in horsemanship.

One interviewee described consumption as part of "human nature," which is signif-icant for two reasons. First, as I have pointed out, this is something humans do that has nothing to do with horse nature; it is about us posturing for each other. Second, ascrib-ing it to human nature makes it seem like it might be something we are destined to do. I would argue that it is more something that we are *socialized* to do as part of the mate-rial culture we inhabit, given that in "the postmodern era, the meanings of consump-tion ... have become tied much more to identity formation" (Sandlin & McLaren, 2009, p. 3). We have been socialized to want to use material objects to express who we are—and who we aspire to be. The horse might let us know that this identity work does not nec-essarily do anything to develop our horsemanship. It may make us look cool though.

"Look at What I've Got!"

When we discussed the influence of consumer culture on VH, a few participants used the word "costume," in that some just wanted to wear it without doing the hard work of horsemanship. Emily S. also observed that "There's an element that goes into this—some people are just doing it because it looks cool." Jeff Derby elaborated: "It's nice if you get a cool hat or if you get a good-looking saddle or some neat gear that you can be proud of and you can spend some disposable income on. Sometimes first somebody sees the silver on a piece of gear, and they're like, oh, that's nice—I have a horse—I'd like to have something pretty like that. Sometimes it's the gear that first gets them." Even though style and taste vary among individuals, VH, arguably, has attractive and distinctive gear; some of it is simply beautiful. The aesthetics tap into the romanti-cism that mainstream U.S. society often adorns the history and culture of the American West with. Although, using stuff to look cool is obviously not limited to horsemanship, nostalgia, or nostalgia about horsemanship:

> Status-oriented consumption, a form of consumer behavior in which possession of
> new and branded commodities is seen as a necessary prerequisite to achieving the
> highly coveted state of "cool," and the idea that membership and higher status in
> peer groups are contingent upon the same criterion, is another concerning aspect
> of consumerist culture. (Cho, Keum, & Shah, 2015, as cited in Fritz, 2020, p. 478)

Having this gear can certainly help to admit you to the VH "club" and be recognized by others in it. One subtheme of this section of the interviews is that some riders buy all of the best (i.e., most expensive) gear in what seems like an attempt to gain "higher status" in the community. This could also be an effort to become better at VH but the "concerning aspect" of it is that it might subtract from actual work with the horse.

While Jeff Derby and Emily S. described what they had observed of others wanting to look cool, Ben reflected on his own relationship with the crossroads of VH and consumer culture, which had undergone a substantial shift. He was not so much concerned with looking cool as he was with keeping pace with his mentor's collection and wondering if he might need *better* stuff (the constant curse of consumer culture). While others I interviewed had also patterned their choice of gear after their mentors', he had reconsidered this after feedback from his mentor, late horseman Peter Campbell. He recounted this for me when I asked about whether VH gear was used to create an image.

> BEN: Yeah. The image—you knocked the nail on the head on that one, and I used to buy into it big time.
>
> JULIANNA: I think a lot of people buy into it.
>
> BEN: I bought into it big time. I've got a tack room for gear—I'm not saying there's anything wrong with that, but you don't need all that. I bought a saddle—I think I might still be paying on it—you've got to pay for it, right?
>
> JULIANNA: Yeah, I know what you mean.
>
> BEN: So, I get the saddle and I was like, man, this thing's nice, and I like it—I really do. But I bought it before I started riding with Peter, and I'm thinking, look at Peter—look at how many saddles he's got—and the bridle bits. Look at all that. And I start asking Peter, if you were going to get somebody to build you a saddle, who would you get? "What's wrong with yours? You don't like it? Why do you want another saddle?" Well, I tell you what, you've got five or six, you know? And I would just leave it like that, and he'd say, "What's wrong with yours? Can't you just be happy?" And Peter made the statement, "Tom Dorrance didn't have but one bridal bit, one hackamore, one saddle."
>
> JULIANNA: Really?
>
> BEN: Yeah. He was such a simple man it was unbelievable.
>
> JULIANNA: So, Peter helped move you past that idea of being a consumer?
>
> BEN: Oh, yeah. I thought I needed—"look at what I've got."

Tom Dorrance lived from 1910 to 2003, arguably a time when there was less of an emphasis on "needing" so much stuff to practice horsemanship effectively. The "look at what I've got" phenomenon might not be new to our age, but I suspect it has kept pace with societal consumerism more broadly. As we have become more materialistic, so has horsemanship. We might be maintaining an image, but it can only advance horsemanship practice so far; we pay for this stuff not only with money, but with our attention and energy, as well. Ben redirected his energy (or, Peter Campbell redirected it for him) by realizing that he did not need as much as he desired.

Tom Dorrance is considered, in the VH community and beyond, a genius of horsemanship and without equal. Two interviewees also shared the story that Dorrance's wife said that his wants and needs existed right alongside each other, with the former not exceeding the latter. He was "simple" in his consumer needs and did not need much materially. But we can also turn that term on its head: In our time, being simple like Dorrance is actually a complex task as it means ignoring the push to buy more and more stuff, especially when we are surrounded by others who buy into materialism. It has become tricky *not* to acquire. Horses are also "simple" in their material needs, so perhaps Dorrance was more horse than human in this regard.

When Looking Cool Breaks Down

Looking like your mentors does not mean much if you cannot ride like your mentors, even at an aspirational level. If you can only get so much done, are you going to work more on how you look or on how you ride? Alicia B. captured this discrepancy between image and ability:

> ALICIA: A lot of people can buy the stuff, and they're like, this is the vaquero tradition—the gear and all that. But they're missing the quality of the true—you can't put that stuff on. If you really don't have it going on, and you don't have the education or the understanding, it's very noticeable—the position on the horse is wrong, and the balance of it is all wrong. So, the people that you watch, and they're truly studying it and understanding it, it's a totally different look. I think that's what's so unique about this style of riding is that you can't fake it. You're not buying your way into it because the horse will tell on you, and pretty soon, you'll have all the stuff and you'll look super cool, but you'll also look like a big idiot because everyone knows you're not supporting your horse and you're not helping him.
>
> JULIANNA: You see that at clinics?
>
> ALICIA: All the time.

Not being able to buy your way into VH, although some try to, can be a blessing for the horse since those who attempt to do this soon find out that wearing the gear without the knowledge is a short road to travel and that they need help with the actual horsemanship. Maggie described this as being a "gearhead"—those who have "all the gear and they ride terribly." She also recalled having a student ask her if she could "be acknowledged for [her] riding skill even though [she doesn't] have the gear." She thought that she could, although she might have to be comfortable shrugging off the influence of consumer culture. In his definition of Discourse, Gee (2015) included that "[b]eing recognized as something . . . is often a contestable, negotiable, and context-sensitive thing (i.e., what works in one setting may not work in other settings)" (np). Being a gearhead does not usually work in the horse part of horsemanship although it may make you *look* like you belong; the flip side of this coin is that not having the gear may make acceptance into the VH community a slower (albeit still possible) process.

What starts out as a more superficial interest in VH can then develop into a more substantial learning journey. Jeff Derby depicted this as switching focus to "the *relationship* that's developed between us and the horse." Seeing the gear in action can be especially motivating, especially if it has been revealed both to the horse and other humans that further learning is needed. As Alicia B. noted, "The horse will tell on you," although, unlike some humans, they will do it in a nonjudgmental way. They can communicate that a rider's horsemanship is lacking, even when that rider otherwise looks cool. In this way, consumer culture must answer to the horse, who has little need of it and yet still, in VH, gets the last word on it.

Clinics as Contradictory Ground

When looking good breaks down, many migrate to where consumer culture creates a place of both benefit and tension. Clinics can be contradictory ground when it comes to consumer culture: They might seem like events where appearances reign, and are undoubtedly places where riders can show off to their mentors and each other ("look at what I've got!"), *but* they are also sites of honesty in that mentors, peers, and horses will see if riders' knowledge includes how to use the gear effectively. Additionally, as I mentioned in chapter three, clinics can be relatively expensive, so they are not necessarily an open option for all. One mentor described clinics as having "become this whole society of three-day horsemanship" that's "marketable." Moreover, the temptation is to make them "human-centered" in order to maintain that marketability. Despite this human-centeredness, attending them does not guarantee improvement: Several interviewees mentioned seeing the same clinic attendees year after year who, in the words of one, "don't ride a damn bit better."

Despite the above tensions, clinics have filled a need in the larger VH community. Gwynn Turnbull brought up that "There's a social element to this style of horsemanship" and that "Clinics offered an alternative to the horse show circuit." She characterized clinics as offering a valuable and "non-competitive" opportunity: "[A clinic] wasn't just about the connection with the horse—it was this wonderful connection between people talking about the connection with their horses. I think that's really why it caught on—it wasn't just that the subject matter was important and interesting and necessary, but it also offered that social in-person connection." Being able to discuss a connection with your horse can also nurture and grow that relationship as riders get validation and share new ideas. Clearly, clinics exist to help both humans and horses, and sometimes that assistance is fused together.

VH practitioners are well aware of the sticky wicket that is educating a horse for a few months and then sending that horse back to, possibly, an uneducated owner; they felt this might be "betraying" the horse. Through offering clinics, Joe Wolter said, "I felt like I was doing more of a service helping the rider than I was helping the horse" because "if you can get the rider to look at things from the horse's point of view, then you stand a chance of them getting along together." Jeff Derby expressed something similar: "I'd rather teach people because I know if I'm just riding the horse, when the horse goes home, what I've tried to do—I've tried to build a relationship based on trust and understanding, and then if I send him home and that person doesn't have that same ability to work through to trust and understanding, I just lied to that horse." Getting horse and rider together, so they can work toward trust and understanding, lessens the need for the horse to have to "fill in for the rider," which, Joe noted, many are willing to do. Several participants referred to the generosity of the horse, and some, like Joe and Jeff, had reflected on ways not to overtax that generosity.

Another way that clinics are contradictory ground affects clinicians more than participants. Greg Eliel remarked that "An important part of the clinics is you can't forget that people are doing this as their recreation." Given this, I asked a few of the mentors, "How do you translate the working tradition of VH into a recreational form that fits into clinics? How do you teach a livestock-based tradition to those who don't work with livestock?" Cody Deering replied:

This can be difficult at times, but a clinic is to understand the "hows" and especially the "whys" of what we are doing. I always try to convey that what we are doing is simulating the real work. Can people practice Vaquero Horsemanship in an arena? Sure, I think so—as long as they do not lose track of why they are doing it. It's job-related, having to do with working cattle, but you have to leave the barn at some point and get to where the cattle are, which could take hours, and it is in that time that you develop a good feel or rapport. That's the goal—building a good relationship in which the horse and rider, and later the cattle, can all understand each other's feelings and ideas very well. So is it possible to teach a cattle-based tradition to people who will probably never work a cow? I would like to think that the person who wants to follow a traditional method would like to be involved in all that entails. However, there are plenty of skills to learn, as I say, on the way to the cattle, so in that way, then yes—why not build a good feel between you and your horse so that it will spill over into the rest of your life?

Cody takes a broader view of VH (even when it seems confined to an arena during a clinic): For him, it is a part of the philosophy of it (which I explore in chapter five), and that makes clinics a modern evolution with traditional ties. Cody enlarged my question by explaining that clinics are part of "the rest of your life," and so if VH can be learned in the former, then it can be practiced in the latter.

Lastly, clinics can be, as social occasions, places that encourage the growth of VH (after all, it was a clinic that first exposed me to it). Mike Bridges commented, "If people didn't have any place to go get with other people wearing the same costume—and do something—you wouldn't have one tenth of the people involved in it." Any gathering like it offers an opportunity to supplement the feedback and education the horse provides with schooling from fellow humans; however, if you wear a costume to a clinic, you had better be prepared to earn it.

MORE POSITIVE ASPECTS OF CONSUMER CULTURE ON HORSEBACK

> *"Why do all vaqueros and buckaroos use silver-mounted bits and spurs?" The old man turned in the saddle, stared at me in surprise and answered bluntly, "Because they have pride. . . . A man transmits his state of mind to the horse. A rider who doesn't have enough pride in his trade to decorate his outfit with a little silver never rides a good horse because he had no pride to transmit to the horse, and a horse that has no pride is never any good."* (Rojas, 2010, p. 450)

In addition to consumer culture being a possible motivator to concentrate on the horsemanship of VH, there were other positive aspects that participants cited. On a pragmatic level, utilizing certain gear can help you get the job done (in addition to, in Rojas' view, transmitting a sense of pride to the horse). Marilyn O. mentioned that "There's a certain functionality of a lot of the stuff," like the wide-brimmed hats and wild rags (usually silk and worn around the neck) that protect you from the elements and can help keep you comfortable. Tack can also greatly benefit horses if it makes them more comfortable while working, and while we might be riding for pleasure or as a hobby, it is always work for the horse.

Work for the artisans and makers of VH matters, too. Susan H. commented that in the VH tradition, "You probably did make a lot more of your own stuff." Since we are not, generally speaking, doing that anymore, this has led to more demand for artisans to fill the gap. Rather than being cheap, or widely available, individually crafted VH gear "is made with quality, and to do a job, and to last a long time" (Alicia B.)—so it can go against the current of mainstream consumer culture. You also know whose hands made the gear and whose life it is helping to support, which is no small feat today when trying to be a more thoughtful and responsible consumer (Greenwood, 2009). Since it is not mass-produced, there is often a long waiting list for handmade vaquero gear. The investment in it is also tempered by the fact that it is made to be used daily as part of a job rather than occasionally as a hobby.

Even though the gear might be practical and durable, it is also considered by those in the VH community to be art. Gwynn Turnbull noted that, "People respond to beautiful things. They respond to the saddles, and the carving, and the silver—the stuff is beautiful.... I think it's fun for them that they can participate with their pocketbook, and buy some neat stuff that is basically living art. I mean, it's functional. It's not just a sculpture that they put on the table. It's something that they can enjoy and get use out of." Bill Reynolds mentioned "our immediate-gratification world" (2014, p. xvi) in his book about the history of the Western saddle. In our interview, he stated that even though VH has evolved, "There are more custom saddlemakers and bit and spurmakers than there ever were. You don't have to go buy a manufactured saddle that will cripple you the first day." You can also buy it from "somebody who really understands the anatomy of a horse's back" and a bit from someone who knows how it "lays in a horse's mouth." Therefore, this increase in artisans bumps up the aesthetic, practical offerings for humans and, hopefully, means the horse's gear fits, and feels, better.

Both Alicia B. and Emily S. linked a rising popularity in handmade gear to a reaction to the business of consumerism, the "more and more" element that can tempt us to continually consume cheaper goods that need to be replaced. For Alicia, an increased interest is both about slowing consumption as well as the pace of life:

> I think it's awesome for the makers—this is their livelihood—making fantastic gear, long-lasting—they're works of art, really. When you look at the romal reins and the rawhide braiding and all of that, and I feel like—just from living in the city and being around the chaos of day-to-day, that there's now a generation of people that are wanting to go back to things that are well-made, handmade—just even the movement of people wanting to do gardening and sustainability.

Alicia's interpretation is supported by Barker and Jane (2016) who stated, "Claims that various aspects of consumption are causing social and environmental problems have led to movements and organizations promoting fiscal responsibility, sustainability and approaches to life which are slower and more simple" (p. 180). If you are not making your own gear, then money will have to be spent, but it can be paid directly to artisans, helping to support the continuation of the traditions (and not to the Amazon equivalents of the horsemanship world). The word *sustainability* connects to the pull of investing in "works of art," although art does not come cheap, so you would need to value the long-term utility of this investment—and be able to afford it; everyone else will have to save for it.

This investment can run counter to mainstream consumer habits; Emily S. mentioned having to save to buy the gear, and so acquiring it had been a sacrifice for her but one that was worth it, considering its lifespan.

> EMILY: Silver bits—those are made by an individual person with their own hands, and then the saddle that I bought that's so expensive, handmade by a guy that goes out in his own little building on his property and builds them. It's really good equipment. It's forever—like that stuff will get passed down to somebody when I die.
>
> JULIANNA: That seems at odds with our consumer culture.
>
> EMILY: Doesn't it? Well that's part of the new age—I'm trying to save some of the old quality as it gets more and more throwaway every year—isn't it?
>
> JULIANNA: Do you think that's part of what appeals to people about this style of horsemanship?
>
> EMILY: I do. I do because it is a throwaway society, and people throw away their animals that aren't good enough, too.

In her view, practicing VH was, at least partly, a reaction to, and commentary on, throwaway society, applying to both gear and the horses that wear it. So, choosing to stick with our horses and our stuff can challenge societal pressures to discard. VH is too much work, if studied seriously, to throw away lightly; it can be materially expensive, if you choose the handmade gear, but is also costly effort- and concentration-wise. The option of learning how to make it yourself remains, although in the southeast it would be difficult to find someone to apprentice to, unless you were willing to travel.

Supporting artisans, a positive side effect of consumer culture, can still have a negative tint since many modern-day makers use the Internet to advertise and sell. Fritz (2020) argued, "Among the socializing functions performed by media culture, perhaps none is more important to the vigor of a capitalist system than indoctrinating the public ... into becoming proficient consumers" (p. 476). While we can praise the support that Alicia B. and Emily S. spoke of, we can simultaneously recognize that social media encourages us to keep consuming (even though that might be mitigated by feeling that we are at least supporting small businesses). While I recognize that all consumerism is not created equal, I also believe that our media-saturated society has increased our perceived need(s) in general, including in horsemanship.

CONNOTATIONS AND RESPECT

Du Gay et al. (2013) discussed the "connotations" of objects as "a much richer set of meanings" (p. 9) than might seem obvious to the eye. What are the connotations of VH gear? As I have argued in this section, the gear has membership potential and also connotes a commitment to the tradition but can be a cheat in and of itself if you bought the look but cannot ride the style. Investing in the gear sends the message that you can afford to do so and may hint that you cannot afford to do so if you lack it. VH traditions are not inherited in the same way they were historically—consumer culture has seen to that. A few of the interviewees, one of whom stated that "anybody can have access to [VH], especially now," were critiqued by others in the community because they had been able to buy all the gear but had not studied VH for very long. Contrary to this example, and as the ideal connotation, the gear is used as "jewelry for the horse . . . to honor the horse for its years of study" (Emily S.). This connotation is similar to the association many historical vaqueros would have had to their gear: It takes years to afford and years to earn.

When Rodolfo Lara Sr. and I discussed the influence of consumer culture on VH, he stated that, "Tack does make a difference. You have to buy quality tack. You have to educate yourself on what you're using, how you're using it." Focusing on learning rather than on possessing more and more is a way to keep the horse at the center of your effort. How many riders own bits that they place into their horses' mouths without knowing exactly how they work? Rodolfo has a horse's skull that he uses to demonstrate to his students what different bits do to, and in, horses' mouths. Depending upon your level of curiosity, you could even read the research of Hilary Clayton (1984 & 1985, as cited in Anthony, 2007), who was the first to make "X-ray fluoroscopic videos of horses chewing bits" (p. 194). She and colleagues documented "just how horses manipulated a bit inside their mouths and precisely where it sat between their teeth" (p. 194). I offer this as an example of how we might utilize knowledge from our time to continue the horsemanship from the original vaqueros' time (when they also likely knew, as Rojas [2010] indicated, exactly how their bits worked in horses' mouths).

In Rodolfo's view, which other participants would surely agree with, buying gear should be a way to connect with VH traditions and further your own education—as such, he believes that it should be treated not just as a commodity: "Don't disrespect it. If you wear it, don't disrespect it. There's a lot of tradition and a lot of years and years of people trying to get better. So, I'm about that. I say don't disrespect it. That's it."

CONCLUSION

Horses are, thankfully, so much more straightforward than consumer culture. Buck Brannaman said that if "your horse says you're alright, you're alright," and what makes you alright is not "how you dress" or "what kind of saddle you put on him as long as it doesn't hurt," but "how you make them feel," including whether the gear fits well and is comfortable. Linda H. added that the horse also does not care how much you spent or whether you are the best outfitted in your group. We should be more like horses in this way.

At best, consumer culture connects us to finer tools to use in our work with horses. At worst, it can be a distraction from the actual practice of horsemanship, absorbing our effort and resources away from the horse; if any sort of horsemanship becomes prohibitively expensive, then it can keep us from practicing it altogether. What we "need" to ride can seem to multiply to keep pace with a society that never gets enough stuff. Even if consumer culture says that VH gear can be a costume, it does not have to be treated as one. As one interviewee noted, if Buck Brannaman were to show up one year wearing pink chaps, then the next year everyone would have them too. Like social media, consumerism can be a distraction—and the horsemanship equivalent of doomscrolling would be to focus on the attainment of more, newer, and flashier gear.

The mentors have some advice on this topic. Greg Eliel feels that we should "keep one thing in mind—this is what we always talk about—and that is put the horse first. What is best for the horse? They can keep human nature at bay, and I think Tom [Dorrance] would be happy with that." Horses can keep the more vexing facets of human nature at bay, including our inclination to consume; however, as cultural objects, both horses and VH can seem mysterious, and that mystery can be exploited. Bruce Sandifer remarked that "marketing people love that mystery because you don't really have to know much. You can sell the mystery of it." In contrast, he looks "at it from more of a scientific or biomechanical process. There's a reason it works. It feels like magic when you do it right. That's the thing—and the horses are happy." The mystery and magic can remain in VH, but getting beyond marketing requires inquiry, study, and, as Rodolfo Lara Sr. said, respect. Respecting the traditions (which scaffold the style and gear) and, most of all, the horse puts consumer culture in its place. Doing so can open up space to foreground the values and beliefs of VH. Working less on attainment and more on developing "an all-encompassing way of regarding the horse" (and fellow humans) leads into the focus of the next chapter: the philosophy of modern Vaquero horsemanship.

INTERLUDE 4

Rodolfo Lara Sr. and Jefe

WHAT I'M GOING TO TELL YOU NEXT IS THE BIGGEST PART OF WHY I'M with horses. The *garrocha* [a 12- to 13-foot-long pole used in riding] is one thing, the classical riding another—also calling myself "Vaquero horsemanship through classical riding." But I'm here to be better to them because they have saved my life more than once. I'll tell you a brief story, and I've shared this only once before, but I think it's important.

I signed up for the military during Desert Shield/Desert Storm. Being in a bunker in Saudi Arabia, having artillery up above, I saw people die; I held people while they died. We were in a bunker one night, and there had been some bus drivers that were from the Philippines and Nigeria. These guys didn't have gas masks, even though we were under the threat of Scud missiles. We had our gas masks, and these guys didn't, so they were digging holes with their hands trying to protect their faces. It was dark, and I remember the light from the moon—I saw this kid—well, we were all kids. He looked at me, and the fear in his eyes is the same fear that I see in some horses when their rider is beating up on them. I've seen that in dogs, too. I've seen it in people. But I see it a lot in horses.

I try to take the negatives out of my life and make them positives. So, that negative gave me a positive—understanding the horse a little bit better because fear in the eye is what changes first. I tell my students, be more empathetic because humans and horses are opposite—one is predator, and one is prey. The nature of the human is such that if you don't get things, you try to take things away. Horses don't. A horse is there for self-preservation, and I had that self-preservation. I wanted to come back home. So, all those experiences have helped me understand the horse better and have given me an understanding of the eye.

We have to let go of our past. Everything that I have done or that has been, I have found peace with it. I have found freedom with it. I have found everything that I needed as far as the therapy that I didn't get when I first got out of the military. I needed my mind to be here, but I wasn't in the now and the present. Now, when I'm on a horse, nothing else matters. The horse says, "Here. Nothing else matters. You're right here."

We need to allow the horse to let us grow. If we don't accept that, and we don't listen to them, and we don't allow them to help us, we're never going to get better. We have to put our vanity away; we have to put our machismo away. That's a big part of what you see most because we're too stubborn, and we think we know it all. So, I tell people, "Learn to communicate better." My clinics are not a horsemanship class; they're a communications class. The most important part of communication is the ability to listen. We neglect the horse's mind and are just focused on "I want a half-pass," "I want a leg yield," "I want shoulders in," and the horse is crying, "Let me go a little bit. Let me breathe a little bit."

By the same token, all of this has helped me understand the horse that I ride sometimes, Jefe. If I'm a little bit worried, I can't ride that horse because he went through some traumatic experiences. He was not even supposed to be here. They were going to send him back to Mexico and put him down, but he's here now. We're working together and having fun. He's helping me every day handle my emotions because if I get on that horse and I demonstrate anger or fear, he would run out of the ring. The fences wouldn't matter. If you get on that horse with fear or anger, it's not a safe place to be. He helps me control my emotions. I can feel when I'm going too far, and I can feel when I can go a little bit further. He's allowed me to go a little further each day, and we're doing some amazing things.

CHAPTER 5

The Philosophy of Modern
Vaquero Horsemanship

*The modern world provides more material goods to us, without offering
us significant cultural values. There is little sense of when more is
undesirable or where 'growth' might mean personal and meaningful
experience rather than material gain.* (Barker & Jane, 2016, p. 194)

*We are speaking of magic, but at the same time of philosophy,
common sense and the world as it is.* (Serres, 2016, p. 47)

IN THE LAST CHAPTER, I CONCENTRATED ON THE INFLUENCE OF CONSUMER
culture on modern Vaquero horsemanship. In this one, I turn to the philosophy
which informs VH. "Growth" in Vaquero horsemanship has a pronounced philosophical (and even spiritual) aspect that includes, not surprisingly, "personal and
meaningful experience(s)" with horses, with no small amount of self-reflection blended
in. As a transition from consumer culture (including the gear) to philosophy, I share
Gwynn Turnbull's thoughts on the relationship between the two:

> I want people to understand that even though the discipline has certain trappings
> that go along with it, that really, it's an all-encompassing way of regarding the horse.
> So, it kind of transcends the trappings. I appreciate the beauty of all that equipment
> because it takes so much time to braid rawhide reins, a rawhide reata, time to engrave
> silver. It takes a lot of time to do these very artistic things, which is in line with the
> amount of time it takes to make a beautiful bridle horse. . . . But I really want peo-
> ple to understand that it goes beyond that, and that we should be looking for this
> connection and this feeling with our horses.

Furthermore, this style of horsemanship has a philosophy that permeates many practitioners' lives, and they described it as accessible even for those who were not working to create bridle horses. Kathleen K. defined VH as being a "thought-through" (and

a felt-through) approach, which corresponds well to the focus of this chapter. Even though the philosophy of VH is its own chapter, it is critical to note that, in horsemanship, any distance between the physical and emotional can collapse: "We have to learn to control our own bodies, understand what's happening with horses—not only biomechanically, but emotionally, because horses are huge sponges of emotion . . . a lot of people don't realize how much breathing and emotions affect horses" (Bruce Sandifer). Practitioners working toward a collapse of distance between themselves and their horses need far more than the mechanics of horsemanship for that to occur.

PHILOSOPHY FROM THE MODERN TEXTS OF VAQUERO HORSEMANSHIP — AND BEYOND

In this section, I turn to the three modern texts that fall into the philosophical category and provide brief, subjective summaries of each one's philosophical elements: Tom Dorrance's *True Unity* (2010; originally published in 1987), Ray Hunt's *Think Harmony with Horses* (1978; dedicated to Tom Dorrance), and Bill Dorrance and Leslie Desmond's *True Horsemanship Through Feel* (2007; originally published in 1999). Readers will see that they shared an overlapping philosophy. I also weave in relevant comments from participants as well as additional research (that is "the beyond" of this section's title). I begin with Tom Dorrance's book because even though it was published after Ray Hunt's, the latter was greatly influenced by the former. Joe Wolter mentioned, akin to Gwynn Turnbull's comments, that the Dorrances and Hunt, although they rode bridle horses and appreciated vaquero style, were not concerned with the particular gear that was used but, instead, there was an emphasis on "communication" and "what your relationship was with the horse." He also noted that "they treated people like they treated everything. They looked at the good and just overlooked the bad. And the good got bigger and the bad got smaller." You will see this reflected in their horsemanship books.

True Unity (Dorrance, 2010)

Some participants specifically mentioned reading *True Unity* over and over because of how "philosophical" it is. Like the two other texts in this section, Dorrance has different things to tell you (or, rather, to nudge you to consider) when you read his book at various points in your horsemanship journey. Bryan Neubert said, "Tom would teach you how to think," and Joe Wolter noted that Tom, like his older brother Bill, was always looking for the good in the horse that could be built upon. Dorrance wrote about the difficulty of using language to capture the more nuanced aspects of

his approach, although he settled on the word "spirit" to convey the need to think beyond the mechanics:

> I felt this in horses all my life, but I don't think I realized how important it was to
> try to calm that inward part down. I was always working on the surface, both men-
> tally and physically—not getting right down to the inside of the horse. No one is
> going to get this without it coming right out of the inside of themselves. The rest
> of it has to come from inside the horse. Mind, body and spirit is what we're talking
> about here. (pp. 14–15)

He let us know that he *progressed* into thinking about spirit, so we need not feel too
badly if we have been stuck working at the physical level. We can also see how his words
inspired participants to work on both the inside of themselves *and* the horse (and therefore not place the whole burden on horses). Dorrance believed that although spirit
might be "the least mentioned," "it is the most important factor to recognize" as part
of "the horse's need for self-preservation" (p. 9).

As Dorrance described it, there is reciprocity available (Dorrance & Desmond
[2007] also mentioned "reciprocal feel") between human and horse, if only humans
will work to recognize it:

> I believe horses *naturally* have tremendous faith in the human being. It is their nat-
> ural instinct of self-preservation that the person needs to understand in order to
> gain the confidence of the horse. Many, many times I have seen where the person
> has missed the understanding of the horse's need for self-preservation, and this has
> caused the lack of confidence the horse is trying so hard to gain. Then, if a person can
> present himself or herself to the horse in a way that is understandable to the horse,
> so it can develop confidence, I find the horse is so forgiving. (p. 6)

He asked us to consider the idea that horses have faith in us and are trying to build confidence, but, also, that this effort coexists with self-preservation; it is up to us to learn
how to balance their willingness with their position as prey animals. The horse will over-
look our failed efforts and miscommunication and continue to work for, and toward, us.
We misread them, he cautioned, and this cuts into confidence-building on both sides.

Reciprocity can be established by a repositioning:

> When you put the horse first and try to work from where the horse is, back to the
> person, it makes it easier for the horse to find. I'd say most people start from where
> the person is and try to get the horse to work back to them. All the time, the horse
> is trying to tell you where he is. Listen to the horse. Try to find out what the horse
> is trying to tell you. (pp. 20–21)

Furthermore, "[t]he horses will tell you if you are listening to them" (p. 115), so you need to learn how to be a specific sort of listener—one that is less human-centered. This requires patience, humility, and cultivation of, perhaps, a new habit of where you place yourself philosophically (rather than just physically) in relation to the horse. Dewey (1902/1990) counseled that "habits ought to be formed with and through attention; not by mechanical repetition but by concentrating our consciousness upon things that bring about our success in any given case" (p. 304). Making a habit of paying individualized attention to the horse, rather than "listening" as yet another mechanical (and thoughtless) exercise of horsemanship, increases our chances of being successful with horses; in Dorrance's view, this includes hearing "what the horse is trying to tell you" as a core horsemanship practice. In Dewey's view, habits should be thoughtfully cultivated and shaped by active minds—in this case, by both human and horse minds exchanging information. Dorrance urged readers to assume that a horse has a mind and to let him use it by "present[ing] something and then let[ting] him figure out how to get there" (p. 128). Joe Wolter affirmed this when urging riders to "see if you can get their thinking changed. And if that changes, their bodies will change." Conceiving as "training" in this way marks this style of horsemanship as forward-thinking, especially by its early proponents. More broadly, the fact that animals have attributes previously only ascribed to humans is an idea that has found some footing in our larger society.

In 2022, both the *Guardian* and the *New Yorker* had articles about intelligence and legal personhood, respectively. In the former, Ball noted, "Until rather recently, philosophers and scientists have been reluctant to grant a mind to any nonhuman entity. Feelings and emotions, hope and pain and a sense of self were deemed attributes that separated us from the rest of the living world" (p. 2). This turn toward "mindedness" also links to two themes of this study: humility and generosity, albeit in different contexts—"Conceiving of a universe of possible minds can discourage human hubris, and advises erring on the side of generosity in considering the rights and dignity of other beings. But it also enables a literally broad-minded view of what other minds could exist" (p. 7). So, science and horsemanship are now occupying some of the same territory. Although the former article focused on legal personhood for Happy, an elephant who has been a long-term resident of the Bronx Zoo, Wright also stated that "Humanity seems to be edging toward a radical new accommodation with the animal kingdom" (p. 2). Similarly, Wright highlighted a societal shift thanks to science:

> Scientific advances have also had a profound effect on popular attitudes. "We understand so much more now about animals' capabilities than we did in the past—how smart they are, how much they can suffer," [Pepperdine law professor] Cupp told [Wright]. "As that knowledge is spreading through society, it is just naturally going to push us to say we need to value these animals more highly." (p. 10)

Specialized horsemanship traditions, like VH, where the horse is valued as more of a lifestyle partner and not as a commodity or competition tool, have been ahead of this shift in our larger society.

Acknowledging that horses have minds, and should be able to use them, can create a space where our desired results diverge: "The horse may not be doing the thing that is the right thing for what the rider's asking him, but as far as the horse is concerned, he is doing the right thing" (p. 130). Giving the horse the benefit of the doubt may mean that it takes us longer to get to the (human's) goal, but it preserves the horse's dignity and spirit along the way. Caring about spirit also includes providing physical reassurance, as Dorrance made a point to mention that "Riders need to realize sometimes that horses need soothing, cuddling and comforting" (p. 126). Ray Hunt also discussed the importance of providing this so that horses understand petting as praise and positive reinforcement. Dorrance offered a moving example of the connection between responsibility, spirit, and physical reassurance:

> A few months ago I was helping a young man with his horse. This was a horse that was real scared inside.... Finally he began to realize what we were offering him was real, that it could be. *There's a big responsibility to not destroy that.* I told the group that horse needed lots and lots of petting. He has found out for the first time in his life he doesn't have to be scared. (p. 116; italics in original)

This is a modern extension of Bentham's (1789, as cited in Derrida, 2008) pivotal question: "Can they suffer?" (p. 27). Noticing that they *can* suffer fear and also attending to, and taking responsibility for, it means that any education done is done so with horses' emotional needs at the forefront.

Bryan Neubert reported that Dorrance "was attracted to the biggest messes he could find" to work with but he "never heard him refer negatively to any horse. The more troubled they were, the more he was interested in helping them." He also recalled that Dorrance's philosophy, and its more pragmatic elements, continued to develop: "I said, 'Do you still feel like you're growing?' and I remember he just turned to me kind of quick and he said, 'Oh, yeah.' I should have known. What he has improved upon was his judgement on what might fit with this individual horse with this individual person."

Even though he was highly accomplished, Tom Dorrance's humility was legendary. Greg Eliel mentioned that he didn't "know of anybody that was more skilled and yet more humble than Tom," and that he "was one of the most ego-free humans [he'd] ever met . . . he was a gentleman, and he was rooted in kindness." Tom Curtin also mentioned that "The ego will get in the way of this way of life and this philosophy, and when ego makes it about you, all this will slip away." Bryan described seeing "Tom Dorrance at a clinic where he would embark on an endeavor; in the middle of it, he'd say, 'Hold up there. Let's try something else.'" Dorrance demonstrated that humility was an inseparable part of his philosophy-in-action.

Think Harmony with Horses (Hunt, 1978)

Ray [Hunt] wanted to see if the horse existed that didn't understand the way he presented things, and he said he never found a horse that didn't understand his philosophy. He was so amazing about communicating with horses. He could just set situations up, and it was just beautiful. (Jaton Lord)

Throughout his book, Ray Hunt, like Tom Dorrance, also presented the horse as a thinking, feeling, and sensitive being who should be free to choose. The horse is described as "an individual" who is "entitled to his thoughts too, just as you are entitled to yours" (p. 2). He advised those working with horses to "[r]ealize you're working with a mind" (p. 6) and to "listen to your horse and learn from him" (p. 43). Work with the horse should be individualized and developmentally appropriate: "The horse tells you where he is. Work with him on his level" (p. 4), and he recommended that we "[s]ee how little it takes to do the job" (p. 11). He also warned that, "If you get into a frame of mind where you doubt your horse, you and he are in trouble" (p. 15). What he depicted sounds like the sort of relationship that we would aim for with a trusted confidante, and, in fact, he used the word "friendship" (p. 83) to capture the ideal horse-human connection.

In the "Equesology" section is Hunt's reiteration of his teaching and learning philosophy: "If you are going to teach a horse something and have a good relationship, you don't make him learn it—you let him learn it" (p. 85). *Letting*, rather than forcing (p. 2), is a key concept in his approach that requires the human to reorient—for so much of horse "training" involves force, if we think of it *not* only as the brute kind, but as also including lack of choice and conceiving of horses as lacking minds of their own (*letting* is a key concept in *True Unity* [Dorrance, 2010, p. 102] and letting horses learn is mentioned in Rojas [2010, p. 395]). Furthermore, he directly linked his conception of horses as sentient beings with our often unrealistic expectations of them as learners:

> We expect immediate learning from a horse. We expect him to go from kindergarten to the 8th grade, to high school, and to college without enough time, preparation, or consideration for his thoughts and feelings. We often don't even get him in a learning frame of mind before we begin to *train* him. We don't even have him relaxed and confident, where he can sit down in class and just listen. We skip all that preparation because we are so superior, or neglectful, or lazy. Because we haven't prepared ourselves to recognize the horse's feelings. (p. 7)

Part of Hunt's point is that we do not even show them the consideration that we show to children, let alone treat them as equals. We do not do the work we should be doing and then blame the horse for the results of that omission. "Expect[ing] immediate learning" is temptingly easy, especially in our impatient, consumer-driven society where horses can be positioned as products. Tom Curtin mentioned that he still, decades later, has "pictures in [his] mind" from seeing Hunt "do things with horses that [he's] never seen anybody even remotely come close to yet to this day" and still "strive[s] for those things every day."

Even the more pragmatic "questions and answers" section contains a summary of Hunt's philosophy:

> [The horse's] attention and his attitude of responding back to you should be a "live softness." This gets back to: you feel of him, you feel for him, then you both feel together, even if it's just getting his attention back with you as you are going down the road. It doesn't have to be doing any particular thing—just being ready to respond to whatever you're going to ask him to do. In other words, it's respond and respect. When you reach for your horse he responds with respect. Respect is understanding, not fear. (p. 56)

These peaceful transactions, rather than dramatic or heated exchanges, take place continually, and the horse understands what is being communicated. Instead of issuing less-frequent, high-stakes commands, this is about the lower-stakes hum of interchange (not to be confused with the constant contact of rein and/or bit pressure). Hunt also highlights what the horse gets from this arrangement: "When he once learns to operate from this place of respond and respect, he turns loose then gives. It's something all horses seem to really like. They like to operate from this place" (p. 60). Overall, he advised, "Be observant, then remember and compare. This is true in every walk of life. . . . I wish it would all fall into place right now for you, but it doesn't because it has to become a way of life. It's a way you think. It's a way you live" (p. 4). Because it "become[s] a way of life," perspective and patience are needed in horsemanship—and beyond. Hunt's philosophy did not indulge abstraction for its own sake but was, and is, tethered, in a constructive way, to the humans who might choose to live it, and, most importantly, to the horses who might enliven it.

True Horsemanship Through Feel
(Dorrance & Desmond, 2007)

Bill Dorrance and Leslie Desmond defined true horsemanship as "when the horse understands through feel what he's expected to do" (p. 362). The very first sentence of *True Horsemanship Through Feel* lets the reader know how they view horses: "Horses are intelligent, and they can make decisions. This is the reason that they can sense what a person wants them to do and will try to understand a person's intent" (p. 1). Horses are, from the outset, positioned as possessing agency (if we will just allow them to exercise it) and willing to work cooperatively with us. The generosity of horses is a point made again a few pages later, and I emphasize it because I believe it is part of their core philosophy: "When the horse understands what you want, he will do what that is, right up to the limits of his physical capacity and sometimes well beyond it" (p. 3). This is reinforced by Jones (2020), a cognitive scientist and horsewoman, who stated, "Horses are generous, but those who are bonded deeply to a true horseman will try their hearts out" (p. 265). Dorrance remarked that, in his then-93 years, "When he understands what you want him to do, through feel, he will do it. I haven't seen any exceptions to this yet" (p. 330). Horses are reliable in their sensitivity to us and await the same from us.

Dorrance and Desmond were clear about what should, and should not, contribute to "feel." To begin with what does not belong, they advised that, "Regardless of the reason a horse is the way he is, if a person can't control him without the use of force or fear, one thing is certain—the person involved isn't yet able to offer the horse a feel that he can understand" (p. 11). People should not "approach a horse with rigid ideas they're expecting him to fit into" (p. 198). We shoulder the responsibility for making ourselves understood to the horse and not the other way around. Along with avoiding force and fear, they believed that "People who use and understand feel in the way we're speaking about aren't mentioning that word 'problem,' not if the subject concerned horses anyway" (p. 173). Instead, a primary goal is to make the horse feel protected: "Be real gentle and patient as you teach your horse to understand that he's safe when he's with you" (p. 72).

The horse's mind and point of view are key to Dorrance and Desmond's approach. Not only should we acknowledge that they have both, but we need to act on this knowledge in all of our interactions with them:

This approach to the horse's mind is the most important part. . . . It [reciprocal feel] *begins* when force and speed are replaced with patience in a different feel that comes when you start to understand the horse's point of view. Sometimes when you miss the chance to reward the horse's efforts by easing off the pressure, it could take a long time before he's ready to try that same move again. That's because he's pretty sure that lowering his head wasn't what you had in mind. If you don't release that pressure when he gives a little try, then he can't be too sure of what you want. But, he'll keep searching in other areas to see what you expect him to do. If you've missed his tries a few times, then lowering his head might not occur to him to try again for a while. Eventually he'll hit on that idea again because most horses want to know what you'd like them to do. It's in their nature to want to get along, and they're curious anyway.

To me, it seems that if a person knew this, they might have more interest in waiting for that horse to figure out what they expected him to do. (p. 81)

Even with horses actively trying to figure out what you are asking for (and, especially with less-expert riders, cues might be muddled), miscommunication will sometimes occur. How patient will we be with this trial and error? Dorrance and Desmond counseled a constant practice of patience, with awareness that horses are trying to collaborate and relying on their curiosity to engage with us. They urged us to approach the horse as capable and thinking his way toward us, while underscoring the horse's (rather than the human's) timeline.

The idea of "reciprocal feel," and reciprocity more broadly, is key to the philosophy of modern VH. In terms of human-animal relations, "reciprocity is not merely cooperation toward a goal, it is a relationship of trust. It is a relationship of belief" (Gibson, 2020, p. 267). It is a two-way exchange where each influences the other, and, even more so, depends upon each other; it is not the cold exchange of consumerism or impersonal interaction. You must be close enough to influence each other, and, with horses, you are physically close, as you trust them with your life, but also emotionally bonded. And they *can* (if you do the work) come to trust you to treat them fairly and with respect. Reciprocity takes time to establish and must be nurtured once it is.

Even in his 90s, Bill Dorrance stated that he was "still looking for ways to improve on how this could be put across to people, because there's nothing more important to the horse than feel. It's what they look for in other living things, it's how they live and, maybe, it's the reason they're still around" (p. 198). He also contended that this philosophy extended further than the farm and ranch and could offer humans a lesson in communication without force or fear:

> With everything nowadays speeded up as it is, I've often wondered if there isn't something real important that people can learn from the way horses interact. When feel is operating in the horse the way it was set up to work, there's no part of it that's got anything to do with mix-ups about force, or fear or resistance. They understand each other—there's no question about that. I'm not sure on this, but I'd rather think there's something the horse has to contribute to this world that's a little further up the line and thought than just having someone sit up there on his back, or having people use him in those other ways they found for him to get their harder work done. (p. 198)

This extension also is evident throughout my interviews as participants generalized their own personal philosophies to include what they had learned about, and with, horses—and about life. They did view horses as contributing profound lessons and value beyond just physical back-up for humans.

PHILOSOPHY IN ACTION

The human-animal bond is a mutually beneficial and dynamic relationship between people and animals that is influenced by behaviors essential to the health and wellbeing of both. This includes, among other things, emotional, psychological, and physical interactions of people, animals, and the environment. (American Veterinary Medical Association [AVMA], nd/np)

All of Life

The American Veterinary Medical Association's definition of the human-animal bond signals the relatedness of "people, animals, and the environment"—hard dividing lines are subsequently softened, and we cross into each other's territory. The philosophy of modern VH also wanders outward from horsemanship into practitioners' lives, and, subsequently, there are no hard dividing lines between them either. Participants' thoughts on this support the idea that "[h]ow we relate to animals is closely related to how we relate to ourselves and to other humans" (Bekoff, 2002, p. 138). Again, this has an historic parallel: "The sayings, proverbs and maxims which are woven into the fabric of California legends and folklore were so much a part of the vaquero's daily life that he applied them in all his dealing with men, horses, cattle and other denizens of the ranches" (Rojas, 2010, p. 390).

Several participants used the phrase "way of life" when describing modern VH; Tom Curtin described it as "a journey" that "you live every day" that is about "how one living thing presents itself to another." Of course, the journey requires ongoing effort on our part. Mike Bridges drew upon a concept that is reoccurring in modern VH—harmony—and combined it with the work we can do to bring harmony about: "We can make adjustments. The horse cannot make an adjustment. The horse is a horse is a horse. So, try to be in harmony with them. I would like to live my life in harmony with all living things."

Like Joe Wolter's statement earlier in this chapter about how the Dorrances and Hunt treated horses and people no differently, Alicia B. observed the same in those she had seen practice VH:

> That's another part that I still find really cool and fascinating is that when you're around the people that ride in the vaquero style and the way their relationships are the same as the way they treat their horses, you want to be around them. They're fun people, and you can trust them. They don't sabotage you. They're just very level-headed and good people to be around, and their horses are the same way.

Alicia had chosen this horsemanship after studying other disciplines, and because she is in an area of the country where she is not surrounded by VH, she has had to seek out similarly interested peers. So, finding "good people," and staying connected with them, has required effort.

Marilyn O. explained how the VH philosophy, which she had learned from Buck Brannaman, had permeated her life: "I really feel like the way that Buck does things is a manner in which I can't just turn myself on when I'm with horses and then be a different person outside of horses. I've had to learn to become kinder and gentler in my own personal life but also more firm. I think it makes you a better person altogether." There is no ring or corral that bounds the philosophy of VH: While the physical work might be done there, the mental and emotional work that fuels it is done all of the time—a lived philosophy, one which will not take hold if it is mechanical or insincere.

Furthermore, Marilyn O. wanted to share her philosophy with others but found that they were not receptive to it until it was accompanied by a practical need. She mentioned that she "used to be kind of preachy about it because I just believed in it so much. I wanted to teach everybody and their mama about this great way to work horses, and people just aren't interested unless they need it." She had learned that "once they see it and can believe in it, that's when I think people start to really ask more questions because if you can get this done, what else can you get done? So there has to be some sort of an open door." Otherwise, the philosophy does not necessarily have anything to attach itself to, which it needs since it is, at a minimum, thought-provoking, and can be quite demanding.

Like Marilyn O., Ben has applied horsemanship lessons to his own life and then reflected on people more generally:

> You've got to have a lot of self-discipline, and then once you have that, you'll find that you'll start putting it into work and relationships. You'll start looking at people differently, I'll tell you that. Once you start picking up how one thing can fix the other, you start looking at people different—at least I have because you start understanding people a little bit, and I've learned by doing this two things about people. One is that people make fun of things they don't understand, and the other thing is that when they run out of knowledge they resort to force.

Extending beliefs outward from horsemanship, and personal experience of it, to all of life was characteristic of participants' responses about this subject. VH seemed to invite this generalization for participants—perhaps because the philosophical facet is so sharp and fundamental. Returning to the idea of Pro-Ams, Leadbeater and Miller (2004) stated that "Professionals are more likely to understand the theory behind good practice, while Pro-Ams might have strong know-how and technique. The stronger theoretical knowledge base of the professionals should allow them more scope for analysis and generalization" (pp. 22–23).

Kathleen K. also spoke about the expansion of her own horsemanship philosophy and more specifically described what this can include:

Then you start to transfer it into your life, and it's the same with humans. I think there's an element of what we're learning that makes us better people.... I think it is a way of being. It is a way of being with your horses. It's a way of controlling your own energy. I've learned you have to center yourself. You have to control what you're putting out there. You oftentimes have people ask you, what is feel? To be able to give an answer to that is difficult. It does have to do a lot with what kind of energy you're putting out there, and with horses it can be turned on quick, and you've got to turn it off quick. I think for humans, that's tough. We take things personally. We hang on to stuff.

This quote illustrates three key points of this chapter: that the philosophy of VH, as participants interpreted it, covers the entire landscape of your life; that as it goes with horses, so it goes with humans; and that the elusive "feel" has a philosophical center. For Kathleen, it has to do with energy that invites a different range of responses; as she noted, humans can be grudge-holders, which can test both horsemanship and life. Several interviewees, including Kathleen, mentioned that horses do not hold grudges, so we diverge from them in this regard. Reflecting on what might hold us back in horsemanship (and life) is the subject of the next section.

SOUL-SEARCHING THROUGH VAQUERO HORSEMANSHIP

Horses perform these amazing athletic feats, and yet they still rest the
weight of their heads gently on our shoulders and breathe softly into
our ears. They stand quietly next to us while we cry. They connect with
all manner of troubled people ... offering their hearts to let people heal.
"Here I am," they imply in peace. "Let's just be." (Jones, 2020, p. 265)

I begin with this quote from *Horse Brain, Human Brain: The Neuroscience of Horsemanship* to let readers know, or to remind them, of the powerful and life-changing connections people find with horses, even, or sometimes especially, during their darkest days. Many of us have found, in the company of horses, a soul-safe place. Due to this, the deeply reflective work that might come about from VH philosophy seems possible. Bryan Neubert mentioned that Tom Dorrance, "put his finger on my chest, and he said, if you want this, it has to come from within here."

Emily S. described VH as requiring "a lot of dedication and soul searching because you have to totally examine yourself to be good with horses at this level." Bruce Sandifer and I discussed how recreational riders, who have often invested much to have horses and attend clinics for fun, can find it "not an easy pill to swallow" when they are told that "this horse is fine, but you're the one that's got to change" (this may make them re-consider their definition of "fun" or at least expand it to include self-examination). Jeff Derby shared an illustration of reflecting on his own practice and teaching:

> For me, it all goes back to the same thing. If we're willing to bang a horse into sub-mission, or just manipulate him into what we want because he doesn't think he has a choice, that's not what I'm after. If that's all we're doing, I'm out. I'll go ride him all by myself, which I threaten to do all the time. Or I won't ride. But again, I'm afraid sometimes that sounds a little sanctimonious. I don't mean it that way. It's not a holier-than-thou thing. I just think about it a lot, and I try to boil it right down to what's actually happening, what my actual motivation is, or what we're actually do-ing out there. Because again, we've gotten really good at coming up with lots of little sayings that sound good, but it doesn't always fit the actions, and so I don't want it to just sound good. I want to question myself. Is that really what's happening? And if it's not, what is happening? And then try to go from there.

As his statements indicate, VH philosophy can be passionate and full of lively reflection. And Jeff was not the only one to express this depth and level of commitment. Ricky Quinn also spoke about his own process of introspection that was sourced in horse-manship and then turned outward:

> The philosophy that I'm talking about is how you present yourself to the horse. It's not what you get out of the horse as far as a result. It's how you manage your own mind, your own emotions, your understanding of what you need from your horse . . . what is appealing to me about this style of horsemanship probably the most is the day that I realized that it really wasn't about the horses—that it was truly about me and how I presented myself to them . . . the answer is understanding yourself, understanding your emotions, understanding how to control your emotions. The human has got to find themselves to even be able to present themselves in a way so horses can accept it. So, it gets addicting because you get better as a person. You go out into the world and the world starts to treat you or view you and accept you dif-ferently, and it feels good. . . . It's really not about the horse. The horse is fine when he's by himself. When you go and catch him, that's when he has problems. So, we've got to stop focusing on that the horse has got the problems and the horse needs to fix this. The human being has got the majority of the work to do.

What Ricky outlined is how he discovered the philosophical aspects of horsemanship, which came after he had been doing the physical work of it. This is obviously different from reading about it beforehand and then trying to attach it to something concrete in the world, but once he started reflecting on it, his horsemanship was forever changed.

Like Ricky, Linda H. referred to how "addicting" this soul-searching could be and defined the spiritual side as wanting "more" from your horsemanship, even though that might place you in the minority:

> These people wanting more are not a huge number compared to what we see in other aspects of the horse world. It's a smaller number, but when you want it, you want it. You kind of move heaven and earth to learn more. When I say it's addictive, it's addictive in a good way because you become more—you become more aware, more empathetic to life—other life, things outside yourself, that other aspects of the horse world do not invite—in fact, might even invite you to become a little more narcissistic—when something's a pursuit of an award and whatever it takes to get there.

Interestingly, she portrayed the spiritual aspect in terms of desire, *wanting it*, and addiction, which seems at odds with what we often think of as the spiritual side of life and an emphasis on values like austerity or self-restraint. But this is not to be mistaken for religious values; instead, it is about being willing to rearrange your soul in order to become better with horses, if that is what is needed. As Linda pointed out, that might come with more awareness and more empathy overall. She also highlighted the difficulty of "commercializing" this kind of horsemanship because "it would degrade it in some way to do that because it touches that deep."

Elijah saw soul-searching as a tense fit with our societal timelines:

> You're going to have to look into your soul . . . and, in this day and age, it's very hard with everybody wanting it *now*. Everybody doesn't want to go deep. Everything is so fast-paced that they don't take time to slow down and fit into the horse's world. Everybody's so fixated on putting the horse in our world . . . there's so many times when everybody's in such a rush that they miss the opportunity to connect with the horse.

Greg Eliel also mentioned our "instant gratification society of constant dopamine hits that absolutely are counterproductive to this way of thinking and living." This looking inward and working outward are comingled in VH, but you have to overcome a parade of distractions to study the philosophy of it. This calls to mind Bekoff's (2002) statement about the soul-searching that animals prompt in him: "Animals continually help me deal with the 'big' question of who I am in the massive but interconnected universe" (p. 192). Similarly, the philosophy of VH involves considering who we are in relation to horses *and* humans—and who we might become. As Elijah noted, this may not fit with the human's timeline, which can unintentionally crowd out a spiritual connection with the horse.

Taking the time for soul-searching is another crooked circling back to historical vaqueros: We have inherited their horsemanship timeline, which has evolved into a philosophy. Bill Reynolds described the philosophy as

> a mindset that gentles you significantly and gives you the ability to look at other people and say, they get to be respected too. There's a transcendence to all of this, and it all really does go back to the fact that these vaqueros two centuries ago simply had the time on their hands where they could say, I wonder if I could get that horse to pick up his right foot and put it here. That's really the origin of it. It's a way of thinking and it's a way of approaching living things in your life.

Vaquero horsemanship is a slow-craft way of thinking with rich rewards through reflection, if you are willing to work on yourself. Johnny C. described this as "bettering yourself, and the rest of the world, through horses." You might not set out to become a better human being by way of VH, but as participants emphasized, the opportunity for it is built into the philosophy. You could not achieve one betterment without the other, which makes it a development of the self, and not just the self in the saddle.

Lastly, I would like to mention that living the philosophy is an individualized, rather than standardized, undertaking. Emily S. likened soul-searching to an artistic process: "The most important thing is working on yourself—self-reflection, self-awareness, and then learning how to use your awareness.... The goals are patience and perseverance.... Then there is just an infinite amount of creativity and art that goes into it." The mention of creativity and art convey that there is no predetermined way to engage with VH philosophy. Philosophical aspects of horsemanship can be daunting, and overwhelming, but thinking of them as an art form is freeing.

Generosity Toward the Horse

> *The best horsemen are quiet and consistent, firmly kind, and, from the horse's point of view, good listeners.* (McGuane, 2013, pp. 10–11)

> *I asked Joe to let his horse know way early. I told him, "He's the type of a person,* that horse is, *that likes to know before he goes to bed tonight what the next day is going to be; instead of waiting until after breakfast and then starting to think about it. That horse is a way early. If he doesn't know way early, it bothers him. He may not sleep."* (Dorrance, 2010, p. 118; italics [reversed here] in original)

Even though Dorrance's quote is humorous, generosity toward horses is an aspect that participants took very seriously as part of modern VH philosophy (Dorrance did, too), and it was one result of their soul-searching. I owe this term to Alex, who mentioned, "I don't know that you can really get with your horse if you don't have a little bit of generosity." That generosity can begin with *how* we try to connect with them. Ray Hunt (1978) thought that we ought to try to communicate the same with both humans and horses: "We can learn to understand one another if we listen to one another, if we respect one another's thoughts; we can work on things, figure them out so there doesn't have to be any hassle in life. And again, we will try to do quite a bit of this with other human beings, but we won't put up much of a try with the horse" (pp. 7–8). Most, if not all, participants see horses as easier to communicate with than people, so putting up more "of a try" might be relatively easy, and horses might actually facilitate this generosity. Johnny C. viewed the horse as especially perceptive: "The horse can seek out the truth faster and see it. You can't hide stuff from a horse—you can't hide who you are. That's one thing I like about horses is they see you for what you are, who you are." If we spend a significant amount of time with a being who sees us for who we are, and continually extend generosity toward them, then the qualities of honesty and generosity can influence our philosophy as part of its practice.

Not surprisingly, part of this generosity includes finding alternatives to force, or as Bryan Neubert stated, "I've tried to make horses do things with no success. I have some ideas about how I can get my idea to become a clearer idea, but I have had zero success making a horse do anything." He *could* use force but does not see that as an option. In a similar vein, Miguel described an approach that is on the horse's timeline and requires patience:

> We're trying to get everyone to understand that they don't have to be rough with their horses. There are certain exercises that we can do that will help you grasp the attention of your horse and bring you and the horse closer together. After practicing, you can have a totally different horse without having to jerk on your horse's face. You could just look where you're going and your horse will go. I'm always repeating to everyone, use a gentle approach, but firm.

What he described entails mutuality, meaning that the goal is two-way communication rather than harsh physical commands. VH philosophy embodies the *opposite* of the horse-as-beast-of-burden approach. Horses are also not treated as objects in service to human ego and vanity. Bruce Sandifer stated, "My philosophy is that I don't allow my pursuit of performance to outweigh the physical and mental comfort of the horse. You can accomplish many things, but it's not for the benefit of the horse—it's at the expense of. It's for the glory of you and not to glorify the horse."

Alternatives to force include not coercing horses into human-sized experiences, designed to fit us rather than them. Jeff Derby discussed not "taking away the horse from the horse" and "trying to find a way that we can work together" without taking away their athleticism and power as it suits us. Instead, he aims to "have them accept what I want rather than make them take what I want." He also used the phrase "trying to leave a whole lot of that in them now," which is similar to what Ray Hunt said in interlude six in this volume; Hunt explained that rather than trying to take a behavior out of a horse, it was better to "leave that in there" and cover it with so many positive experiences that the horse would not feel the need to resort to that behavior. Not forcing horses to be reduced to our comfort level or to quit behaviors we find troubling is, in participants' views, a generosity that we can afford.

Generosity can also mean *not* continuing to work with humans. Maggie recounted how she had come to view training situations where horses would do better without further working relationships with us:

> There's a quote from Ray Hunt, "That horse is going to be fine, but he's never going to be the horse he could have been." I saw that a lot with the horses I was working with—they weren't going to be what they could have been if something had been different earlier on, and I also believe the horse has a choice in this. If he doesn't want to ride into the sunset as a unicorn pooping cupcakes underneath a rainbow, then who am I to make him? He has a choice here too. Maybe his choice is, I'm ruined enough. Why don't you just leave me alone and let me graze out my days? Why don't you just leave me alone instead of trying to fix me? I really don't want to be fixed. Fixing sometimes costs way more to the horse.

Some of the participants, like Maggie, had worked with horses who had been trained with other methods and had inherited the fallout of these approaches. While they were often able to remediate these horses, this was not always a complete fix. Giving them the choice *not* to participate might not be what first comes to mind when pondering generosity toward horses, but in VH philosophy there is an overarching awareness of, and respect for, horse agency.

Failure and Compromise

In this section, I explain how failure and compromise assist in finetuning the philosophy of modern VH in action. Joe Wolter recalled that Ray Hunt "used to say, 'You've got to do too much to find out how much is enough.'" His longtime friend, Bryan Neubert, sees failure as "a very big part of success" because "you're learning what doesn't work." He also noted that there are "times with horses you allow them to fail, or as Tom [Dorrance] put it, help them be miserable"; you do this not to punish them but so that they will seek out an alternative of their own accord. For humans educating horses, key is that horses "have different personalities, different memories, different sensitivities; they're as different as everybody you know" (Bryan). If they were all the same, we could just follow a step-by-step method to educate them, which, participants made sure that I understood, is definitely not how VH is lived. Educating horses (I also discussed this as "differentiation" in chapter two) necessitates flexibility—and with that comes the possibility of failure.

Cody Deering outlined his philosophy as "using a feel-based approach, inside of the traditions, meaning that you are always adapting to fit the horse." He called it being "ever adjustable, respecting the traditions, but never being so dogmatic that you can't change when you should." He also "base[s] this on what a horse might think about a situation from their perspective." I have already referred to the philosophy of modern VH as a lived one, and it also is negotiated with individual horses along the way. The traditions of VH, in Cody's view, also need to be reflected upon; he gave the example of not using the gear you are "supposed" to use in the bridle horse progression if it is not the right fit for that particular horse at that time.

Flexibility is the cousin to compromise. When I first asked Bryan Neubert about his horsemanship philosophy, he shared the following story about his, at the time, little humans:

> I said to the kids, "I want you to gather the wood for the stove and put it on the porch." So, when I get home at the end of the day, put my horse away, put my dogs away, but saw no wood on the front porch, and here are gobs of tracks from a little red wagon, I see that they had gathered wood. When I get to the *back* porch, I'm thinking how did they put this wood so high? I mean they must have had wood on their heads or something to put it up that high, and here they are just little kids. I was a little annoyed that they put the wood on the porch that's on the other end of the house. I thought, I've got to commend them for this. I *wanted* to say, what are you thinking putting the wood on this end of the house? But it's more important to commend them for their efforts. I thought, just keep your mouth shut. I said, "You guys have got a heck of a pile here. How did you get it so tall? You must have made 20 trips with the wagon." Then, two or three days later as we're packing the wood through the kitchen and through the living room, I said, "What do you guys think—you did a good job here, but wouldn't it be easier if the wood was packed on the porch next to the wood stove?" "Yeah, that would be a good idea."

The way he dealt with his young sons' "failure" was not to acknowledge it as such, especially since they had completed the task, but to let it stand as a success and then to suggest a revision a few days later. He protected their feelings. He does exactly the same with horses:

> There are so many times when you're working with a horse that the answer he comes up with may not be the one you were hoping for. I assume it's because of a desire to

please you, to help you. An example would be when you're first training a horse to go from a walk to a trot, but he goes into a lope. There's going to be times when you need a lope, so you don't want to be too critical when he lopes when you're asking him to trot. Don't criticize him but just tell him, that's a nice effort but not quite what I had in mind. Then, you don't kill his desire to please you—the same with those kids.

He lets them "do it their way" and then suggests something else while bearing their sensitivity in mind. A notable postscript to this story is that his two sons and daughter, who all have careers in horsemanship, have told him that they have taken "the theory" that he taught them and extended it into new territory.

Moment to Moment in Vaquero Horsemanship

Horses seem to stand for freedom not just to ride out of town or toward a distant horizon, but freedom from ourselves and our imprisonment and things that take us out of our own time and place. (McGuane, 2013, p. x)

I characterized this section as "moment to moment" to highlight the mindfulness feature of VH philosophy—or paying undivided attention to the horse and "being in the moment" (Amy G.). This has its parallels in the primary texts of VH; specifically, Ray Hunt (1978) advised readers that, "You've got to be awake and alert every minute, every stride, because you're working with something alive that thinks and feels. He makes decisions. If we're not there to help him, he may make a decision we don't want him to make. Then we blame it on the horse. But, I grant you, it's not the horse's fault" (p. 26). Mindfulness is not just practiced for its own sake but in order to treat a horse more fairly *and* to assign blame fairly.

Both Bryan Neubert and Joe Wolter shared anecdotes about this subject. Bryan remembered that Tom Dorrance had told him when making the drive from Nevada to California, "I never turned the radio on. I would just meditate on experiences that I had had all the way from Battle Mountain to Salinas." Dorrance's book is the most philosophical of the bunch, so it is not surprising that he spent much time contemplating his experiences. Joe recalled that Ray Hunt had told him that he shouldn't worry so much and reassured him that he was doing well and that "In the later years, I got to thinking he was right. He was exactly right. When you worry about stuff, you keep it from happening." Worry often occurs when looking backward with regret or forward with trepidation, so mindfulness in horsemanship can curtail that; of course, many look to the horse for an example of being in the present.

Mindfulness is cultivated in VH to deal with human worry and other pesky emotions that get in the way of connecting *quietly* with horses. Bruce Sandifer mentioned that he and Jeff Derby teach mindful breathing and "meditative stuff" to address fear and anxiety in their students. Bruce has observed that riders are often focused on their physical movements being correct, but they try to get them to realize that "really being able to control your [emotional] center is the key" and that "you cannot hold tension in your body" because "tension is always the enemy of engagement." Tension is particularly tricky because it can *seem* to create engagement but is "forceful and not guidable." Horsemanship is perhaps unique in its blending of physicality and philosophy, and so educators like Bruce and Jeff encourage students to attend to both—simultaneously, if you can manage that.

To continue with the idea that VH contains a philosophical and pragmatic loop, I share Bryan Neubert's statement that

> The measure of a rider's talent is in his ability to detect from the horse the slightest hint in the direction he may want to go so that he may be able to ease the pressure, thus influencing the horse in that direction. To me, that's horsemanship in a nutshell, right there. That's it. Basically you are applying pressure until the horse thinks in the direction you want him to and take the pressure off. So he thinks he's the one that's applying and taking pressure off, not so much like a reward for doing the right thing.

I would argue that his description takes what otherwise might seem mechanical to the level of philosophy due to the amount of presence of mind, thought, and reflection involved. Rojas (2010) described the need to "synchronize the thoughts of the rider to those of the horse" (p. 439). "Pressure and release" can sound like another phrasing of "stimulus and response," but in VH the critical element is that, as Bryan noted, it merges with the horse's response instead of the human's. The rider has to be fast in thought and movement, which requires moment-to-moment awareness, and the aspiration would be one mind riding. Melanie A. commented that VH "really allows you to be educated and be so much more aware of your interactions with the horse, and that's what is, I think, key. It helps you really to get into a horse's mind. Because if you can influence a horse's mind, you can influence the body." You can see the chain reaction here: Humans influence their own minds, which affects their bodies, and then, as you become skillful at this, you attend to the horse's mind, which affect the horse's body. When you become practiced at it, it becomes circular.

Experience-wise, riding can become safer and riders more capable by increasing awareness. Jones (2020) reminded readers that "Our equine friends do not have goal-driven brains with bloated frontal lobes. Horses' brains are stimulus driven. In other words, instead of being motivated by internal plans and goals, horses are motivated by the sights, sounds, and smells in their immediate external environments" (p. 194). Because we so often ask them to overcome their natural flight inclination, we need to pay close attention to their signals, which requires in-the-moment focus. Tony noted that, around horses, people often fail to notice what the horse tries to communicate, resulting in "getting themselves into some trouble and into wrecks because they miss those little details." The antidote for this is more thoughtful focus on the horse (slow-craft horsemanship). Even if a lack of attention does not result in a wreck, it can still impede progress. Linda H. mentioned riders who, because "they're not thinking" and "ride without observing," continue "without getting any better." This description is similar to the remark of another participant who had observed that some attend clinics year after year without advancing their skills—approaching horsemanship as a recreational, consumer experience rather than a philosophical one.

Bill Dorrance (Dorrance & Desmond, 2007) remarked that, over the course of his long career, "In most cases, it's the slowness part that I see getting left out. It's a real disadvantage to a horse when this happens.... Most people just want to go way too fast" (p. 277). As Elijah mentioned earlier in this chapter, the popularity of being "in such a rush" naturally affects our interactions with horses. Kathleen K. portrayed a similar tension in her own horsemanship by stating that her "ultimate goal" "is to ride every step ... but we're in a hurry. We're always in a hurry—in life in general." For her, time with horses is far more than a job: "This is a place that, for me, grounds me and slows me down. If I'm having a rough day, if I can just be next to a horse, stand to a horse, or ride a horse, I'll be alright." As I discussed in the last section, the philosophy of VH is a way of life for some. Accordingly, the roughness of life can be smoothed out by shifting your full focus to horses, who uniquely embody the physical and philosophical in VH.

Approaching horses as philosophical partners could lead to unexpected results. Linda H. illustrated this in her explanation of the mindful approach to horsemanship:

> We can all work hard, but are we willing to do thoughtful work? For me, it's like walking meditation. I'm fully present when I'm working the horses—I'm not somewhere else, and they deserve that from me.... That's part of its gift. Sometimes, with a horse, if your mind wanders, nothing like a horse to bring you back! The person's like, I'm back--fully present! ... A lot of people are trying to just make horses fit into their life. It's like, this is all you need because this is all I have to give. That's what we'll say but that's really not always what they need.... Sometimes a horse says, it's not enough.

Thoughtful work requires more of all involved, and the horse telling you that what you are giving is not sufficient can lead to bruised egos and even injury. Not being sure what to bring to the situation next can lead to a crisis of philosophy and a search for a better and different way. In VH, the horse helps to set the philosophical agenda of the human—an agenda that, on balance, often demands more of us.

CONCLUSION

In Vaquero horsemanship, philosophy connects mind, body, and spirit in order to protect the same in the horse. Participants equated VH with an opportunity to connect on a deeply personal level with the horses and humans that they worked with throughout their careers. As Greg Eliel noted, everyone has "their own filter" and "their own recipe card" in formulating their horsemanship philosophy, but this still results in "common themes," which have been the focus of this chapter. Amy G.'s definition of VH foregrounds some of these:

> It's just a harmonious, connected partnership that's equal. You are not superior to that horse. You are equal partners, and when you are able to give them that, that's when they give you so much of themselves, and they're happy and willing to do it—like you know that they are willing to do whatever you ask and they are. It depends on how you ask though.

In general, the world tells us that horses, and all animals, are inferior to us so repositioning them as "equal beings" is a philosophical move. Giving them the option to *choose* willingness and putting thought into "how you ask" requires pairing knowledge with an awareness of pragmatic consequences. Amy's central goal of "a harmonious, connected partnership that's equal" echoes Rudy's (2014) portrayal of the work of Mary and Claudine Andre, who study and live with bonobos:

> They're also inviting humans to become a different kind of creature, a being that is enmeshed and interconnected, that intuits or feels the experience of the other, and in doing so recovers or reinvents some forgotten animal talents and senses. The ways they are engaging animals—by sharing their space and bodies with them—pull us away from our minds and back into our senses. (pp. 213–214)

"Reinvent[ing] some forgotten animal talents and senses" recalls Bekoff's (2002) wondering "if humans view animals as having some qualities that we have lost—their mindful presence, their unfiltered emotions, their zest for life" (p. 104). While there is obviously a cognitive component to VH philosophy, it is more sensory than the academic sort of philosophy since it must be experienced and felt as a striving for interconnection. If well executed, the result is *not* that the horse becomes more like the human, but that they are "equal partners," and work as "a different kind of creature."

Linda H. described her horsemanship journey as her "spiritual path in life." She viewed VH as entwining horsemanship with all of life, which captures the other main emphasis of this chapter:

What's an unintended gift for us is that we become better as humans. It really becomes a journey of self. That's what Vaquero horsemanship is encouraging. There's
the tradition of creating a bridle horse, but then along with that as you become better with the horse, you become better as a human. . . . It's an inward journey, this
vein of horsemanship.

As someone who first learned about horsemanship and riding via mechanics, with no
inclusion of philosophical aspects, I did not necessarily expect philosophy to be such
a significant aspect of this study; I found though, that once I started asking about it,
and following up on participants' comments, that modern VH cannot be fully realized
without its philosophical facet, and that participants highly valued the soul-searching
that ensued, even though they had to take a hard look at their own beliefs and behaviors.
This reflection can also occur even if you are not following the traditional goals of VH,
as Linda H. noted: "Making that ultimate refined bridle horse is important if you're
going to that destination—the bigger issue is that we keep the philosophy of honoring
and understanding the horse . . . that needs to be brought into every discipline because
we're troubling horses faster than we can help them." If studying the philosophy of VH,
and cultivating your own iteration of it, even without the ultimate goal of creating a bridle horse, results in fewer troubled horses, then this philosophy justifies its existence.

INTERLUDE 5

Linda Hoover and Ally

Years ago, I ran across a quote that said something like, gift giving is an opportunity to show someone how little you know about them. We all have given gifts, but have we really thought about how the other feels when receiving them? Did we give them something they really wanted, or did we simply think that our intention was enough? For me, how this pertains to horses goes back to the mid-1990s. It was the first time I was participating in a Ray Hunt clinic. I had taken a sensitive filly to start in the colt class. Being quite new to Vaquero horsemanship, there was so much I didn't know.

It was on the second day of the clinic, and I was brushing the filly in her stall. A man in the next stall, who had been following this approach to horsemanship for a while, looked over and commented, "You pet her like you're scrubbing a floor." Wow, I was taken aback. That was the furthest thing from what I would have expected someone to say to me. I wish I could say that I had clarity in my intention, but I can't. What I can say is that it wasn't to be intentionally unkind. However, clearly this man saw something that I didn't. As I pondered his words, I tried to find the truth in his observation. As much as I hated to admit it, I was petting her mindlessly while really thinking about my needs. I was nervous about starting this horse. She was struggling with being in an unfamiliar environment and was scared. I was struggling to understand the concepts being offered by Ray and had my concerns about safely riding her. She needed comfort, but then so did I. As the clinic continued, I kept hearing the words "You pet her like you're scrubbing a floor." What did this really mean, and what was I going to do about this?

I'd like to say that the insights I needed were readily found that weekend; however, my lesson in petting had only just begun and was a gradual unfolding. The filly stayed with me for a couple more months. This gave me time to explore how I could offer my physical touch in a way that was more fitting to her. It offered me the opportunity to be more present and not simply go through the motions of a mechanical gesture. I've never been one to slap a horse's neck as is often seen when riders are "petting" their horses; however, beyond that, I was never given insights into how best to pet a horse. I found the need to reflect on what I did want to offer when I petted a horse. What was its real purpose? I started to delve into some of the science about touch. Physical touch is something that mammals, including humans, need and crave. The bonding of a mother with her offspring is what creates the ability to emotionally attach to others. Deprivation of touch wreaks havoc on the emotional well-being of the individual. I became so much more aware of what I offered a horse, be it through petting or really in any of my interactions. It all started with my intention. What did I want the horse to feel? For me when I pet, I want a horse to feel comfort, contentment, and security in my leadership.

I began to think about touch as it relates to people. Even as a person, while I know that being patted on the back usually means I did well, I would much prefer for someone to offer a much softer touch or to simply put their hand on my shoulder and say something meaningful. One of my goals became to replicate what another horse would offer. Slapping on the neck isn't it. I'm working to build on what an emotionally balanced mare would offer to her foal with a caring, reassuring nuzzle or even a scratch. And how convenient it is that a favorite place for a horse to be scratched is near the withers, which is easily done while riding.

For some horses, touch hasn't always brought a good feeling—either because the mare wasn't able to provide that or because rough handling by a person occurred. For those horses I found that initial petting was too much. They simply needed me to give them space during our interactions. These horses can struggle to accept that touch is a good thing. There are so many attributes to gaining rapport and offering comfort through touch. There is the amount of pressure, a rhythm, a tempo, and where the touch is applied. Each is unique to the individual. What feels good to one horse may be offensive to another. As my understanding deepened, I grew to look more closely at physical changes in the horses. A touch that gains rapport will bring about subtle and sometimes profound changes in the horse's demeanor. I noted if there is a softening of the eyes, a lowering of the head, a relaxing of the lips, a change in breathing, or a lick and chew as tension is eased.

I learned how essential it was that I be in as grounded an emotional state as possible. If my head was filled with other thoughts beyond the comfort of my horse, as it was at that clinic all those many years ago, I am very likely to miss the mark of helping my horse feel like I have their best interest at heart. I learned that my intention is one thing; however, the horse's perception is their reality. I grew as a person to have more empathy, more clarity, and to show up first with the intention to give what the horse needed and simply not what I wanted to give. To this day, I am forever grateful to the very sensitive filly who brought me to that Ray Hunt clinic. I carry that experience with me and share it with others. I can often be quoted as saying, "If you can hear your hand, you're petting too loud," and so begins me sharing the tenets of the art of petting.

CHAPTER 6

The Cultural Roots of Vaquero Horsemanship

The vaquero has stood for centuries in the shadows—not the spotlight—of history. He has lived his life in remote areas doing what he has always done—working with horses and taking care of someone else's cattle, often under primitive conditions. No Hall of Fame touts his accomplishments, as do those for the cowboy and buckaroo. (Clayton et al., 2001, pp. 62–63)

My father enjoyed westerns, just for the sake of westerns; he didn't want messages, cultural lessons, political statements—just good old-fashioned shootouts. I do too. (Figueredo, 2015, p. xi)

T
HESE QUOTES ENCOMPASS TWO KEY IDEAS OF THIS CHAPTER, WHICH IS about the cultural roots of Vaquero horsemanship: (1) acknowledging those roots and (2) the appeal of taking "cultural lessons" out of horsemanship. In *Revolvers and Pistolas, Vaqueros and Caballeros*, D. H. Figueredo (2015) recounted how his father wanted to watch westerns as entertainment, a desire he shared until he started to think more deeply about them; horsemanship has a similar pull and an even more immediate one. Learning to work with horses will keep you busy enough. No need, or time, to add in critical thinking about cultural background. But VH has a distinct cultural history—apart from the mainstream Western one—and one that has not received its due in popular culture (Figueredo, 2015, p. 3). This latest "renaissance" of VH, as one participant described it, is an opportunity to remedy that by recognizing the cultural roots of it. In this chapter, I discuss how participants shared and supported this idea, and I also explore the words that keep "vaquero" company: buckaroo, Californio, caballero, and charro. The word itself, like the horsemanship, is also faceted like a Montana sapphire; you have to hold it up to the light to fully appreciate it.

Before sharing what interviewees reported about the cultural roots of VH, I will first briefly summarize printed sources about this topic. Recall that in chapter one, I cited Morris' (2014) statement that vaqueros "were of Spanish, Mexican, Indian and later of European blood" (p. xi); there is consensus about this in the texts that mention vaqueros. Early vaqueros who came from Mexico, and later ones who were perceived to be Mexican, were obviously not immune to the racism and prejudice of their day.

> The Mexican vaquero, as a person without land, had faced discrimination in Mexico and faced it again in the United States. In Mexico vaqueros had an accepted place in society. In the United States they were interlopers who faced discrimination, violence, and racism. Despite the antipathy Anglos showed about working with Mexicans, they admitted, if only grudgingly, that vaqueros were the first cowboys and that they had excellent reputations as ropers and superior bronc busters. (Monday & Colley, 1997, p. xxiv)

Monroy (1990) argued that racism toward Mexicans and Mexican Americans contained "the notable exception of the skilled vaqueros" (p. 194), arguably because their skill in horsemanship had been recognized and valued. I will return to the question of whether VH somehow transcends culture later in this chapter.

There is also, across sources, credit given to the highly significant role that Native American vaqueros played. Rojas (2010) depicted them as cultivating the same characteristics that modern VH practitioners esteem: "The Indian vaqueros respected their horses and showed great patience in handling them. They believed that a man cannot deprive a horse of his dignity without losing some of his own. Consequently, they never did anything derogatory to the horse's dignity" (p. 448). Elsewhere in his writings, Rojas (2010) stated that they became the most skillful riders and silversmiths of their time (p. 135; p. 138). When I asked Bill Reynolds how Rojas had acquired the nickname of "Chief" and whether he was Native American himself, he said that Rojas had earned it because "he knew all the stories of the old vaqueros and would impress people with his various knowledge"; he was born in Southern California (his family had migrated from Mexico) and was of Yaqui, Mayo, and Spanish descent. However, despite the fact that Rojas documented their influence, other "testimonials" from the era of historical VH did not, "except in occasional passing remarks" (Sánchez, 1995, p. 179). Suffice it to say that VH history is no different than other histories in that it is embattled ground, vulnerable to omissions, master narratives, and human failings.

CULTURAL ROOTS ACCORDING TO
SOUTHEASTERN PARTICIPANTS

During our interviews, I asked southeastern participants whether they thought there were different cultural traditions at work in VH, and if they thought of it as having roots in a certain culture. Not surprisingly, they all said that they associate it with

California; except for two who did not go further back than its Californian roots, all also said that they think of it as coming originally from Spain (two traced the roots back to the Moors). While there was commonality in their responses, there was also varying amounts of detail offered as well as some unique answers, which I discuss below.

Four elaborated on their responses about the Spanish cultural roots of VH by specifically adding that it traveled through Mexico to arrive in California. Matthew answered that "It came up through Mexico, originally from Spain, into Mexico, up through California, and into the Great Basin in Nevada ... and then it splintered off—the Texas cowboy, very different." [Several made a point of mentioning, akin to Matthew's comments, that the vaquero was distinct from the Texas cowboy.] Both Alex and Alicia B. also mentioned the influence of Mexican vaqueros and charros as well as their roping skills as part of their responses to this question.

Two participants highlighted the role of Native American vaqueros. One participant stated that she thought that "The Spaniards, the Mexicans, the Native Americans all played a big part in forming it, and I think there's a whole lot of that that just goes right into the mill. Naturally, everything gets Americanized and gringoized." I believe that what she meant by going "right into the mill" refers to the dominant culture absorbing, and to some extent erasing, distinct cultural origins and influences and turning it into a more mainstream "American" brand of VH. This can lead to uncertainty about the cultural sources of VH. When I asked about the roots, Alex replied that, "A lot of the first cowboys as I understand it were actually Indians, Native Americans." He wondered whether the development of VH "was from the Spanish culture or the Native part or a mixture of all of it." He also shared how his perception of the cultural roots of VH had affected his horsemanship:

> I always felt like if I was working with a horse, I'm trying to fix up a situation and then let him find it. He might find it right away—it might take him days upon days. It didn't really matter. I think that idea came from maybe some of that California culture and where they had a lot of country and a lot of time and a different view. That's the way I always thought of it. I don't know if I'm right or not.

I appreciated his honesty in stating that he was not sure, and I suspect that many modern VH practitioners share his query. So much of horsemanship happens in the moment, so needing to know whether you are "right or not" about the cultural origins is admittedly not essential to the daily practice of it. Furthermore, to know about Native American vaqueros, you would have to either read about it or have been told. Academic texts aside, which the general public does not generally seek out, there is only mention of them in Rojas' and Morris' books. If your favorite clinicians happen to discuss the history of VH, then they might highlight it.

IMPORTANCE OF CULTURAL ROOTS
ACCORDING TO THE MENTORS

I did not ask the mentors which cultures they associated historical VH with; instead, I asked them if they thought it was important to know its cultural roots. All said yes. As I have discussed earlier in this volume, many southeastern participants were introduced to VH by Buck Brannaman, and as I quoted in chapter one, he acknowledges the presence of Native American vaqueros, "which really messes with the history of the whole cowboys and Indians thing because Indians were some of the first cowboys" (personal interview). While I did not ask the other mentors if they agreed with his statement (because I felt that it would be too leading), the overall consensus was that modern practitioners should know the history of VH. Tom Curtin said that he thinks that

> It's extremely important. If you want to understand the value of what you're trying to accomplish for the benefit of your horse, I think it's very important that you understand the history of it and the culture of it and why you're doing what you're doing. It's like I tell folks at my clinics all the time, don't do what I ask you to do because I asked you to do it. Do it because you know why you're doing it. I'd want to know why.

For him, learning about the roots is part of being a critically engaged student—asking from whence it comes to better understand the modern "why" of it. He also commented that he had studied it because it "was offered" to him by his mentors. Cody Deering framed "considering where the horsemanship and the stockmanship came from" with questions: "Why were things done the way they were? How are things different today? Or what things remain the same? Do the principles ring true each time? What is necessary for me? What can I learn from this? What is fitting and what is not so that I can understand the situation I am in?" That both mentors emphasized questioning can encourage their students to learn the history beyond the "Americanized and gringoized" form of VH referred to above.

There were two mentors that had much to say about the cultural roots of VH. Bruce Sandifer and Jeff Derby, who usually coteach, each talked at length about the role that Native Americans played. Bruce's website states, "These early Californio vaqueros of mostly Indian blood have developed one of the most brilliant and sophisticated systems of handling horses that I have ever seen or read about." Bear in mind that being a vaquero "was considered a pretty low-level job," and that, with the exception of vaqueros, "It was illegal and punishable by death for Natives to ride horses" as part of the Spaniards trying to maintain control (Bruce Sandifer, personal interview; see also Monroy, 1990, p. 78). Bruce attributed part of Native Americans' horsemanship abilities to their transferring what they learned from working with animals on the ground to horseback (since they were not allowed horses):

The Spanish had them herding stuff around the missions afoot . . . if you've ever moved cattle in a wide area afoot, you realize that forethought and planning ahead is important because you cannot out-muscle them—you can't outrun them—you have to think. You have to work inside their nature—not yours. So, it forces you to see things from a different perspective. . . . You learn patience and how to observe things. And, you're at a time when there's no outside influence at all. You have so much time to focus on the little things. They became amazing at just understanding not how much to do but how little you could affect things with the smallest movement.

Jeff expanded on Bruce's comments by further explaining why he thinks Native Americans became such skillful riders: "I don't want to speak too generally or too overly romantic about Native American cultures, but if you have a belief that animals have a spirit, have a soul, have things to teach us—that they can be our friends, our partners, our mentors—you value the animal at a different level than if that animal is a piece of meat or simply a piece of chattel that you own or just a tool." Valuing horses in the way Jeff described is clearly evident in the culture of modern VH.

A COLLAPSE OF CULTURAL DISTANCE — OR NOT

The vaquero was a Spaniard, a mestizo (halfbreed) [sic], a pure Indian, or a Gringo, that is to say, a man of one of the other European races other than Spanish. (Rojas, 2010, p. 430)

Rojas' quote is intriguing in that he grouped all vaqueros together, regardless of race and ethnicity (foregoing the need for the word *buckaroo*, which I explain later in this chapter); elsewhere in this writings, he does refer to "Gringo" riders separately. Buck Brannaman echoed Rojas' quote: "That's what was interesting—in the early days of the vaquero in California—if you were a vaquero you made your living on a horse and you were part of that culture and tradition and all the other vaqueros were your brothers and it didn't matter what color you were." VH, as all forms of horsemanship, exists nested within our larger society, itself made up of many cultures. The focus of this section is to explore the question of whether, in modern VH, a collapse of cultural distance is possible—or not.

After I asked southeastern participants about the cultural origins of VH, and all had replied that it came from a cultural distance, I then asked the follow-up question of whether this distance matters (I did not want to ask *how* it matters, since it would be leading, so I settled on whether it *did*). Some expressed that the distance did not matter and, furthermore, described being "interested in" and "embracing" the distinct cultural roots of VH. Alex felt like "if the ideas are the same," then differences in cultural origins did not matter. Overall, they did not see VH as too distant from their own cultures—at least not so much that it would impact their learning of it. Their receptivity to VH might also be due to seeing it as coming from a not-so-relatively-distant California, which mediated their conceptions of cultural origins.

Several southeastern participants interpreted my follow-up question to be about whether cultural distance *should* matter, which led to statements about horsemanship transcending culture, that is, "good horsemanship is good horsemanship," regardless of the cultural context in which it is practiced—and that culture in VH "is all lumped into one," which is similar to Rojas' quote. One depicted it as akin to being open-minded: "It shouldn't [matter] because all cultures—no matter what, we're talking about horsemanship—everybody's got something to offer, and I think people ought to be really receptive to that. If you close that off, you've closed off learning." Relatedly, two other answers were about this sort of receptivity to learning, which culture was collapsed into: For example, we *should* be open to cross-cultural influences. One wonders if this is an instance of what Geertz (2000) described as the "tendency to see diversity as surface and universality as depth" (p. 59). Mixing cultural knowledge was viewed as a path to further understanding, although one could argue that the cultural aspects take the backseat since learning VH often means doing so from someone with the same cultural background as the student.

Claiming that "good" horsemanship is somehow above human culture is a double-edged sword. This claim means that VH can be practiced by anyone from any cultural group, arguably to the benefit of the horse; it can also mean that we ignore or minimize the actual cultural roots of VH. One southeastern participant commented, "It [cultural distance] is not even an issue because they don't even know the roots. . . . I don't think people even give it enough thought. They don't know the history enough." Not giving "enough thought" to the cultural origins of VH can be dangerous when it signals a collapse that flattens cultural distinction altogether. As an example of this, I had the following conversation about the cultural roots of VH with one southeastern participant; this followed his statement that "we owe everything to the Mexicans for bringing it [VH] through. So, there's that. We don't look down our nose at them, that's for sure."

> INTERVIEWEE: I tell you what got to me was, when I first started, I started with the reining, then the team roping. I kept wanting to gravitate more and more to the real deal—what I consider the real deal—the true cowboy and, in my mind, the true cowboy is the vaquero.
>
> JULIANNA: But there's a distinction there. I mean, the white American cowboy is not the Mexican vaquero.
>
> INTERVIEWEE: They are now.
>
> JULIANNA: In your mind, they're one and the same?

INTERVIEWEE: Dave Weaver, Martin Black—they're all part of the same frater-
nity, and they all work together. Do you know who Mary Williams Hyde is?
Well, she travels in that whole circuit. Go look at her pictures. There's plenty
of white guys. She's got folks obviously of Mexican descent, and those that ar-
en't. . . . She's not Mexican.

Notably, this exchange was the only one of its kind and so is not representative, but I
still share it here because it leads to what I feel are crucial points about the intersection
of horsemanship and culture. While we can certainly disagree about whether horsemanship can be practiced in a cultural vacuum, what struck me about his response was
citing as support white horsepeople and a white photographer who, by her own definition, documents buckaroo culture.

But how is this participant's response different from Rojas' (2010) description, cited
earlier in this chapter, that historical vaqueros were actually multiracial and multiethnic? I would argue that these statements have to be taken in their respective cultural contexts: It is outside of my scope to fully analyze what Rojas' comment meant
in his time (although I will turn a more critical eye to the labels themselves in a following section). What I can do is offer a note of caution about my participant's comment.
Maintaining that cultural differences do not matter in our current context is seriously
concerning given inequality, racism, and prejudice: These exist in our society and so
must be considered as part of the larger cultural setting in which VH is *now* practiced.
Furthermore, in his claim that "we owe everything to the Mexicans" for bringing VH
to the United States, he ignored the contribution that Native Americans made, which
is one aspect of historical VH that is actually well-supported by research.

Our societal landscape is deeply scarred by denial of tribal communities' knowledge
(which continues to this day), even in horsemanship. Diné scholar and horsewoman
Kelsey Dayle John (2018) pointed out that

Anthropologists write that the horse was introduced through Spanish colonization
in the late 1700s; however the horse exists in Diné creation stories. In the commonly
written phrase, "the horse was brought over by the Spanish," Diné face a very subtle form of epistemic violence—one that delegitimizes Diné creation stories where
the horse was present from the start. This commonly accepted horse origin story
positions the horse as a non-"Indigenous" newcomer to the Americas and, thus, un-
dermines the sacred relationship between Diné peoples, horses, and land. (p. 56)

Furthermore, John (2019) noted that "livestock reduction policies" (i.e., animal slaugh-
ter) were used historically to force the Diné to assimilate (p. 54). Horses and horsemanship have long been political matters and sites of injustice—because that was forced
upon the Diné and other tribes.

John (2019) described her own father's approach to horse education as "embody[ing] patience, kindness, empathy, and relationships" (p. 62), which sounds exactly like what modern VH aspires to be. Even though "Diné love and relate to horses unlike any other people" (p. 63), mainstream Western horsemanship does not often recognize this—or how other tribal communities relate to, and care for, horses today. Some of this knowledge is not ours to have, or to appropriate, but depicting horsemanship in the United States, and beyond, as an acultural, apolitical space (as if we have simply evolved beyond both) is simply inaccurate.

In sum, although I can appreciate the argument that these cultural issues do not matter *to the horse* (and we can be thankful for that), we can also remain aware that culture does matter in *horsemanship* because the latter obviously includes the former but is also, always, practiced in cultural and historical contexts. Even though he did not include Native American ontologies in this statement, I find Dewey's (1938) judgment to be relevant here: "Mankind [*sic*] likes to think in terms of extreme opposites. It is given to formulating its beliefs in terms of *Either-Ors*, between which it recognizes no intermediate possibilities" (p. 17; italics in original). Considering that, both human culture not mattering to the horse *and* that it does matter in human horsemanship can be true at the same time. Resorting to the dominant culture to describe VH can erase the cultural origins that are faint enough to begin with. I argue (and I am thinking beyond my own small study) that we have to be careful about a possible progression of that erasure until we only see VH in light of our current culture of practice. Furthermore, this flattening of culture can establish VH experts as only, or primarily, coming from one cultural group, and what seems to be tolerance is more like homogeneity without equality.

PURISTS AND BASTARDS

Another cultural distinction that came out during interviews was between "pure" VH and "bastardization" (note that I am playing with the grammatical form of it in the section title, which I will explain below). There was recognition among participants that purely historical VH is not what most are practicing today, especially in the southeastern United States. One interviewee deliberately did not label herself as a vaquero because a high-profile devotee (not part of this study) had stated that the name was for those who "can only genetically be a vaquero," and she did not want to "draw the criticism of people like" him. What she described is obviously a very small pool of possibility, unlikely for those living in the southeast. The mentors that I interviewed did not mention this distinction, except that one told me that I could be a vaquero, given my cultural heritage; I replied that the horse might disagree, given my lack of skill. Some of the mentors, however, did refer to themselves as traditionalists (not purists) and added that this meant they were open to learning from other disciplines.

Along with questions of "pure" claims to VH, came acknowledgment that modern VH has been "bastardized." This was a concept that both groups of interviewees mentioned. Jeff Derby described it as occurring "every time it travels, every time it changes hands, every generation—it's likely to be a little changed." When interviewees mentioned this, it was matter-of-fact and presented as unavoidable; I would argue that most, if not all, interpretations of modern VH are a bastardization of sorts since there are relatively few primary documents about it, and practitioners reserve the right to adopt some elements and not others (e.g., the snaffle bit). Furthermore, even purists today are vaqueros in contexts (including cultural) that are different from those of their historical counterparts. While we might think of bastardization as negative, it can yet give rise to more possibility: The traditional rules do not have to apply.

In fact, the word *bastard* is more nuanced than it might seem. Even its traditional reference to a child born out of wedlock "has not always been offensive . . . it was a relatively neutral term until as recently as the late 20th century." Per *Merriam-Webster*, it can also mean "of mixed or ill-conceived origin" or "lacking genuineness or authority." What does bastardization mean for cultural acknowledgment, though? Being a bastard can indicate that you are illegitimate—or that your parents do not claim, or want, you due to social stigma. To use a vintage phrasing, you are not a rightful heir. This ties into my caution about modern followers of VH not knowing from whence these traditions came. Even though bastardization might be viewed neutrally, it is very much about power—and who acknowledges whom. Again, to return to cultural studies, Williams (1983) reminded us that, "It is true also that a tradition is always selective, and that there will always be a tendency for this process of selection to be related to and even governed by the interests of the class that is dominant" (pp. 320–321). In this view, a cultural tradition, as it persists over time, is shaped and determined by those with the power to do so—and not by all equally; accordingly, the survival and popular use of the word "vaquero" is due to its adoption by the dominant American culture—like a bastard given up at birth due to the aforementioned "social stigma." We should be careful about VH being handled as horsemanship that does not know who its parents are.

THE WORTH OF THE WORD

To outsiders, it really matters little which label is applied. To the individuals involved, however, it is of crucial importance. To apply the wrong term is an affront, proof that the observer does not understand the culture at all. (Clayton et al., 2001, p. 223)

In *Vaqueros, Cowboys, and Buckaroos*, Clayton et al. (2001) take each term in turn and explain its history and cultural significance. As the quote above illustrates, which word you use "is of crucial importance"; even though they overlap, they are not synonyms. I had a conversation with one participant about another clinician (not part of this study) who uses the word "vaquero" in her promotional materials.

> I think I know why she's using that word. It's a positive thing—in that people need something to give them a frame of reference of who they think you are. The people who know her don't need a word. That word is really for the people that don't know you . . . it doesn't say Natural horsemanship, which is a term that's really on the outs and an oxymoron anyway for anybody who truly knows the English language.

In her view, "vaquero" was used because "if you asked the general public, I bet they would say they associate it with gentler methods." She also remarked that she thinks of Buck Brannaman as more of a buckaroo than a vaquero, although this is not how his website describes him, and his Vaquero Pro-Am Roping took place (until 2022), as she called it, in "the hotbed of the bridle horse tradition." I include these details to demonstrate that the word itself is contested. And if you are not yet convinced that word choice in horsemanship matters, consider how many I include in this section that border the word vaquero: buckaroo, caballero, Californio, and charro.

Vaquero versus Buckaroo

> *He had recently been traumatized by hearing that American*
> *cowboys called Mexican vaquero "buckaroos." It made him*
> *feel sad, philosophical even.* (Urrea, 2005, p. 40)

Mike Bridges described the word "buckaroo" as "an Anglo corruption of vaquero." Another interviewee said that not knowing "how to pronounce vaquero" or "roll our r's" resulted in it. According to Clayton et al. (2001), vaquero culture produced geographical variations: "[W]hen Anglos took up the practice of herding cattle in what was to become California and southern Texas, they adapted the vaquero pattern into a culture that can be divided into two distinct versions related to specific areas of the United States—the cowboy and the buckaroo" (p. xvi). They also stated that because the "buckaroo traces his origin back to the California vaquero," "time and aesthetics . . . became so important to buckaroo style" (pp. 189–190).

Some participants believe that what we call VH now is more buckaroo in practice. Tom Curtin outlined this idea:

The vaquero style was very much alive and well in California and up that western coast, but then it broadened out as California became more populated and the ranches expanded and moved out into Nevada, Oregon, western Idaho—basically west of the continental divide. That's where your buckaroo-type tradition has come into play. And so, today what a lot of these people speak of vaquero tradition has descended from that.

As I have mentioned earlier in this volume, although vaqueros and buckaroos are clearly closely related, one difference is the use of the snaffle bit. In addition to the modern example of different gear used, there is also the fact that, for some, vaqueros and buckaroos refer to distinct cultural backgrounds. Rojas (2010) has a section titled "Buckarooing in Nevada" (p. 491), and Clayton et al. (2001) reported that "Ernest Morris (in his book *El Vaquero*) associates the term *vaquero* in California with Hispanics, the term *buckaroo* with Anglos, the two titles (and nationalities) melding through pronunciation (and sun tans) into *baqueros*" (p. 157). In a similar vein, Mike Bridges stated that once historical VH grew beyond the original vaqueros, Anglos were called buckaroos rather than vaqueros. I also observed that if I tried to apply the word *vaquero* to current practitioners who are not of Mexican, Spanish, or Native American descent, then some let me know that this would be inaccurate. Like the quote that opens this section indicates, names matter.

Vaquero versus Californio

The word "Californio" is unique as one of "vaquero's" relations because there is scholarship about its historical usage and meaning—and it has been revised, and revived, by one of the mentors in this project, Gwynn Turnbull. I will begin by summarizing some historical references and work my way forward.

Monroy (1990) described how those who wished to separate themselves from Mexicans (and Native Americans) found a way to do so with the word "Californio":

People and things deemed Spanish (food, music, horsemen, and so on) were acceptable to Californians, whereas those deemed Mexican carried negative connotations, a pattern that has persisted to this day.... Thus flattered, these Spanish Californios paid allegiance to the Americans, rode horses with them, and further distanced themselves from Mexicans. (p. 207)

He also mentioned that this was a way "to distinguish themselves from the disparaged lower classes, whom everyone began calling derisively Mexicans regardless of their origin, economic condition, or moral quality" (p. 206). Because "[t]he horse expressed the gentility of the Californio elites" (p. 138), horsemanship of that era would be collapsed into this expression of prejudice. Anecdotally, this reminds me of my mother's generation (she was born in 1942), including my own family members, who would call themselves "Spanish" even though our lineage was both Spanish and Mexican.

In his *Decline of the Californios*, Pitt (1966/1994) compared California's romanticized past to what its descendants might experience:

> The Mexican-American discovers that "Anglos" are far less kindly disposed toward the living Mexican-Americans than toward the imaginary Californios, and he claims that Yankees fawn over the clay caballeros sold in Olvera Street [an historical neighborhood turned tourist attraction in Los Angeles] but tend to show contempt for the people who sell them. Live people constitute a forgotten minority, while the mythical ones are remembered only too well. (p. 293)

Pitt has himself been accused of presenting "only a homogenized Californio identity" (Gutiérrez, 1998, p. viii) and "perpetuating a romantic fiction of the Californio past" (p. ix); however, the point he makes above, that there was, and is, a discrepancy between how California's past and present Mexican and Mexican American residents are treated is a valid one. Californios, in its current iteration, no longer refers to a particular racial or ethnic group, despite its history.

Now we have the Californio Bride Horse Association (https://www.californio bridlehorseassociation.com) and the Original Californios Ranch Roping & Horsemanship Clinics (https://www.thecalifornios.com). Gwynn Turnbull, who created the Original Californios, explained why she chose this name:

> I thought, let's go one evolution away from the vaquero because I was trying to find something that took our modern-day sensibilities about how we feel horses should be treated and kind of take the old traditional maneuvers that they had from the vaquero era—cleanse out the stuff that was hard on horses and try to end up with something that kept the good from the old but also brought our modern sensibilities about, ethically, how we treat our horses. So, I started the Californios Ranch Roping and Stock Horse Contest in 2000, and that was my goal.

There are two distances at work here. Gwynn chose "Californio" because she *wanted* to separate what she created from what she feels are VH's less-desirable traditions. The other distance is cultural: This was historically a term that reflected a part of California's contentious past, which included racism and prejudice. Now that it has been distanced from the past and has a more neutral existence, I wonder if we will soon forget that VH was entwined with these failings of human nature, which are still with us today.

Vaquero versus Caballero

The word "caballero," which non-Spanish speakers may be tempted to link to the Spanish word for horse, "caballo," also has, like "Californio," a history that was very much about societal and economic division.

> There were vaqueros. And there were caballeros. And though both were horse riders, the act of riding horses did not make them equal.... Caballero was a statement of honor, a symbol of nobility regardless of the financial situation of the gentlemen in question. "In that single Spanish word . . . there was all the history of their people," essayed New Mexican novelist Ruth Laughlin. "It implied pride of race, aristocratic recognition, innate courtesy, and punctilious formality. As the oldest European title in the Americas it merited respect." (Figueredo, 2015, p. 44)

A word as heavy as "caballero" might have needed to be carried around on horseback—so much did it convey, apparently. Both Rojas (2010, p. 129) and Monroy (1990, p. 78) confirmed Figueredo's depiction. I include a brief mention of it here since it was a very, very distant cousin to "vaquero," although it is not used in modern VH as far as I could tell.

Vaquero versus Charro

> *There's not a whole lot of people out here that know what a charro*
> *is. Everywhere we go, we're always referred to as vaqueros.* (Miguel)

> *A vaquero is not to be confused with the Mexican* charro, *a*
> *performer who participated in the* charreada, *or Mexican rodeo, nor*
> *is he a* caballero, *a gentleman on horseback. He is a* paisano, *or*
> *country man, a tough, working man, not a genteel sort of fellow.*
> (Clayton et al., 2001, p. 2; italics [reversed here] in original)

"Charro" is perhaps "vaquero's" closest cousin, although, historically, it contained "a clear and distinct difference" of being applied to a "gentlemen rancher . . . a landowner, a person of wealth, a person of prestige, a person who expected respect" (Monday & Colley, 1997, p. xxiv). Clayton et al. (2001) elaborated on what separated a vaquero from a charro: "The basic difference between a vaquero and a charro is that the charro must have all the skills in riding and roping of the vaquero but also have fine clothes, excellent gear, and a fine horse. Above all, according to Díaz's wife Rosa, 'He must be a gentleman.'" (p. 45). Bennett's (1998) depiction also outlined the boundaries between the two terms, which continue today.

> Within 100 years of the conquest, to be considered a charro was already a mark of distinction, and those who become charros today are heir to a way of life as heavy with tradition as the charro's saddle is heavy with carved silver. Asked what the difference is between a charro and a vaquero, champion charro Gerardo Díaz of San Antonio, Texas replied, "Every charro is a vaquero but not every vaquero is a charro. The charro has to set an example by his skills and also through his whole way of life." (p. 312)

These statements were supported by Rodolfo Lara Sr.'s explanation of charro "attire," which is "dressing as Mexico" and has "almost 500 years of culture, tradition, and evolution" behind it and so carries "a lot of responsibility."

I asked both Miguel (who noted above that it is not a well-known term in the southeastern United States) and Rodolfo Lara Sr. why "charro" is not as popular a term as "vaquero" is. Miguel and I speculated that, even though historical vaqueros would have been working cowboys, today many of those following VH would more closely fit with Miguel's description that "Charros originally were wealthy individuals or they owned haciendas" and would ride for entertainment donning "formal attire." We agreed that it was "curious" that vaquero had won as the label of choice. Part of this might be due to non-Spanish speakers lacking knowledge or familiarity enough to question the difference. There can also be a less benign explanation. Charro-as-Mexican makes it a target for racism and prejudice. Rodolfo and I discussed that "vaquero" seems like a more neutral, "friendlier" word because "we can all be vaqueros and vaqueras." The word *charro* might hit a cultural wall because "we as humans sometimes are quick to criticize and judge rather than understand." "Vaquero" also evokes "working with cows," which has cultural resonance for Americans, while "charro" is more closely associated with Mexican horsemanship and competition.

Both Rodolfo Lara Sr. and Miguel have participated in *charreadas*, which Rodolfo informed me were formalized and federated in the 1920s. Rodolfo explained the roots of this competition: "One hacienda would gather up their charros and vaqueros, and they would say, we're going to go compete against the other hacienda. It would be who did it better. That's why instead of being out in the open as a job, they took it to where the town could go in and watch this ranch compete against that ranch." Miguel commented that now, even though the two are related, "That doesn't mean the charros, necessarily, can do what these vaqueros could do outside of the arena. You know, outside of the arena is a little harder." In his own career, and knowing the differences between the names, Miguel was able to move between them: "I do it all—charro, vaquero, cowboy."

THE WORTH OF THE WORD IN THIS STUDY

Miguel's comment above makes this an appropriate place to bring in ideas about the turbulent nature of language. What I characterized earlier as faceted, might also, if anthropomorphized, be called restless; the restlessness of the word "vaquero" corresponds well with Bakhtin's (1981) portrayal of all "living" language:

> But no living word relates to its object in a *singular* way: between the word and its object, between the word and the speaking subject, there exists in an elastic environment of other, alien words about the same object, the same theme, and this is an environment that is often difficult to penetrate. It is precisely in the process of living interaction with the specific environment that the word may be individualized and given stylistic shape. (p. 270; italics in original)

The critical thing to note about the word "vaquero" is that even though it has the straightforward English translation of "cowboy," that is where the straightness ends. It is currently layered with meaning from different cultural contexts, and has been brought into, for English speakers, a modern conception of horsemanship distinct from its historical origins. We can see how it has been "individualized" by single speakers (who might use it interchangeably with buckaroo, cowboy, or even Californio) but also by its use in mainstream American horsemanship culture. It has been "given stylistic shape" by connoting certain elements of horsemanship to some of its audience—namely, replacing some of the characteristics of "Natural horsemanship," which has fallen out of favor. Furthermore, there is some disagreement about what exactly it means and the cultural roots it entails, which is part of, I would argue, Bakhtin's "elastic environment." I share this connection to theory to suggest that the word's restlessness is perhaps not so much problematic as it is predictable (as part of the nature of language more generally). And we do have "meanings [that] are temporarily stabilized" (Barker & Jane, 2016, p. 124) of vaquero and its extended family.

Another crucial thing to bear in mind is that many horsepeople prefer *not* to use descriptive labels that would place them in any sort of group that would, by definition, then exclude other descriptors that might apply to them. They simply shy away from semantic boxes altogether. This might also be due to the fact that modern VH has become a product to be bought and sold, so some do not want to be part of this marketing effort. As I have mentioned, there are several interviewees who would not call themselves vaqueros although they have learned or been influenced by VH.

The meaning of the word "vaquero" shifts according to the speaker, audience, and situation. Since I study literacy and language in context, I always think that particular word choices are significant, but I also recognize that in the actual presence of horses, labels have little, if any, utility (unless, perhaps, other humans are around). Surely the horse doesn't care whether we call the subject of this study "vaquero" or "buckaroo" or just "horsemanship." Moreover, human comprehension is expansive enough to understand all of the somewhat interchangeable labels and how messy, perhaps even inaccurately, the word "vaquero" is used today. Vaquero horsemanship means something different today than it meant historically, and it also seems to mean something different depending on where you use it in the United States and beyond. Those that I interviewed for this project understood that it was a definitional starting point, with specific cultural and geographical roots, and that it provided common ground from which to travel forward into more complexity.

CONCLUSION

"Honoring the horse" is a fairly common phrase in modern VH. Considering what participants expressed about the cultural roots of VH, with some specificity *and* some ambiguity, and as someone schooled in sociocultural approaches to education, I believe that we also need to honor knowledge of the cultural roots of VH, so that they do not fade away as we get further from them. As Bill Reynolds asked, "What happens to all of this without people who write about it and say, don't forget this is where it came from?" I have a simple answer: We will forget where it came from. In addition to writing about it, we can talk about it, making it part of the learning of VH; that might actually be the easiest part of VH to learn. Otherwise, VH might become more of a modern consumer construction, something we have created with our desire to be distinct in horsemanship.

Furthermore, I would argue that cultural distance should *not* be collapsed if it means an absence of culture(s). This is a separate issue from viewing VH as open to those from all cultural backgrounds and embracing the idea that on horseback, we are not judged by race or ethnicity (not by the horse, at any rate). Horsemanship can feel like it takes place in a sort of special dimension where elements like society and culture hold no sway. I do believe that horsemanship crosses (but not erases) cultural boundaries and can bring a diverse group of riders together. Culture both does and does not matter in horsemanship: It does not matter *to* the horse although it does still very much matter in the world *surrounding* the horse and so is deserving of thought and reflection as part of the practice of horsemanship.

As far as the word "vaquero" itself, we can play devil's advocate (Haraway, 2012) with it, having hauled it forward into a modern, somewhat foreign context (and that is one thing I have attempted to do in this chapter). Haraway proposed that "devil's advocates can work within uncertainty, doubt, and skepticism and still remain passionate and committed, open to knowing more, enacting better, without losing respect for doubt ... devil's advocates can take the heat of conflict, contradiction, and overflowing complexity" (p. 24). Horsemanship enacted by humans is always complex because we have a tendency to corrupt it with ego, greed, and our own shortcomings. Perhaps "vaquero" should remain a contradictory and complex word—and let the philosophy that has evolved from it continue to shape itself to better fit the horse.

To outsiders, the gear of the vaquero, the charro, and even the American cowboy who practices modern VH (like some in this study) can seem extreme or unusual; taking it out of its horsemanship context subtracts its cultural roots and traditions, and these traditions in turn reveal the purpose of the gear. Even though I agree with Williams' (1983) statement that "A culture can never be reduced to its artifacts while it is being lived" (p. 323), it is through VH gear ("its artifacts") that some of its accompanying cultural traditions have been, and can be, preserved. I would like to end with an exchange Miguel and I had about the misunderstanding that can occur when the gear is viewed as isolated from its cultural context.

> MIGUEL: A lot of people don't understand what a bridle horse is supposed to look like. The first thing they're going to pick apart is your bridle, a little bit longer shank—that's the first thing that catches their attention. Then they go over and see your spurs. I know there's some stereotyping going on because of that. Really, the gear is only going to be as severe as the rider using it. So, there are a lot of places where people kind of look at you funny.
>
> JULIANNA: Because of the gear that you're using?
>
> MIGUEL: Because of the gear. A lot of people are like, "Look at that big saddle horn." That's the way they make them, and that's the traditional way of riding. We'll keep using them that way.

INTERLUDE 6

Tom Curtin and Dusty

THERE ARE SEVERAL HORSES THAT HAVE REALLY TAUGHT ME A LOT. ONE particular horse was one that Ray Hunt got me involved with. I was 29 years old and was just starting to spend actual time riding with Ray. I was at one of his clinics, and there was a young lady there riding this particular horse in the colt starting, and he bucked her off seven times in four days. She went to Ray at the end of the clinic and said, "I'm in a lot of trouble. I know I'm in trouble. What do I need to do?" He said, "Talk to that young man over there," and he pointed to me. "He would be able to help you." So, I took the horse and rode him for a month. He wasn't what I would speak of as a rank horse or mean or aggressive. He could get easily scared and extremely bothered when he got scared. I didn't know how to keep him from getting scared.

At that point in my life, I could get a horse to do what I wanted him to do because he would be scared not to. I'm not proud of that—it's just what I knew at that point. So, as time went on, I got this horse where I could ride him. I'm not saying he wasn't a little bit fractious or a little dangerous for other folks to ride. I told the owner, "This is definitely not going to work for you. You need to do something different than to think you can take this horse home and ride." So, she said, "Would you keep him another 30 days? Let's try him 30 more days and see how he progresses." I said, "Sure." He did get somewhat better, but this horse could really get scared, and when he got scared, he got really bothered and really came apart. Again, he only did it because he was scared. We were getting by, and I got to where I could rope off of him and do different things with him. I could work cattle on him, but I spent more time getting him scared than not being scared.

At the end of the 60 days the owner came, and I told her, "This still isn't going to be any safer or better for you." That's when I realized you've got to be truthful with people. I could've kidded her through it and said, "Oh, he's fine. He'll be all right. You just have to figure it out." I thought, no, you've got to tell this lady the truth. So, she said, "Let me ask you this. Would you be willing to just keep the horse and ride him?" I said, "Well, I could use an extra horse right at this time." So, I committed to taking the horse. I got to where I could do a lot of stuff on him. He was a lot of fun, but if you weren't paying attention and you did one little thing, one little mistake, you'd have him where he could really come apart; when he came apart, it was difficult to get him gathered back up again.

I had had him almost a year and a half, and I've got this horse riding pretty nice. I'm not saying he was safe, but I could kind of force him through some things and survive it. Then we went to this branding with Ray; he always loved to go to a branding and head and heel calves. At the end of the branding, there was one calf left. Ray and Trina, my wife, dragged the second to the last calf up there, and then there was this last calf. Several people had thrown and missed and thrown and missed. This calf was pretty sharp, and he came whipping past me, and this is where it doesn't take long to get humbled. I mean, you get to thinking you're somebody. I reached and roped that calf, and I mean I snagged him and caught him right quick. I just really aggressively did what we speak of as dallying my rope around my horn very quickly. I gave that horse a little jerk, and I mean—the wreck was on, and we were in this huge corral. This horse went to bucking, and he could've bucked anywhere he wanted to go in that pen. Where do you think he went? Straight to Ray. He went straight bucking down there toward Ray, and he had seen him coming and wasn't going to move intentionally, trying to get him to stop. This horse ran right into Ray, and I looked up at Ray, and I said, "I've got to get that out of this horse." And he said, "I believe I would leave that in there" and just rode off. I didn't say this to him then, but several years later I brought that particular moment up and told him that I had thought to myself, "You know, you're not the one that's got to ride this colt, I do. And I've got to get that out of there."

So, six or eight months went by, and I rode the horse, but it never really got any better. Ray asked me if I would come to California and help him start some of his colts. I thought that that was an honor for me to be able to do that, so I jumped on a plane and flew out there. Ray always would ask you how you're doing and how's your family. I got to the airport, and Ray came to pick me up. He didn't say hi, how are you, how's Trina, or anything—first words out of his mouth were, "Did you ever get that out of that horse?" I said, "No sir." He said, "Well, I believe I'd just leave that in there," and he turned around and walked off. We had a 30- or 40-minute ride from the airport to where we were going, and I thought, "I'm going to wait until I get him in that truck and we're going down the road where he can't walk off, and I'm going to quiz him about this." So, I said to him, "Mr. Ray, I don't know what you mean by that." He said, "Tom, a horse is a lot like an onion. He's made in layers. If you get a bad spot in an onion and you go to picking at it, it's just going to keep getting worse and worse, and it's going to work down into the middle. So, when you have a place like that on a horse or a situation like that, if you keep picking at that, it'll never go away. It'll always be at the surface on that horse. If you try to stop that and get that horse back to feeling good about himself, those places will heal. You can cover them up with so many good things that that spot won't come out in that horse. That's that horse's nature. It's in there—you'll never get it out. As long as you try to get it out, it'll never get any better. But you can cover it up with so many good things that it doesn't ever come to the surface."

So, I went home and really went to work on that. Every time that horse felt like he was going to get into a little bit of trouble or a little unsure, instead of me forcing him through it, I just backed up, and I'd go back to doing something that I knew he understood. I'd use that to my advantage, and I would build up from there. It wasn't three to four months later, our little girl was about three years old at that time, and I got in a situation where I needed that horse, and I had enough confidence in him that I could put her on him, and he'd take care of her. It was unbelievable how that horse changed when I changed my train of thought. So, that horse was so valuable to me because he was difficult for me at first. I could ride him. I grew up riding saddle broncs and bucking horses; I was thrilled to ride a horse that bucked. So that wasn't what bothered me so much, but I knew that horse when he would get like that didn't feel right and didn't feel good inside. That horse was really influential in my life.

CHAPTER 7

A Virtual Gallop: Using Technology to Learn Vaquero Horsemanship

THERE IS NO PLACE FOR A COMPUTER IN A HORSE CORRAL. WHILE YOU could hold a smartphone while working with a horse, you place yourself at risk by being distracted from the half-ton animal accompanying you (and you can forget about the social media scrolling that so many of us do—the horse will have none of that). Although the common and accessible tools of technology (video and the Internet, including social media) might not be a natural fit with the in-the-moment work of horse education, they can play critical and unique roles in learning Vaquero horsemanship. In this chapter, I explore these roles, and how they affected those I interviewed as they learned Vaquero horsemanship.

THE INTERSECTION OF VAQUERO HORSEMANSHIP AND TECHNOLOGY

One initial goal of this project was to understand how technology might both help and hinder learning this particular style of horsemanship, especially since participants have to rely upon it given the distance separating them from VH's geographical and cultural origins and nearby communities of practice. As I will share, horse educators of a variety of ages assimilated technology into their individual learning trails in ways that they reported as empowering and sometimes life-changing. To employ a riding metaphor, technology meant that they could gallop toward learning Vaquero horsemanship; however, while technology played a significant role, it was not as simple as being wholly transformed by digital participation since the presence of the horse mediated whatever trainers learned virtually.

Relatively recent research on adults utilizing technology for their own learning has included studies of digital writing (Sharp, 2017); collaborative practices in university courses (Sharp, 2018); online discussions in graduate-level courses (Vogler et al., 2013); digital storytelling in literacy education (Prins, 2017a & 2017b); and critical literacy projects that include digital literacies (Ajayi, 2015; Albers, Pace, & Odo, 2016). Furthermore, learning with digital tools now includes participatory culture, which Jenkins (2008) described as the "culture in which fans and other consumers are invited to actively participate in the creation and circulation of new content" (p. 331). This has become a canonical term in the field of digital literacies—one inheritance from an expanded and socially situated definition of literacy (Barton & Hamilton, 1998; Kress, 2010; New London Group, 1996; Street, 1984; see also Leander & Boldt, 2012). Even for those who did not grow up with an omnipresence of technology, as users we all now expect to be active participants when we engage with digital worlds. Our ability to communicate has expanded to include posting, creating, filming, and commenting, amid other actions that have moved us beyond just passive screen-watching and scrolling. Learning horsemanship with technology lends a new nuance to participatory culture as hands-on work with the horse must be a substantial amount of it. Furthermore, as Jenkins et al. (2009) noted, "Participatory culture shifts the focus of literacy from individual expression to community involvement" (p. xiii), and so learning about VH on the Internet connects us to far-flung and ever-shifting virtual—and often specialized—communities. In this project, the digital is available to participants when more traditional literacies (i.e., books) and more immediate physical communities are not, and so they benefit from this availability. Some assimilated technology into their individual learning trajectories in ways that they reported as empowering and sometimes life-changing.

In virtual communities, more peer, rather than teacher- or expert-centered, learning occurs (Balkin & Sonnevend, 2016, p. 11), so this digital learning often looks very different from the formal learning most of us experienced in school. Authority rises and falls according to particular situations, and the parameters of participation are not necessarily defined by age. Notably, the younger interviewees did not seem to be, insofar as their interviews conveyed, inherently more proficient, enthusiastic, or comfortable than their older counterparts. Instead, all participants demonstrated a kind of "eclecticism of digital practices" (Costa et al., 2019, p. 575) (even as they shared common elements, which I will detail in this chapter). Note the use of the word "eclecticism," which is also part of the title of a popular magazine in the VH community (*Eclectic Horseman*); this word is certainly a brand of this horsemanship style in that learners, in my observation, do a sort of digital cherry-picking, which is encouraged by the enormity of the Internet. Indeed, one's journey with technology would almost certainly have to be heterogenous to be meaningful, especially in an out-of-school environment. Digital investigation driven by interest is unique to each learner.

THE VERNACULAR AND THE DIGITAL IN LEARNING VAQUERO HORSEMANSHIP

I find it helpful to view participants' thoughts about technology and learning VH through the lens of vernacular literacies (Barton & Hamilton, 1998), and its spinoff of vernacular digital literacies (Barton & Lee, 2012). Barton and Hamilton (1998) defined *vernacular literacies* as being "rooted in everyday experience and serv[ing] everyday purposes" (p. 251) and "more likely to be voluntary and self-generated" (p. 253; see also Heath, 1983, and Purcell-Gates, 1995). What participants learned via technology was "learned informally" (p. 252) in their everyday lives as they relied upon their own interests and comfort with technology. Barton and Hamilton also made the point that vernacular literacies are "rarely separated from use" and instead "are integrated in everyday activities" (p. 252). Although vernacular literacies usually exclude the workplace (p. 252), in this instance, the workplace is an extension of the home, since many participants are self-employed.

In particular, participants shared two characteristics of vernacular literacies that Barton and Hamilton (1998) identified. The first is that of sensemaking where "people consciously carry out their own research" (again, they may do this eclectically) and "become local experts" (p. 250). This aspect can be marked by "a tenacious imperative to learn, to find out more" (p. 250). Since this is not a style of horsemanship that participants could easily study in their own physical communities, a desire to learn about it motivated their development. They had to "find out where and how to get the resources they need[ed]" (p. 250), using, in this case, technology to further the search. Next, the "social participation" aspect is present in that social activities often accompanied the individual learning trails that I describe in this chapter: Participants consistently interacted with others online as well as in person at clinics and through lessons. All interviewees spoke of this social dimension, as their comments in this chapter reveal.

Vernacular literacies also have been predictably affected by the digital. Barton and Lee (2012) described how the Internet has given rise to new forms of vernacular literacies as "many practices of reading and writing are being transformed by people's participation in online activities and, as a result, the dynamics of everyday life are changing in profound ways" (p. 282). In their study of Flickr use, Barton and Lee (2012) argued that as digital access has increased, so has the value that we ascribe to vernacular literacies:

> [V]ernacular practices have been less valued socially than more dominant practices which are sponsored and supported by education and other external institutions. In the case of Flickr, these local practices are now more valued. What was personal and often private is now put into the public realm. People are making public and giving greater circulation to activities which previously were local and where

people could regulate access and use. These activities are no longer confined to the local sphere. (p. 297)

The digital continues to fuel self-sponsored education as learners utilize what they find to change themselves and their lives. If participants in this study were "confined to the local sphere," then their learning trails would have been shortened (or perhaps not have occurred at all); instead, they were able to learn about VH in a particular geographical region far from its roots and local practice, aided by technology. The digital spread of information about VH has also increased its value through exposure and accessibility: More want to learn about it as more come to know about its existence.

GEOGRAPHICAL DISTANCE, COLLAPSED

On a fundamental—and perhaps unsurprising—level, technology has helped to collapse distance and "to spread what Vaquero horsemanship is" across geographical boundaries (Riley). There was consensus about technology helping significantly to overcome geographical distance: "I think it's helped people learn more. It's more accessible. Somebody like me who's on the East Coast could never have access to this stuff. If I just went out West and I was like, 'Hey, teach me some vaquero stuff,' they'd probably laugh me off the ranch" (Amy S.). Technology might well step in as a virtual teacher in the absence of any others, especially when you are just starting to learn about VH (I think of this as the Wikipedia phenomenon in that so many of us turn to the Internet to first find out about a given topic, and the Internet can be depended upon to give us at least *some* information, although it may not be balanced or correct).

For Natalie and Miguel, YouTube provided their introduction to Vaquero horsemanship. Although they both had backgrounds in other styles of horsemanship, and Miguel was acquainted with VH from his family, they did not have a pronounced interest in it until they encountered a certain video:

> What attracted me really—Miguel and I were watching YouTube one day. He saw a video, and he's like, hey, come here and watch this. And I was like, how are they doing that with their horses? Did his hand move? And I think that's kind of when you discovered it too, right? You've known a little bit about it before that maybe. (Miguel agrees.)

In their experiences, they did not seek it out so much as stumble upon it after becoming curious about what they viewed. Without technology in this instance, which allowed them to wander amid this collapsed geographical distance, they might not have then started to study it more formally since they were unlikely to encounter it locally. In another example, Jeff Derby described learning about Bruce Sandifer's work after having "stumbled onto some things Bruce was writing on social media." This led to a professional collaboration where they regularly co-teach clinics.

Technology was a significant part of the learning process for Emma, who described the relationship between VH and virtual information in the following way:

> I definitely think it's made it more accessible. And, like we were talking about earlier, if you weren't born into it or in an area where it was thriving, you didn't really know about it. So, now, you can read articles online, there's tons of websites that are about traditional Vaquero horsemanship, and the gear, and the people to talk to, and the books, and everything.

Technology provided a wider range of resources than print books alone and functioned as a component of "relating to the world in new ways" using vernacular digital literacies (Barton & Lee, 2012, p. 295). Participants did not express that they favored digital literacies over traditional print but communicated that they utilized technology to find books as well as multimedia sources to continue to learn. In this way, technology acted as a kind of librarian who might help learners plan their journeys across geographical boundaries.

CONNECTION AND "SOCIAL PROOF"

Another common function of technology is connection across borders (the positive side of participatory culture), or as Miguel described it, "With technology nowadays, you can communicate with anybody," and participants in this project expressed that they, too, utilized it to find others also interested in Vaquero horsemanship. Maggie stated that, when describing practicing VH in the southeastern United States, "It's just hard to find your peers and then the people interested in this are so few and far between anyway—and we're geographically separated. So, maybe the only connection that's really practical to have is that online connection." They used "online connections[s]" in one of two ways in this regard: (1) to find others close by; and (2) to find others with the same interest throughout the world. Pragmatically, the Internet is a forum to find out when a given clinician is coming through, but that alone would likely not constitute enough of a community, as none of the interviewees mentioned relying on clinics alone for VH education. On a local level then, technology helped them "realize there were people out there that wanted this" (Noah). This shared interest motivated them to keep searching for community, virtual and local.

As Alicia B. described, the Internet could fill a vacuum: "I feel like the community is very spread out. If it weren't for Facebook, I would feel very alone because there's not a lot of that community around here. But it's a great community as far as social media now." In this sense, technology delivers what has come to be one of its recognized functions of providing links across the boundaries that would otherwise keep us separated. Like the participants in Costa et al.'s (2019) study, "Engagement and identification with digital practices becomes a form of self-inclusion in a modern society and by default a strategy that brings them closer to the practices of other groups with whom they co-exist" (p. 575). In a wider, global sense, technology has made "the world smaller," as Melanie A. noted, who also added that it "gives us a way of communicating with people of like minds who aren't in this area . . . and makes us know that we're not alone." Again, I believe that we arrive at our phones and keyboards with the expectation that technology will do what Melanie described, and so it makes sense that those who know they are geographically alone would turn to it to moderate that isolation.

When I asked Linda H. how technology and digital literacies have affected her learning Vaquero horsemanship, her response included a larger societal context:

> We have suffered as people because we've lost that sense of community. Social media has been good to bring a sense of community back. . . . Sometimes you do feel like you're the only one out there, and either you're comfortable with that or you're not. I'm comfortable walking my own path and always have been. That's easy for me, but I realize that a lot of my clients are going to be more comfortable in a supportive environment which makes it easier for them to be the only person in a barn being the odd man out on this path. They need that social proof of the others around them.

Those studying VH in the southeastern United States would not be able to depend on a neighbor sharing their interest and so social media expands the neighborhood in a necessary way for those devoted to what was, and still is, in their region an unusual style of horsemanship. For participants, it can provide an opportunity "to be a part of something" in both the horsemanship and larger social worlds.

For one participant, Johnny C., who described himself as an "outsider" and felt like he had been shut out socially from the few around him who shared his interest in Vaquero horsemanship, technology made a crucial difference. He described his virtual community as the "only" one that he had access to and as one that "really helped [him] get somewhere faster" in his learning of VH. In his particular case, the "somewhere" he got to was remarkable. He described obsessively researching horsemanship, including VH, on YouTube specifically, and subsequently making contact with one of the "old guard" of VH, Mike Thomas, who happened to be living in Georgia at the time. They began communicating online and then met in person—the beginning of an enduring friendship that was, and is, extremely important to Johnny (Mike passed away in 2023). In addition to providing practical and philosophical advice, this well-regarded elder regularly praised Johnny's abilities in online forums, like Facebook, thereby raising his social standing in significant ways; this then led to him being sought out to provide lessons and clinics. He felt like he had hit a solid and highly frustrating wall with people in the surrounding physical community until technology—and the mentor that it led to—stepped in and subsequently enlarged that community and his professional opportunities along with it. His story is an illustration of "the ways in which vernacular activities can give access to resources and provide a voice which may otherwise not be heard" (Barton & Lee, 2012, p. 284).

Even though technology made a significant dent in the isolation that participants might feel, it meant confronting the specific challenge of connecting with your direct competition in virtual environments. So, for example, if you belong to a Facebook group with others who practice a particular style of horsemanship like VH, then you are posting to connect but also to promote yourself. While the two are not mutually exclusive, the mixing of the two means you might have mixed motivations for maintaining a social media presence. Maggie described this dilemma by asking: "How do we make [social media] a more effective time together of the community and networking device where instead of everybody using it to promote their own stuff, which is great that it's there for that, but knowing these people are so isolated, how can we use that to help fight this isolation?" While participants used social media to counter isolation, they would not be able to avoid this tension since *all* of them mentioned using the Internet to advertise themselves to some degree. This dilemma was ongoing and unresolved, as far as I could tell, due to the nature of participation in social media that encourages a digital blending of professional and personal lives. This may well be part of another aspect of Maggie's description of a nuanced digital advantage: "There's this isolation that happens that technology can help replace, but not fully replace." It can also help you connect but also unavoidably places you in competition with your peers. In the next section, I turn to a more straightforward technology that predates the Internet: video, which held a specific appeal to most participants.

THE CRITICAL ADVANTAGES OF VIDEO

Video is such a commonplace part of our daily lives now that we take its presence and accessibility for granted, and the reader may wonder why this aspect even merits a mention. After all, wouldn't we just assume that videos would be used by horse educators to expand their knowledge? Video, of course, provides a unique opportunity as it can often be easily accessed, for free or for a relatively nominal fee. All participants mentioned watching videos, DVDs, or YouTube as part of their learning experiences with VH; Elijah labeled them as his "best source." Participants appreciated the widespread access to video as well as being able to watch when, and how often, they saw fit, either alone or with company. So, video served a critical role for some, a supplemental one for others, and was a distinctive resource for those with learning styles that required repetition and for those looking to share in real time what they observed while watching.

As Alex described, this kind of literacy addressed a significant gap in print availability about Vaquero horsemanship: "I'd read an article where someone had interviewed Bill Dorrance. He was talking about throwing some of these vaquero roping shots. It was killing me because I couldn't pick that up from the description. How would you describe it well enough in print? You need to see the whole thing in motion." For learners, "see[ing] the whole thing in motion" was an essential element when dealing with a thousand-plus-pound live animal who responds in real time and sometimes unpredictably. Bill mentioned that the techniques of VH are

> hard to describe. To teach somebody how to throw a houlihan [a certain rope shot] and do it in a narrative, you'd have to be pretty good with descriptive language. Even then, I think it'd be darned near impossible. You either have to show them how to do it, which would be great, but if there's nobody around to show me, videos—definitely videos.

Access to videos "makes it [VH] just right at your fingertips, so you don't have to travel out West" (Kathleen K.), which resolves a fundamental challenge of studying a subject that has its roots thousands of miles away.

Kathleen K. also pointed out that she was initially overwhelmed by how much information can be contained in videos but that she returned to them as needed: "But then when you start approaching it and having moments where you're like, oh, I remember that was in that video—and then you go back and pick it up." In addition to access, being able to repeatedly view videos was also an elemental aspect of their helpfulness. This feature was one that Elijah elaborated upon:

> You can probably watch it 300 times and find something different to do every single time. And that's right there at your fingertips—you don't have to go anywhere. You can just sit there and study and write notes and rewind it. With a lot of these clinics, stuff is so subtle and happens so quickly that you can't just say, hold on just one second and go back right there. . . . You're working hard so you can't stop for a

second and go, hey, can we go back and look? With these DVDs, these video clips, the Internet, you can go back and see what you might do differently.

The fast pace of working with animals means that the more meditative parts of your learning process, the "subtle" aspects, might need to occur in a space removed from practice or as a different part of that practice. In a way, studying video stands in contrast to the fast-paced and attention-deprived nature of technology that has become so commonplace—meaning, many of us are quickly consuming and never returning to what we see. We look for novelty and new information, but working with horses requires a different sort of concentration. Instead of technology making us more impatient throughout our lives, as our attention spans become shorter, we might become more patient with technology for the sake of our horses. Furthermore, being able to watch a video at your leisure, and as many times as you want to, provides a balance to the more immediate part of working, and learning, with horses. It also means that video serves visual learners (as some described themselves) as well as those who benefited from repetition, especially when this led to new realizations.

Accessing videos was not always a solitary endeavor; there was, for Emma, a social dimension as the video worked in a kind of dialogue with her experiences:

> The DVD doesn't change, but your way of thinking changes. We might watch the DVD once, and we'll notice the lead-changes part. And, a couple weeks later, we'll go ride with somebody, and talk about something, and see something happening there, and then you'll go back and watch that DVD and go, oh, wow, look—it's there. You just didn't notice it before. So I really like to watch it with other people because everybody gets something different and sees something different.

In this scenario, video functions as a tool that might be unchanging but remains in conversation with those who engage with it. Even though we might be tempted to think of a sole viewer in front of a screen, and while that undoubtedly occurs often, Emma's remarks highlighted the intersection of the lone and the communal, which applied overall to learning VH.

In addition to seeking out access to others in both real and virtual settings, participants needed continual access to many forms of media, both traditional and new, as no single one was exhaustive enough to provide the information they might need or want to seek out. Continual accessibility was a characteristic that marked positive learning experiences in participants' descriptions, and multimedia resources were at the top of this list. Not all digital resources are created equal, however, and figuring out the value of each one, and which resources came from actual experts, became vital skills.

IDENTIFICATION OF FALSE EXPERTISE AND LEARNING TO CRITICALLY EVALUATE SOURCES

Although we are now into Web 4.0, Web 2.0 brought a decentered expertise as part of our digital engagement. Lankshear and Knobel (2011) described how one change from version 1.0 to 2.0 was that authority and expertise became "distributed, collective, and hybrid" (p. 41). Rather than being concentrated in one source, or individual, expertise is often flattened in digital worlds (still another kind of collapse) as many contribute to the accumulation of shared knowledge. Just as in real life, we might be perceived as an expert in one online context and not in another. Authority shifts as we move through our day, although technology has arguably made it easier to assume, or present ourselves as possessing, shades of expertise. Even though technology made it in some ways easier to learn Vaquero horsemanship, interviewees could go from not having enough information in their local communities to too much information in virtual ones. In this way the information galloped toward them, leaving them to judge what to take seriously.

Riley remarked on her feelings about social media: "I particularly don't like Facebook, but I find that if you have a question about anything, all you have to do is write it and boom, you've got all kinds of opinions." Other participants also mentioned having mixed feelings about social media but continuing to use it even though some information might subsequently be "cast out" (Charlotte). When asked if she thought that technology has affected becoming an expert at Vaquero horsemanship, Kathleen K. responded, "I think that it creates people who think they're experts, right?" Participants, unsurprisingly as experienced users of technology, realized that "Everyone can look at it [VH] online and get some information—enough information to form an opinion—but not necessarily be qualified to perform it" (Emma). Amy S. stated that technology had made VH "more accessible," but this "also in a way cheapens it" because "to some degree, anyone's posting videos and they can all claim something... there's more information available, but there's also fewer people willing to research it, I think. They just kind of take it at face value." She concluded by saying that there are still "more pros than cons" to this. Therefore, more responsibility is placed upon the learner, a reality we see more generally with technology, as a critical eye is needed to sift through information-rich contexts.

A danger that Emily S. acknowledged is one that might come from false expertise, when people do not "understand the level of knowledge needed to be good with any animal, but especially a horse, because what you're trying to ask of them, and how big they are... it's like learning a foreign language." Those working closely with horses realize that their lives depend on how well they speak that language, and so identifying false expertise is critical as they build their own knowledge base. Jeff Derby expressed a similar idea: "There's some danger in technology because it's easy to give a false impression of how much you know. You don't watch a YouTube video and then know how to ride a horse. . . . But that doesn't mean there is not good information there—you have to be a discerning participant or discerning student of that information."

Alicia B. described the importance of having knowledge *before* turning to technology:

> I definitely, from the second that I was able to access [technology], I was using it and searching and weeding through. I'm grateful that I had the knowledge and the education on Vaquero horsemanship before having that thrown at me because there's so much out there now that when I watch certain things—you can actually see the ones that are doing it in a correct way, and I'm really glad to have it because I feel like it exposes you to so much more. But I feel like if you didn't have the right fundamentals first, it could really mess you up.

She also described watching with her daughter, who is "growing up with Facebook and YouTube and all of these things that are very accessible to her," and realizing how important it is to teach her to view critically what might otherwise seem desirable—she does this by "show[ing] her something else" that would then illustrate its shortcomings. She views part of her ongoing job as an educator "to research and be skeptical and to really find what works and what doesn't." While Alicia's daughter has her mother for guidance, participants more often had to rely on themselves to know when to "move on," which likely meant no small investment of time as filters were cultivated. Of course, the most significant filter for them would be horses themselves, and so they had the advantage of getting to apply digital suggestions to non-virtual lessons and experiences. Overall, a Vaquero horsemanship expert cannot be created online or digitally but *can* integrate digital information to help develop that expertise (although, remember that "expert" was a title everyone was reluctant to adopt, as discussed in chapter three).

LIMITATIONS OF TECHNOLOGY AND THE NEED FOR "FEEL"

Even though "technologies provide ways for people to engage in new activities, ones which they have not engaged in before and which have not been possible before" (Barton & Lee, 2012, p. 284), the last theme from the interviews that I will discuss captured the limitations of technology in this horsemanship context. There is a need for "feel"; recall that Ray Hunt (1978) stated that "[t]o digest these [horsemanship] goals in the capsule form a person need only know 'feel, timing, and balance.' But the truth of the matter is that just those three small terms take a lifetime of chewing before they begin to digest" (p. 10). The more mysterious aspect aside, there is a physical component that would have to get beyond being a "spectator" (Linda H.). Even non-horse people will surely understand that working with horses effectively requires that you "ride, ride, ride" (Natalie). All participants conveyed that learning VH must have this dimension of action and "feel" as its ultimate test.

In describing vernacular literacies, Hamilton (2000) stated, "Everyday literacies are subservient to the goals of purposeful activities and are defined by people in terms of these activities" (p. 5). The overall purposeful activity in this context was to learn more and more about Vaquero horsemanship in practice, a progression that participants each defined for themselves, although they agreed that this was a step with no digital substitution possible. As much as technology can communicate about Vaquero horsemanship, it is this dimension of "feel" that simply does not translate to a virtual environment. Amy G. captured what she considered to be the dividing line between what can be studied via technology and what has to be accomplished in the physical world:

> What kind of feel are you getting out of your screen? Nothing . . . so, it's not getting to the place where it really resides. I think you have to have the feel, and then you have to know that you want it, and then maybe you can get some help on the computer, but you can't start there. . . . This is an art. It's creative. It comes from some other high place, in my opinion. It's definitely more refined than anything you just see on a screen.

Technology served a pivotal, yet partial, function. That VH was, and is, an art form, was supported by print and digital literacies, but how to *be* an artist practicing it would come through working with a horse in real time.

Furthermore, the passionate tone of Amy G.'s statements marked an overall characteristic of participants' descriptions of their individual interests in VH. They were drawn to the "art" of it, even if they did not all use that particular term. They *sounded* like artists when they described a commitment to a style of horsemanship that they had to actively seek out in order to learn about it since it was not geographically, or culturally, readily available. In a sense, they needed an artist's focus and discipline to be able to pursue this particular path, which included wading through an abundance of digital information. So even though technology provided an essential connection, part of learning its utility in this context involved knowing where that potential ended.

We tend to think of the volume of information available digitally as a positive thing; however, Ricky Quinn had an intriguing take on this. He speculated that having so many options can lead to us *not* working on something long enough because we know we can find someone else explaining it yet another way online. Our horsemanship attention spans suffer. He shared that, "Anything I've ever learned from [Buck] Brannaman, if I stuck with it and adjusted myself, it's worked 100 percent of the time. Did it work right away? No. Because over 20 years, I've had to figure it out. That's what I think technology gets in our way with. Too much information." It would be better for horsemanship students to "find somebody they really respected so that they had one train of thought for a while." Technology can discourage the adoption of a mentor, like Ricky described, because we are encouraged to look for "the bigger, better deal" in the expanse of the Internet—there will always seem to be someone, or something, better "out there." A valuable part of the process is subtracted when we keep jumping from one explanation to another, and he thought it could be detrimental "on the human side—on the soul side" if it prevents us from "get[ting] it on a more of a horse level." Ricky concluded by pointing out that Tom Dorrance and Ray Hunt did not have access to technology and yet still developed their philosophies and became "legends" of this horsemanship. It was an "old-school" approach of "going through the process in tangible ways and feeling it." They also did not have the distraction of social media and instead spent their free time "working with horses in the evening as their entertainment." He reminded me that the gift of information comes at a cost, and that being protective of how we spend whatever amount of time we have to learn horsemanship is wise.

LESSONS FROM THE DIGITAL WORLD OF VAQUERO HORSEMANSHIP

If there is an overall motif that runs throughout this part of my findings, it is that technology might make learning VH possible across a vast distance, but it cannot provide the whole journey; what interviewees learned in a virtual environment had to be created and recreated in their physical worlds. This is not to say that they did not move back-and-forth between the two—often, according to their descriptions, without tension. The individualized nature of the learning trails that each participant spoke about signaled a kind of eclecticism in that each learner leaned upon digital and print literacies in a variety of combinations. Barton and Hamilton (1998) stated that "The texts of everyday life can be more fluid, inventive and hybrid in their discourse characteristics" (p. 258). Participants' descriptions of learning VH with technology reflect this fluidity and hybridity, necessitated by the online needing the offline for application.

Furthermore, three elements were key to learning on participants' own terms while utilizing technology: accessibility, flexibility, and criticality. For some participants, this was a significant way to learn about Vaquero horsemanship because clinics can be prohibitively expensive and occur infrequently (although you can audit for a much lower fee, and, as Kathleen K. mentioned, the pandemic resulted in an increase in virtual clinics, which are usually a fraction of the cost of in-person ones). Given the geographical constraints, technology therefore filled a void in a singular way. Flexibility was noteworthy because participants could access these tools when, where, and how often they wanted. Adults learning in a context such as this is anything but uniform as each learner searched out what they needed and wanted in any given moment rather than being dictated to by another authority. Participants also developed a critical eye on their own timelines, recognizing that this aspect was crucial to comprehending what to take seriously given so much information. Criticality was part of learning what to pay attention to regarding VH's digital presence and what to be skeptical of as they continued learning. They needed to develop a critical eye to be able to sift through the immense nation of information that the Internet contains—one of the drawbacks of *everybody* being able to post and participate. As learning progressed, one would have to know what to heed and what to ignore to be able to continue to acquire knowledge that proves useful.

CONCLUSION

*I think, with all of the resources available, it would be silly not to
exhaust every option possible because there is Internet, and social
media, and books, and DVDs, and clinics, and local trainers. I
think if you're passionate about it, you'll take all of it.* (Emma)

In this project, all participants had spent years, often decades, studying Vaquero horsemanship, and, despite their various motivations for doing so, had all utilized technology to some degree. Living and working in a part of the United States where there might be few to no others in the surrounding community with the same interest meant that a virtual community might be the only option; however, even if that was the case, digital and virtual sources of information could only go so far as the need for "feel" was the ultimate test of what they had learned. Given that we rely more and more upon virtual learning and may be tempted to view it in increasingly positive terms, we would do well to remember that it extends only so far in one's learning trail and that this reach varies among individuals.

Participants described utilizing technology in highly individualized ways that defied prediction and pattern, and so, in some sense, a resource was a resource, whether it was physical or virtual, although nothing trumped the ultimate resource of the horse. As Emma pointed out, "If you're passionate about it, you'll take all of it." You'd gallop toward knowledge, "real" and digital, with as much energy as you could if it means a better working relationship with your horse, but—and this is crucial—you would have curated a critical filter to protect yourself and your horse from inadequate and ineffectual knowledge.

Lastly, Tom Curtin expressed what I would characterize as the attitude typical of all participants: measured acknowledgment of technology as a resource with pronounced limitations. He feels that, when it comes to technology, the "bottom line, though, goes back to Ray [Hunt]. Ray would say, either your horse is with you, or he's not. My bottom line is either it works, or it doesn't. You can learn all this stuff on the Internet that you want, but when you go out and use it, does it work? Is it alright with that horse?" Lest we get too romantic about the learning opportunities that technology seems to provide, he also cautioned against accepting virtual studying as a substitute: "Nothing is ever going to take the place of spending time with the animal.... This [VH] comes to you by spending as much time around and riding as many horses as you possibly can." In Vaquero horsemanship, the horse, an ancient form of technology, holds sway over the newest iteration of it.

INTERLUDE 7

Kathleen Kelley, Red, and Twinkle Toes

THERE ARE MANY HORSES THAT HAVE INFLUENCED ME IN MY ONGOING horsemanship journey, but two have played pivotal roles in influencing who I am as a horsewoman today and directed me on my path. One was a filly, Red, and the other, Twinkle Toes, is the horse that holds my heart.

The filly was a red-headed pistol who quickly taught her humans that she was large and in charge—traveling on her hind legs, front legs striking in the air, with her teeth bared. This became her way of being. She was well on her way to becoming aggressive, and I was terrified of what she could do if allowed. It was the first time I had seen what "overloving" a horse could do to them. She was a very smart, fat, and sassy treat-monster, whose only job was to be cute. She had zero boundaries and would charge any human who came into her pasture or stall. She was my true beginning to wanting to understand a better way to work with horses because there was no amount of love or force that could harness her spirit; tapping into her brain was the only way to navigate. I studied, found guidance, and worked on mastering better timing. I had a few round pen sessions where I calculated in my head how many strides I had to climb out to safety. I worked through the uncomfortable, and she helped me to start to understand that no amount of love or force can will a horse to be what you'd like them to be. They crave our guidance, consistency, understanding, and nonemotional boundaries. We got to the other side together. The filly is now an upstanding citizen well into her wiser years, living a wonderful life, teaching humans about proper boundaries, and I'm still working on me.

The horse that continues to this day to teach me to be better as a human and a horsewoman is my own. He has been in many hands—some great hands. He has been greatly misunderstood and over the years labeled as insecure, too sensitive, hot, overly reactive, too vocal, disrespectful, having clinic baggage (that was the first time I'd heard that one), and dangerous. In the wrong hands I guess I could see where these labels might have come from, and in the beginning of my journey with him, I may have agreed with a few. Before he became mine, for five dollars and a whole lot of rehabilitation miles, he was sent to "trainers." He was started, restarted, and restarted some more well into the prime of his life by some well-known names in the industry, but he always went back to what he knew, which was to handle it all himself because the human on his back hadn't offered anything consistent or confident. I had known him for years and watched from the sidelines, and I finally got an opportunity to work with him a bit. He was like working with a feather on the ground—light and responsive and a smidge squirrely. I went to swing a leg over, and he so graciously cantered off while I was landing my rear in the saddle. So, we started there. I fell in love on my first ride.

He has sensitivity and awareness like no horse I had ever ridden. You asked for too much, then you got too much. You had poor timing, then he let you know that you had poor timing. You were not too sure about the situation, then he wasn't too sure about the situation. He refined me and taught me the ambiguous term "feel" as clear as could be and in its full spectrum. He taught me that, in this horsemanship, what works for one may not work for the next. He taught me that curiosity is a good thing in a horse. He taught me not to redirect an inquisitive mind, but to harness it to help guide the mind to the feet and then back to a confident mind. He taught me that the past is the past, so ride where you are, and blame no one and nothing; forward motion works, and the excuses of the past are just that—excuses. He taught me that I need to get a handle on my human emotions, and that there's not much room for them in horsemanship. He taught me not to take it all too personally. He taught me that there is zero room for ego in horsemanship—zero. He taught me how to gracefully eat humble pie. He taught me to navigate, investigate, and to keep on learning, and that the end result will be harmonious when you find it. He taught me that just because "they" say so isn't enough of an answer, so keep investigating and exploring. He taught me not to give up on a horse. He is my dance partner. He is the horse that if I am asked to slay a fire-breathing dragon, then I'd choose him to ride into battle with. Retirement is knocking on his door, but he still enjoys teaching and that he will do well beyond his years on this planet because what he has taught me, I will honor by passing along to every horse and human that I help guide on this horsemanship journey.

CONCLUSION

Evolution, Blending, and a Hopeful Future

In the 1930s, the widely respected medicine man Nicholas
Black Elk famously phrased it thus: "everything [a Lakota]
does is in a circle [because the world] always works in
circles and everything tries to be round." (Halder, 2002, as
cited in Praet, 2014, p. 161; parentheticals in original)

Now to the very heart of wonder. Because species diversity was created
prior to humanity, and because we evolved within it, we have never
fathomed its limits. As a consequence, the living world is the natural
domain of the most restless and paradoxical part of the human
spirit. Our sense of wonder grows exponentially: the greater the
knowledge, the deeper the mystery and the more we seek knowledge
to create new mystery. . . . A quiet passion burns, not for total control
but for the sensation of constant advance. (Wilson, 1984, p. 10)

I N THIS CONCLUSION, I WILL FOCUS UPON THE THEMES OF EVOLUTION, BLEND-
ing traditions, and the hoped-for future of Vaquero horsemanship while reiterat-
ing some key ideas of this study. Vaquero horsemanship has come back around:
We have returned to an historical form of horsemanship, albeit with updated sensibilities and a different economic context (since so many do not use it to work livestock). It
has also evolved into a form — not without controversy — that has been changed to accommodate recreational riders. I purposely utilize both concepts of circling back *and*
of evolution (which connotes a straighter line of progress) because the discrepancy between the two captures the friction that I have also explored in this volume, especially
in regard to VH's relationship to consumer culture and its cultural roots. "Evolution"
also comes from the participants themselves and so represents their viewpoint about
how VH has changed from its historical version to our modern one. VH has not come

back *full* circle, so much as it has continued its journey in a circular way, and the journey itself has collapsed some amount of distance between historical and modern forms of VH and between its western roots and southeastern practitioners—and perhaps the greatest amount between horse and rider.

I will also concentrate on one of the themes of the interviews: possibility and "constant advance" fueled by passion, mentioned in Wilson's quote above. VH is very much about what is possible between the horse and the human—and the sort of bond that might be cultivated and nurtured over time. Perhaps what we now consider an extraordinary horse-human bond can become ordinary. As Rodolfo Lara Sr. described, "Every person and every experience has prepared me to understand horses better because we have not tapped the surface of them"; other interviewees made similar statements about this potential. Another way that participants "advance" is by combining other horsemanship disciplines, which I will discuss later in this chapter.

One of the questions that I added to my interview protocol and asked the mentors was what they hoped the future of VH would be. This question came to mind simply because they were many decades into their horsemanship careers. In thinking about the intersection between horsemanship and hope, it occurred to me that the study and practice of modern VH is indeed a hopeful exercise. While it may be easy to view VH cynically, as a form that often does not resemble its traditional one, subject to the corrupting influence of consumerism, I do not want to end on that note. The tough horsepeople in this volume would have to be hopeful to invest themselves in a form of horsemanship that they have to dig out from history, possibly practice in isolation (at least part of the time), hustle hard to make a living at, and constantly meet and educate one new horse after another. I also observed that when handling horses, even the toughest of them turned gentle—and that, too, is a sort of hope—that "manhandling" is not needed and that gentleness will suffice. There is also a strong strain of pragmatism in VH since maintaining the lifestyle demands it.

Therefore, I find the idea of pragmatist hope (Stitzlein, 2020) to be relevant here. Stitzlein defined *pragmatist hope* as "always tied to what one *is* doing and feasibly *can do* in the present, especially when equipped with knowledge of the past" (p. 29; italics in original). It is action informed by realistic possibility (which is itself informed by precedent). She also advised, "Pragmatist habits of hope, however, are better understood as a verb—hoping, an ongoing activity we do, often, with or alongside others" (p. 44). Modern VH is centered around the immediacy of interacting with horses (an activity that is a collection of verbs) and is populated not only by personal histories, but also by a larger historical context. What we know about historical VH is tenuous and so some measure of hope is helpful in the work that it takes to learn, and preserve, what survives of the tradition.

THE EVOLUTION OF VAQUERO HORSEMANSHIP

I owe the characterization of modern VH as an evolution to Tom Curtin, who mentioned it during our interview; Mike Bridges, in a subsequent one, used the word as well. Gwynn Turnbull also noted that as "people's sensibilities change and evolve" so does horsemanship; she believes that we need to

> continue to distill this horsemanship so that the good keeps getting better, and the parts of it that don't work or no longer fit our sensibilities can pass into history, and I think that that's supposed to be what's taking place. You have to put a little heat on it and see what stays and what ends up being vapor. . . . I really think the beautiful part of it, the part that works, the part that brings this amazing connection between a human and an animal helps us understand our world better. I think that that's the part that we need to keep.

Similarly, Jeff Derby acknowledged that tradition can be "dangerous" as it can mean that "we do this because this is how we've always done it," and even though there can be "some real power in knowledge of experience and consistency," we should "continue to try to learn and to improve." Both Jeff and Linda H. mentioned Maya Angelou's advice when we discussed how VH might continue to evolve: "Do the best you can until you know better. Then when you know better, do better."

As I have discussed earlier in this volume, a central characteristic of VH is a willingness to continue learning in order to improve for both humans' and horses' sake. Linda H. would like to see us

> keep time-honored traditions that serve the horse as we embrace new ideas and scientific findings that offer expanded stewardship. To keep traditions only because "that's the way we've always done it" is shortsighted. We should periodically reexamine what we are doing with an objective eye. Horsemanship should always be viewed as a journey as there is always more to learn.

Kathleen K. made a similar statement about new knowledge regarding how horses' brains work: "I think being able to study the horse's brain and what is happening when we're asking these things of the horse—that is, for me, putting proof to why this horsemanship works. It puts scientific evidence behind how we're working with horses. I think [equine neuroscientist] Dr. [Steve] Peters [Peters & Black, 2012] teaming up with other great horsemen has been really fascinating."

Recall that in chapter three, the consensus of participants was that expertise was not necessarily a goal due to VH being a journey; you never arrive at expertise even as you became more knowledgeable. Being (humbly) knowledgeable was also distinct from being authoritative, and I believe that participants would agree with this portion of de Certeau's (1984) portrayal of the role of the expert in modern society: "Ultimately, the more authority the Expert has, the less competence he has, up to the point where his fund of competence is exhausted" (p. 7). Participants were more invested in their horses perceiving them as competent (rather than as experts).

Furthermore, if VH continues to evolve, then expertise is an ever-moving target. Bruce Sandifer offered a specific example for students who want to keep learning, even given the fact that not all will want to make bridle horses, when he stated, "What we do with people is we clear up misunderstandings about pressure—how things actually work inside a horse's mouth—give them an opportunity to see these things and how different bits work." This is certainly something that historical vaqueros knew given their daily and prolonged contact with their gear, so if this part of evolution is actually a circling back, all the better for the horse.

Part of the evolution of VH (or any form of horsemanship, really) takes place in spite of us, in a way. Both Gwynn Turnbull and Greg Eliel talked about having to fight our own natures to *let* horsemanship evolve. Gwynn stated that she thinks "that the people that are drawn to this want to be fair to their horses" but humans can be sidetracked: "If we can stay open and try to maintain some kind of moral, ethical compass, which is difficult to do—I mean, that takes a tremendous amount of effort because our ego is always tapping us on the shoulder." Greg observed, "The encroachment of human nature in this is going to degrade the relationship with the horses if we're not careful, so we have to constantly keep it at bay, and that's where the learning comes in. You've got to keep your mind fresh, and I don't want to become a stagnant brain if I can help myself." I believe that *all* of the participants saw continual learning as a powerful antidote to the negative side of human nature, including arrogance, impatience, harshness, and thoughtlessness in horsemanship.

There is something in VH that attracts people who are open to learning over a span of many years and who appreciate a challenge. Evolution does not just happen but must be facilitated by a willingness to learn and to use that learning to counter our own shortcomings. Joe Wolter, as one who has seen the digital age change horsemanship dramatically in his lifetime, remarked, "There's more stuff out there now to learn.... We've never been in a better time." Greg Eliel expressed something similar: "There's more education out there now than there's ever been." Tom Curtin added that he has "no doubt it'll keep evolving." The fact that they emphasize evolution rather than dilution into disappearance is, again, an act of hopeful pragmatism—a hope that "is not just about a vision of the future, but rather a way of living purposively in the present that is informed by the past and what is anticipated to come" (Stitzlein, 2020, p. 29). I did not hear participants express a blind optimism about the future of VH but, instead, I heard hope tempered by reasonable expectations, given what they have experienced in their lifetimes of horsemanship.

Ray Hunt had a well-known saying about how we should "make the wrong thing difficult and the right thing easy." Both Joe Wolter and Bruce Sandifer discussed turning this phrase around to foreground making the right thing easy so as to encourage riders to focus on that piece of it. Bruce said, "I think people get hung up on the wrong thing difficult part and forget about, how do I make what I want the most natural and easy thing for the horse to do?" Joe, who prefaced his comments by stating that he was not being critical (which was evident, as his esteem for Hunt is as clear as clean glass), said that he

> would turn that around . . . because to me, when I heard "wrong thing difficult, and the right thing easy," it was like I've *got* to put him to work. But the problem with that is I'm so busy putting him to work that I missed the right thing easy part. . . . Horses are searching right off the bat, and I tell people, if we'll just look more at what he's doing right, then it's easy to see what he's doing wrong. But the human—we're not conditioned to look for the right thing first. That changed me quite a bit when I turned those words around.

Because the order in the phrase mattered to him, he thought it might also matter to his own students. He has evolved his philosophy so that it might more easily nudge others to make positive assumptions about horses.

Although "evolution" has a positive connotation (and Gwynn Turnbull's "distillation" a more neutral one), a related term also came up: dilution. Tom Curtin mentioned that he is "already one generation diluted" from the Dorrances and Ray Hunt; this is inevitable as many of those I interviewed are in what will be the last generation to have known them personally; however, even dilution can be a site of possibility, as it may well lead to a positive transformation prefaced by intense change (Seneca, 1969/2004, p. 181). Seeing this dilution firsthand is what inspired Bruce Sandifer to dedicate himself to reviving VH. He observed that it had been "diluted from its original form, and I think, in that dilution, it lost a lot of its really neat aspects." He was "struck by the fact that, in the cradle of this style of horsemanship [California], nobody was applying it anymore. You saw a few people doing it in a show pen and using some of the gear, but really the style and the essence—the working style was gone." While living in California (which he still does), he decided he "would try to bring that back." He has been successful, but no doubt finds it a challenge since he is still "always trying to refine this." Indeed, dilution is not dissolution.

Lastly, on a more global scale, we are living in a time with profound concern about climate change, and so cattle raising has come under scrutiny. Many now studying VH are not raising livestock for a living, and so it is perhaps fortunate—and timely—that it has shifted away from cattle specifically. When we discussed the future of VH, Bill Reynolds stated, "I fight my head about it pretty seriously because this enters into environmental questions." He does, however, feel hopeful about the continuation of "the philosophical side and the illustrative aspects of how you can use this to become a better human . . . as well as how we relate to the environment and how we relate to the animal world that we share this planet with."

THE HOPED-FOR FUTURE OF
VAQUERO HORSEMANSHIP

There is a strong subculture of those dedicated to preserving VH. As Bruce Sandifer said, "It's not going anywhere. It's evergreen." Stitzlein's (2020) definition of hope as "most essentially a disposition toward possibility and change for the betterment of oneself and, typically, others" (p. 42) applies here, although the "others" must include horses, whose existence is woven into this hope. VH has had to evolve to survive societal and cultural changes, and so those who have learned its modern version have had to recreate it while keeping its traditional core—how much of that core is preserved varies among individuals.

Part of hope for VH's future involves continuing to cast a glance backward. A common theme in this topic was that interviewees hoped that the efforts of the Dorrance brothers and Ray Hunt, who had "a better way of getting the job done," "be perpetuated." Buck Brannaman mentioned that he has "tried real hard to do what would make him [Ray Hunt] proud." He also shared that Ray "would always say that they wanted to find a way to work with the horse as if the horse got to make up the rules." Gwynn Turnbull mentioned that she thought that these

> principles need to continue on, and I plan on trying to perpetuate that because it's such a good way to live. I hope that The Californios continues to carry that on, and I really want it to be a meeting ground or a place where like-minded people can get together and talk about their passion for horses and their passion for the connection that they can one day have with their horses.

Gwynn's statements exemplify how each horseperson working within these principles has found their own individual ways of carrying them on. As part of this, there was, unsurprisingly, a desire to see the next generation do the same. Tom Curtin stated that his "desire would be to see some young folks keep this stuff alive and going on." Mike Bridges said that he hoped "that it can continue to be taught. It won't be taught on a wide range because it's only going to have a limited amount of interest. It does require quite a bit of work and understanding if you're really going to try to take the horse to a high level of development. I'm very much interested in seeing that as much of it gets preserved as possible." Alicia B., whose daughter is now riding her bridle horse, thought of her when responding to my question about hope:

> I watch all these horsemen, and I see how they're so thoughtful in the way that they talk to people, and they're so thoughtful in the way they reach and touch a horse—what I would love to see for future generations and the younger kids coming up, like Riv, is that they can see that and go, okay, this is a totally different feeling. It's not something that's forced and jammed down the horse's throat. It's something that you do with your horse, but you do it with humans too.

Her comments connect to chapter five, about the philosophy of modern VH, and how it encircles participants' lives, including horses but not limited to horsemanship.

In addition to appealing to a smaller group within horsemanship, as Mike Bridges noted above, another challenge is that VH can be hard to learn and see in practice, especially in the southeastern United States. Cody Deering had this take on the issue:

> Make no mistake, the traditions still live on the best they can, but sometimes you can't see them from the road. You have to go deep into a canyon or way out on the sagebrush sea somewhere perhaps. You can seek out a mentor to speak with who knows some things about it. At the time of this interview, the older generation who had the knowledge firsthand from the 90-year-olds they learned from when they were young have almost all passed away, but the passing down of knowledge and the ties to the past are still there continuing on.

Most of those who knew the Dorrances and Ray Hunt personally are now the elders of our time. The road back to the historical vaqueros grows ever distant, so whatever causes that distance to collapse better be held fast.

As I mentioned in the evolution section, some interviewees expressed hope for a future that includes blending traditional knowledge with new understanding, from both human and horse sources. Amy G. stated that her "hope is that the future of the vaquero tradition will use this new evidence and continue to seek out an even softer approach with horses, even if it means doing away with some practices of old. We must always continue to strive to put the horse first." Amy looks forward (evolving) while Emily S. looks back to classical horsemanship (circling): "My hope is that quality horsemanship utilizing the principles of classical education of horse and human has been reawakened and with it, an understanding of how to learn from the horses themselves." Horses provide an ever-present possibility to learn, no matter in which direction we look.

Several interviewees mentioned hoping to see an increased awareness of biomechanics in VH. I asked Bruce Sandifer how people should learn about this. He replied:

> I think a lot of it is just your own body—to understand when you look somewhere what it does to your hips and your shoulders—the movements that we know influence a horse.... And so, once we figure out that the control comes through the core and through the center—people have been talking about doing lateral flexions for 500 years pretty seriously to develop strength and collection. I think that's one of the big things—understanding yourself, but also look at the masters. They have been continuously doing it, and then apply it to your situation, to your principles.... I think what we need to do as horsemen is not just copy people, but figure out what principles we want to ride in and then learn to work inside the parameters of those principles.

In a similar vein, Linda H. hopes

> there will always be those seeking to follow the path of making a bridle horse as it is valuable to the development of the stock horse. Additionally, I would like to see people learn more about applied learning theory to better understand how horses learn and about holistic horse-keeping practices along with adjunctive therapies to better care for their horses.

Being willing to expand into learning theory and holistic care addresses both the mind and body of the horse, and an increased awareness of both is one hoped-for next step of evolution.

Awareness also can be intentionally developed into increased generosity and compassion toward the horse, as I highlighted in chapter five. Ricky Quinn hopes that, in the future, more people will be willing to reflect on how they view "problem" horses:

> I hope people start to understand more and more that the horse has a brain and that people would also understand and accept that horses do not want to be in trouble. That's why you can get so much from them. They do not want trouble. I wish they would understand that even if a horse kicked them, bucked them off, pulled back, or does things that people don't like and that's when they label horses as being bad or ruined—that horses do not enjoy that behavior. If the human could remove themselves from that behavior, not label the horse as one way or the other, completely remove that thought process—and just work with the horse where the horse is and help that horse think and find a way out of trouble and start to succeed emotionally and mentally. That would be where I'd hope this horse world goes in time. And, I think it is actually.

What Ricky detailed is a mindful shift in how we view a horse's behavior, which sounds reasonable enough to agree to but can be a challenge in the heat of the moment (e.g., when bucked off or kicked). We need to realize that we are engaging with another *thinking* being; this includes tweaking the easy assumption that horses are "misbehaving" or reacting without a logic behind this behavior (in addition to not taking it personally). This requires discipline of thought—especially until it is practiced enough to become a philosophy.

A central sentiment of all interviews was that the horse matters—period. The idea that the well-being of the horse is markedly more important than VH itself also came out in some interviews. Joe Wolter stated that "I don't care what kind of bridle he's got on him. If he looks like he's happy doing his job, that's beautiful to me." Jeff Derby placed that idea in the context of VH but also acknowledged that it transcends any given discipline:

> This part of valuing the horse—of trying to see things from the horse's perspective and trying to change our approach to better fit the horse—I hope that continues. If the best way for that to continue is talking about the culture, the heritage, the traditions of this, that is to me the important part. It's not about the spade bit or the type of saddle or the style of our spurs. I don't think it matters if that disappears. Being able to ride and interact with horses and learn from them a way to interact, not just with them, but with people in our world in a manner that's a little more fitting, a little more beneficial to everybody—meaning seeing things from the other's perspective. So that's the part that I want to share and hope that it continues, whether it's connected to bridle horses or Californio traditions. To me, that's just a teaching tool.

Like Alicia B., Jeff highlighted the philosophy, which he hopes will continue. And there is humor in this philosophy, too; in a sentiment that perhaps only horsepeople can fully appreciate, Joe Wolter shared that he hoped to see his grandkids riding "with grins on their faces and the horses have grins on their faces, too."

THE HORSE AND HUMAN IN A PLACE OF POSSIBILITY

One of the things that people need the most is hope. They often come pretty dejected to clinics. I've got to keep them alive, and I've got to be direct, but I'm going to be encouraging. I learned a long time ago that putting more pressure doesn't always work on a horse that's

struggling. I'm going to do the same thing with people. So, I want them
to know that there's hope, and that it's attainable, and that if they
take this study on, their lives will never be the same. (Greg Eliel)

When I think about the intersection of hope and possibility in VH, what first comes to mind is that you would have to be hopeful to willingly undertake a teaching and learning process that will span many years with no promise of success—and often for fun, no less. Also, I am aware that "hope" and "possibility" may sound like naïve and idealistic notions to apply to the sometimes-gritty world of Western riding; although, one of the rather gruff horsemen I interviewed described horses as "so real and so pure," and this feeling is undoubtedly shared by all who contributed to this project.

The central tenet of this section is that getting glimpses of what is possible in horsemanship, including VH, promotes hope. Gwynn Turnbull described it as, "Sometimes you'll just get moments of this amazing connection where you really do feel like you're one living, breathing body—the two of you together." She elaborated: "Life is a painful proposition, and so there's some kind of healing that comes from that connection that we make with a horse, be it ever so fleeting. So that can be as broad as you want it to be. I mean, we're really just trying to connect with other living things in a positive way." Interviewees have turned to modern VH because they believe (and hope) that it will facilitate a certain caliber of connection—one that is not about compliance from the horse but, instead, is a bond that is more like one between two family members (well, family members who respect, and listen to, each other). Jeff Derby illustrated this goal: "What I want (from VH) is that feeling of connectedness where I can basically think something, or maybe there's something physically subtly going on there, but I feel like I can just decide what I'm wanting when I'm riding, and we flow together to it, within their physical capabilities." This might be the aspect that looks like magic to observers in that the rider can just be *thinking* a cue, which leads to subtle physical movement, and the horse responds. This phenomenon was, according to Olmert (2009), first named "the ideomotor principle" by British physiologist William Carpenter in 1852: "He proposed that the mere idea or expectation of an action can produce, inadvertently, the motor behavior of that complicated act" (p. 99). This explanation reinforces the efficacy and value of the subtle (i.e., gentle) cues that are at the heart of VH; force is overkill. Possibility in horsemanship can be rooted in science—science to come and even science from the original vaqueros' time (there is that circling again).

Some of the hard work that hope and possibility require can be done to repay horses for their generosity. Bruce Sandifer talked about how "we force them to accommodate to us—where if we learned to accommodate to their nature, even a little bit, they're so appreciative . . . we look at thousands of years of horses doing things that they shouldn't be doing, like riding into battle, but they do them. And so, they are an amazing animal."

Jones (2020) supported this idea: "Hollywood sells that romantic myth of horse whispering, but the best trainers don't whisper —they *watch, listen, learn, and think*. The horses do the whispering. The human's job is to rivet attention to their faintest hints. Let's try to connect with animals at their level, instead of demanding that they constantly adjust to us" (p. 8). Learning about their anatomy is a relatively easy way for us to better connect with them. Tom Curtin recommends that riders

> definitely do a certain amount of educating themselves on the anatomy of a horse. That would help you better understand the value of this horsemanship and what you're trying to accomplish with it. Don't ask your horse to do something he's not physically able to—and know that there's something there that you could have if you're more aware of how anatomy works.

I wonder how many beginning riders are allowed to climb onto a horse's back, as I did as an adult, without knowing the basics of how bits work or how the horse's senses, like eyesight, actually work. As Tom further explained, we need to learn "what these animals need from us to be able to better understand their way of life so that we can get them to do what we would like them to do because they want to do it and not because they have to do it." For him, this is "what intrigues and drives [him] in this day after day after day."

Greg Eliel, after decades of being on this horsemanship journey, stated, "Horses have an amazing way of building better people.... They were very generous with me, these horses, and they allowed me to learn and make a lot of mistakes.... I don't know anywhere better for developing a human than around a horse." In fact, this volume contains the testimonies of those who feel that they have been built into better people by horses, and part of that has been facilitated by historical and modern VH.

EXAMPLES OF EVOLVING AND CIRCLING: BALANCE AND SIGNAL; VH AND VETERANS; AND THE *GARROCHA*

In this section, I would like to share three detailed examples of modern VH in diverse settings. These are illustrations of how practitioners are taking the traditions of VH and individualizing them—generating new interest in this horsemanship even as these examples circle back and evolve forward. These brief accounts are about active and curious engagement, bracketed by dedication. What I heard from these horsepeople is that they are passionate about the *process*, which takes hope to sustain.

The Balance and Signal Approach

Bruce Sandifer has devoted decades to studying and preserving the "early Californio bridle horse methods," and has been joined in his efforts by Jeff Derby. They recognize that many who attend their "workshops" are not working vaqueros, but Jeff observed that VH

> offers a relationship that is counter to the rest of our modern world. We're in a 'you can order it off Amazon and have it here tomorrow,' 'everything right now at our fingertips' society. This is based on developing a relationship with an animal through trust, understanding, knowledge, and education, and you can't cheat that, and it takes time to develop—it takes care and consideration.

Recall that in chapter one, I characterized VH as "slow-craft horsemanship"; participants see it as being attractive to those who understand that and are willing to invest in it. They have, I argue, made a conscious change to break from instant gratification in horsemanship and seek something meaningful for the long haul.

Jeff was drawn to what Bruce had developed as an alternative to the popular "pressure and release" approach. Instead, as Bruce described it, this alternative involves "the shifting of balance and the disruption of balance as a signal to create things and then the return of balance to reward." Jeff defined the component of balance first:

> There is a strong neutral position where things are level and can go either way just as easily. . . . I think when you watch a foal, the very first thing that a horse does when he's born is he tries to get on his feet and find his balance and then tries to find the security of the mare. Then he's doing nothing other than practicing and working and playing to improve his balance. I think balance really, really matters to horses.

In his description, we can see that they have formulated their approach based on what they believe the horse seeks and needs—not just the human agenda. The second part of signaling is

> trying to communicate with the horse and to give the horse an idea. We're not trying to make the horse do something. . . . The signal is going to be a disruption of balance or a shift of my balance, but even in that, it's only going to be a signal. I'm not going to hold myself out of balance until the horse does what I want and then get back in balance. . . . It's not a physical manipulation. It is presenting an idea. So, it's

like a signal on a car. The blinker doesn't make the car go left. The signal says, "What about left? What about left?"

Note that Jeff emphasized two-way communication; this is the difference between dictation and dialogue. Bruce formulated this after many years of experience as a cowboy, and Jeff mentioned that he "taught pressure and release for decades" until he met Bruce. Jeff also acknowledged that they could be accused of dealing in "just semantics" but stated, "We're not waiting for the horse to do the right thing to get back in balance. We're getting back in balance whether he does the right thing or not." Jeff characterized what they offer the horse as "trying to become, in a sense, that mare—meaning, here's a place that you're in balance. There's a lack of tension, and some safety, some leadership here." The horse's first "partner" is the mare, and in historical VH, vaqueros spent so much time with their horses that they arguably formed a partnership that might well have been a close second. So even though this is an evolution, circling back to that primary connection between mare and foal echoes at least part of the historical version of VH.

Working with Veterans

While discussing "the culture and the stewardship" of modern VH, I asked Greg Eliel about his work with military veterans. He comes from a military family and stated, "I don't think we've taken good care of our veterans coming home, and I don't think we can afford to lose any more of them." He shared that because his mentors had "invested time and energy" to help him, he decided that "somewhere in this [horsemanship] culture, there's an opportunity to pay it forward," but he wanted to do this "in a way that is contributory to the well-being of the horse." Within "the transition from being a warrior to being a civilian again," he saw an opportunity for the horse to help.

This recognition came from his experiences working with struggling clinic participants while he was still Buck Brannaman's apprentice. This is what he observed:

> In any given clinic, say you had 20 riders there, one or two people are there for the sole reason that they have had some sort of trauma, and their trauma is probably based on something to do with one of the ugly sides of mankind. They surround themselves with horses because they get something from them that they no longer get from people, and I recognized that early on. I started to work with them to help enhance their journey towards eliminating or minimizing the trauma in their lives. . . . I can work with them in the clinic and nobody would know they were traumatized. I let the horse do what the horse does well, which is when you let the

horse be themselves and the people see this, it starts to have an amazing effect on the human heart.

My impression is that Greg turned his attentive eye, often oriented to horses, to human participants and identified those who were struggling—just as he would spot a troubled horse (although horses will not hide being troubled like humans who are socialized to disguise it). Horses are also in a distinctive position to help us; Ekholm Fry (2019) stated,

> As a prey animal, horses pay close attention to self- and energy-preservation, and as a social animal, to interactions with others. Their sociosensual awareness, a concept first introduced by anthropologist E. Richard Sorenson (1978) and which is shared with humans, means that they benefit from orienting and responding to the states of others. (p. 270)

Horses' status as prey animals, combined with their awareness of "the states of others" (including, crucially, emotional ones), makes them relatively easy to relate to for some people; our shared sociability and vulnerability connects us.

Greg then crossed paths with a Vermont veteran who had started a nonprofit and was interested in how horses might help other veterans as they had helped him with post-traumatic stress. The two organized a clinic and "spent three days letting the horses do their thing, and the results were astounding and gratifying." This caused Greg to think, "I can just tag a three-day clinic for veterans on the end of my public clinics, and that's how it started." Even though he often gets the most recognition for these efforts, he cited "this amazing group of open-hearted, wonderful local people" who create an informal "infrastructure," including giving veterans gas money to get there, making meals for them, and providing places to stay during the clinics.

During these clinics, Greg lets the horse take the lead (although I suspect that he is being modest, which is characteristic of those who follow VH): "All I would do is get them in proximity to the horse and point things out, and I'd let the horse do their thing. They just have this amazing ability to fill in the voids in the human heart." There are both mysterious and pragmatic elements to this approach: mysterious because who can fully describe what is possible between horse and human, each as unique as DNA, and pragmatic because horses, although prey animals and often gentle, are still capable of injuring and killing us so a sophisticated amount of skill is needed to get to the heart-exchange that Greg described. It cannot be done safely or expertly by a beginner. Vaquero horsemanship might seem, on the surface, to have very little to do with this, but it is another modern evolution of the studied, and practiced, *reading* of VH combined with stewardship of fellow humans. Lastly, Greg views assisting in this way as fulfilling "an obligation to try and help where [he] can" as all he needs are "three gentle horses in a round pen" to help veterans, and he can "affect their lives." Because historical VH was based upon military riding traditions, this is, also, a sort of circling back.

Working with the *Garrocha*

Rodolfo Lara Sr., as a native of Mexico and long-term resident of the United States as well as a military veteran (as you have already read about in his interlude), has spent his horsemanship career blending traditions, having been influenced by classical horsemanship as well as the charro and vaquero traditions. He currently utilizes the *garrocha* (a 12- to 13-foot-long pole) in his clinics, a tool historically used in Doma Vaquera ("Doma" is Spanish for "dressage"). He shared that the *garrocha* was used to work cattle and also as a weapon (although it does not have the tip of a lance) when you have a bull "that's trying to kill you" and need "to be able to outmaneuver that bull." Rodolfo gives the *garrocha* a very different job with his students. He lets them know that "if you don't have the horsemanship part, it could be a struggle, and that's the beauty about this. The *garrocha* really demands a rider to be better and to be aware of how powerful their seat is." So, the job of the *garrocha* is to clarify a rider's abilities and is also, arguably, an external litmus test of the "health" of their horsemanship.

Rodolfo discovered the *garrocha* on his own horsemanship journey. He happened to see videos of riders working with it, was not intimidated since he "was able to handle a rope pretty good," and it sparked his curiosity:

> I started watching, and I thought, I can incorporate this tool into my riding to help my horses out. If we use this with all the roping and ranch horses, they will be much better. Why? Because you're really connecting with a horse to be able to move him around, and you would be getting him used to things—being on both sides and getting the rider *not* to micromanage the reins.

If you become skillful enough with the *garrocha*, then it can become more of an art form (no small feat for a human handling a very long pole and a 1,000+ pound live animal). Rodolfo knows how challenging this can be, for some more than others, so he has become mindful of how he begins his clinics and of what might get in participants' way:

> The thing that will come in between a person and getting better is the person's ability to block herself and not go forward, but if I could get out of the situation that I was in in those dark places—I used to start with, tell me a little story about yourself. "Oh, I can't do this" and "I have the worst way of doing this." In order for us not to go

there, now I start with, tell me a positive thing about you, and a positive thing about your horse, and maybe one thing that you want to get out of this clinic. Because if we take, from the get-go, the negative out of the vocabulary, chances are that we're going to end up with something a little bit better, but put the positives in there.

In line with the focus of this concluding chapter, his approach helps the rider envision new possibilities of both skill and connection. Rodolfo explained that the *garrocha* cannot be approached cold but *can* be implemented with the same sort of curiosity he felt when first seeing it in action: "It's a test of the development of your horse because you can't just go out there with a *garrocha* and say, I'm going to do it. There are things that have to be there for it to be successful. I want to tell the rider, get your artistic side out. Let's dance. Let's dance with the horses." He expressed that what he cares about is being "good to [his] horse" and "becoming better to him each day" and believes that working with the *garrocha* helps him and those he teaches do this, regardless of discipline. His goal is for his work with the *garrocha* to "be a beautiful thing, and it shouldn't be a forced thing. If we go against nature, we're not developing art. I want to one day develop art."

THE IMPACT OF GEOGRAPHICAL DISTANCE

At this project's end, I can draw some conclusions about learning, and living, VH in the southeastern United States. The learning of it can be somewhat affected by geography, in terms of opportunities to do so, and the living of it might be lonelier, given less of a consistent community presence (although not so much if you prefer horse company to the human kind). As I mentioned in chapter one, southeastern participants specified these two considerations of opportunity and community but still felt it was possible to learn this style with its distant roots. Not surprisingly, being born in a certain geographical area does not contribute to any sort of natural talent in learning this style. Also, in our current time, globalization has made global and local "relative terms" (Barker & Jane, 2016; see also Storey, 2021, p. 230), and this has affected consumerism and "cultural" production since we are able to buy what only used to be local.

The mentors also contributed responses to the question of whether geographical distance matters. Greg Eliel pointed out that stereotypes can come into play:

Here's another thing I think is important to understand. When I come to the East Coast and do clinics, they're always asking what the guys in the West are like. Are they all like Ray Hunt? Do they all ride like Buck? And then I go to the West Coast, and they think everybody out here has got a teacup in their hand with their little finger up and they're chasing foxes, and there's actually amazing commonalities between the East and West Coast. . . . The bulk of the human-horse population—they're not that much different everywhere you go.

One theme of this book has been the troublesome habits of humans that get in the way of connecting—with each other and with horses. Interestingly, Greg's term, "the human-horse population," reflects one of VH's goals: to become a hyphenated combination in real time with both parts joined on equal terms.

While VH has evolved from a livestock-working tradition (even though it is still that way for some), it has also gained new life in clinic-based education. This does not mean that it has become easy to teach—or to learn; people often arrive at VH after some struggle. Joe Wolter mentioned that "The fact that they're at the clinic usually means they're searching, and so, they're more ready." As I discussed in chapter five, he believes that having encountered some trouble is a motivating factor, no matter where you happen to ride. (Although, it is "a little easier" to teach, he noted with a smile, if he does not "have to worry about them falling off.")

Along with a searching mindset, there was another element that matters in learning modern VH in the southeastern United States (and beyond). Tom Curtin, who spent over two decades in Florida, called it "desire" to "want to work with this lifestyle and live this way of life" no matter where you happen to live. Greg Eliel believes that "passion is the primer" "that sets people apart," and he has observed that those who are successful, across the United States, are "passionate about learning, and they can go beyond mediocrity." So, being in the southeast did not stop those determined to learn and was not seen as a hindrance by their mentors. To take Joe Wolter's notion of trouble and amend it: Because southeastern participants might have had some trouble finding resources, they then could have become even more resolute. In fact, there might even be a benefit to being in an area where you practice a less-popular form of horsemanship since you might then be more open to a combination of horsemanship styles, without a nearby community to pressure you into conformity. A passion for horsemanship can roam across disciplines.

BLENDING DISCIPLINES AND TRADITIONS

In the spirit of possibility, I share one topic that participants saw as a positive and necessary evolution of VH: blending horsemanship disciplines; this came from them as I did not specifically ask about it. Blending different disciplines may not sound like an unusual act, but some participants reported that it was not as common as it could be, and that riders, especially amateur ones, were often hesitant to get out of their horsemanship comfort zones. Melanie Smith Taylor, who, as I mentioned, was an early supporter of Ray Hunt in the southeast, shared, "Once people are in their own world, they kind of tend to stay there. There aren't as many people who are curious about other areas of the equestrian world and the other areas of horsemanship that I would hope would be." Furthermore, this lack of curiosity can be disastrous for horses: "A lot of people don't know what they don't know, and I think a lack of education causes a lot of horses to be ridden verging on abuse, but it's not because people intentionally want to harm them." Joe Wolter shared that he did not find it common, during his many years in California, for VH and dressage riders to exchange ideas and that "the lines of communication weren't open." He was encouraged when I told him that, in this project, there was evidence of near-universal openness to other disciplines from participants.

All of the mentors thought that VH could mix with other disciplines. Mike Bridges reported that he "use[s] a lot of classical influence," having taught in Europe for almost 27 years. This has shown him that "It's all related," and he believes that "There's no end to the possibilities of you learning about your particular discipline and then the other disciplines and how they might relate to or help you in yours. There might be something there that might help you make a better cow horseman if you'll just keep your eyes open and have an open mind about it." Similarly, Rodolfo Lara Sr. mentioned, "I respect everybody's style of riding, and I learn from it. I don't close myself off into one style of riding. I'll always be open to any suggestions of how I can better myself."

Blending horsemanship traditions is a pragmatic move as it is the result of evaluating different ones to ascertain what might help you and your horse advance. Part of Stitzlein's (2020) depiction of pragmatism is that it includes "responding with inquiry to understand [challenges], ingenuity to experiment with improving them, and vision to craft a better future" (p. 23). The combination of different disciplines and traditions is, I would argue, the result of inquiry—asking how VH might be improved and/or brought into new arenas—both physical and philosophical. The better future benefits individuals, of course, but can also serve as an exemplar for the next generation of riders and their horses.

Mike Bridges quoted a friend from the Spanish Riding School who said that "There's only good riding and bad riding. The horse doesn't care what kind of saddle is on his back." Gwynn Turnbull also mentioned being "open to all disciplines" and that the gear stops mattering at a certain point: "You do something long enough, and you reach a certain level of expertise, you start to understand the universality of it. You know that this horse might be wearing a spade bit, but it's really just a prop at this point. It really just becomes an adornment." Echoing this universality, Tom Curtin commented that VH "ties into all different types of disciplines," including dressage as well as other Western ones like reining and cutting.

Overall, the other discipline mentioned most often was dressage. In the southeastern group, it was not uncommon for riders to have studied dressage and even competed in it. Both Maggie and Greg Eliel talked about how VH has roots in classical dressage, and, due to that, VH has the intrinsic ability to transcend disciplines since it was a blend from the beginning. Maggie outlined how the elements that are important in VH are leading to a greater appreciation for the bridle horse tradition: "It's understanding timing and feel. It's a really cool thing to share, and I think people are starting to realize that it works for any horse. It doesn't matter if you're working cows or you're jumping fences or doing dressage. I mean, the basis is in dressage." Greg Eliel would like "to see some people riding FEI [*Fédération Équestre Internationale*] levels of dressage start to incorporate some of these elements into it—not only because it would make their dressage better, but their horses would become so much happier and more comfortable in their jobs." My overall sense was that interviewees were motivated to learn whichever approach(es) would help them and their horses progress, no matter its name.

Even though VH "has its roots in classical riding," Bruce Sandifer made a distinction between the two:

> In classical dressage, you would think about the contact on the bit. It's a direct contact from your hands to the bit, and it's not supposed to be harsh. It's supposed to be a very light, fluid contact to help the horse balance. Vaqueros took that and put it into the equipment so that the weight and the balance of this equipment gave that horse the same balancing confidence and the same ability to help them collect without the rider having to hold contact. But they also developed that through the processes of the hackamore into the two-rein into the bridle.

What is important for the reader who is unfamiliar with different disciplines to understand is that those who follow VH see it as being a continuation of an historically established horsemanship that branched out but did not lose its refinement.

Reed E. had also noticed that VH had more in common with dressage *timelines* than other Western ones:

> That's one thing I like about the dressage progression is that you don't expect to have an FEI or a Grand Prix horse when they're four or five years old. Typically, you're in the double digits by the time they have gone through the progression to teach the signals and develop the body so that they can do that. If you look at the Western competitive world, all of the big money to be won is at two, three, four, and five. You're showing a young horse at a very high level, and it's a lot of stress on them, and they have to push them to make sure that they get them there in that amount of time. You end up with a lot of joint, knee, hock issues, and a lot of those horses just don't last to make an older horse. Whereas if you're going to create a bridle horse, it's more along the lines of a high-level dressage horse, and you've also developed musculature and carriage so you're probably going to have him longer.

This is not to say that all competition horses break down early—but it does mean that, as participants perceived it, modern VH, and the value it places on the horse, does not *generally* include horse-as-commodity; this is part of what is attractive about it. It is not necessarily that VH is incompatible with competition but is less of a fit with the kinds of competition that treat the horse as something to be used for financial gain or human vanity. What Reed described is about investing time into a horse so that they are able to partner with you for many years. Morris (2010) described how "the old vaqueros" had "caballos [who] were still in good use when they were 25 or 30 years old" due to how they treated them, and seeing them work together was "a sight to see. The scene has all but left the earth" (p. 51). It has not left the earth quite yet.

THE WORTH OF THE WORD — ONE LAST TIME

I am almost hesitant to admit how much time I spent thinking (and sometimes agonizing) over the word "vaquero" in this project: What of its history does it still carry for modern users? Has the metaphorical distance of the word somehow collapsed? Has the meaning of it circled back? How should we acknowledge its cultural roots? And how would I explain my agonizing to a horse, who might wonder why I was spending my time on something that does not matter to them? Then I had what I would characterize as a clarifying conversation with Joe Wolter.

Joe expressed that he was hesitant to use the word "vaquero" because "people stereotype people, and if someone else hears that word, then they shut the door, and think, well, they've got nothing for me because I do this other [style of horsemanship]." He felt that human nature edges in and prevents us from being open to what we think lives in a box separate from the one we have placed ourselves in—including being willing to learn from clinicians outside of our discipline. However, he acknowledged that "people want to belong" and "people want to be part of a group;" this made me realize that "vaquero" gives us a loosely organized group, even if we do not completely agree on its nuances. It provides a conversational starting point, or as Joe said, "Maybe it's just a way to communicate."

Furthermore, Joe and I concurred that words can be vexing. When I asked which word or phrase he would choose to describe his own approach, he replied, "I can't get past the word 'horsemanship.' Horseman. I'm hoping I'm looked on as a horseman someday." An "open" word like "horsemanship" contains possibilities that more specific ones might foreclose. I then asked Joe what his experiences had been with the label of VH during his time in California, and he said (as I quoted in chapter one), "When I was with the Dorrances and Ray Hunt, they called it 'this thing.' 'This thing with the horses.'" I elaborate upon what I termed its "spaciousness" in chapter one: The further

I got into this study, the more appreciation I had for calling it "this thing with the horses" because its vagueness becomes its strength. "This thing" can contain specific approaches, like VH, but also can remain open to other disciplines and ideas; it can grow and change its mind, a hallmark, by the way, of modern VH. Any single word or phrase may be fated to fall short when it has to cover not only the horsemanship practice itself, but also the philosophy—and hundreds of years of history. My conversation with Joe elucidated for me that I appreciate the phrase "Vaquero horsemanship" and especially the working origin of the word "vaquero" (not least of all because it is still used today in this way in Mexico and so is a direct link to its past in what is now the western United States). I also think that the romanticism that the phrase has attained may benefit horses in that it attracts humans to what is today a fair-minded discipline and one that aims to elevate their well-being.

FINAL THOUGHTS

I have attempted to, in this volume, portray the "shared worlds" (van Dooren, 2014) of humans and horses learning and practicing Vaquero horsemanship in the southeastern United States and beyond. Van Dooren defined a shared world as

> the way of being with others that, as far as we know, is unique to some mammals and birds: a particular sociality rooted in our being *emotionally* at stake in each other's lives. This possibility, this way of being with others, is a complex biosocial achievement. . . . It is not enough for two such beings to have lived alongside each other and in proximity to one another; rather, they must also in some way have become *at stake in each other*, bound up with what *matters* to each other. In other words, they must in some sense, more or less consciously, have come to inhabit a meaningfully *shared world*. (p. 283; italics in original)

In historical VH, those who lived and worked with horses as closely as vaqueros did surely shared worlds, and some of the appeal of modern VH includes circling back to that close bond with our horses. I suspect that participants in this project would agree that they are "bound up with what matters" to their horses. Furthermore, being "at stake in each other" in horsemanship includes being dependent upon each other for both physical and emotional safety; the reader should recognize this description as being a close match to VH.

If VH is traveling back around, then its circle has expanded along the way to include contemporary knowledge. The circle needs "great scrutiny," as Amy G. noted, so that we do not "fall into the trap of carrying out a custom just for the sake of tradition";

she also mentioned, "There is a growing body of evidence-based research in areas of equine neuroscience, anatomy, and biomechanics that should be causing us all to call into question our traditional approaches with horses." Indeed, this was a theme of interviews when participants talked about what they hoped VH would evolve into. This includes what we have learned about how the horse's brain and body work; an example would be Jones' (2020) *Horse Brain, Human Brain*. Her statements about horse intelligence line up with elements of VH philosophy: "Horses are not just smart; they are learning *machines*. They scout for cues everywhere and soak up information. Once acquired, new knowledge sticks to a horse's brain like superglue. If there's a problem with equine learning, it's that horses learn too quickly—and forget too poorly—to accommodate human errors" (p. 132; italics in original). Fortunately for us, as Tom Dorrance (2010) stated, they are forgiving of our errors (p. 6).

Bearing in mind that this is both a reporting of an academic study and a book for those who are interested in horsemanship more generally, I also hope that if readers find what I have reported appealing, then they also have acquired resources for further learning about the actual practice of VH from those who have devoted their lives to it. As Temple Grandin (2009) argued, "If everyone could train and handle horses the way the horse whisperers and the old-time horsemen do, lots fewer horses would be put down, sold, or neglected because of behavior problems. But that can't happen if people don't understand what the horse whisperers and horsemen are actually doing" (p. 124; she also mentioned Tom Dorrance on page 123). Vaquero horsemanship has been developed by "horse whisperers" and "old-time horsemen," and while the historical practice is becoming ever harder to trace, there is a robust, if smallish, community in the United States and beyond who are dedicated to it still—and they hope to pass on what they know to the next generation of riders.

Horses are at the mercy of both what we know and do not know, which should be motivation to continually increase the former in a perpetual cycle of learning, practice, reflection, and revised practice. Near the end of this project, I observed a few of the mentors riding their own horses. What I saw was quiet and continual negotiation rather than the rider mandating a "shared" language. Instead of a jarring form of stimulus and response, which I have seen in other sorts of horsemanship, VH is more transactional, with each side having a say. This aims to be human-and-horse-centered horsemanship. As VH continues to evolve, the possibility of ever better connections between horse and human remains. My hope is that I have held Vaquero horsemanship, with its many distinctive facets, up to the light for a moment.

APPENDIX

Participants Identified by Name

Fred Allen
Melanie Allen
Buck Brannaman
Mike Bridges
Alicia Byberg-Landman
Johnny Crooks
Tom Curtin
Trina Curtin
Cody Deering

Reed Edwards
Greg Eliel
Amy Gaddis
Linda Hoover
Susan Hopkins
Kathleen Kelley
Rodolfo Lara Sr.
Jaton Lord
Bryan Neubert

Marilyn Obie
Ricky Quinn
Bill Reynolds
Bruce Sandifer
Emily Shields
Amy Skinner
Melanie Smith Taylor
Gwynn Turnbull
Joe Wolter

ACKNOWLEDGMENTS

I AM VERY GRATEFUL TO PARTICIPANTS IN THIS STUDY, BOTH NAMED AND ANONYmous. Thank you for trusting me with your stories and experiences, even when you were not initially sure why I arrived at your farms and ranches with so many pesky questions; thank you for your patience and willingness to share.

Alan Beck, editor of the New Directions in the Human-Animal Bond series, was unfailingly kind and supportive. A sincere thanks to Justin Race and Andrea Gapsch at Purdue University Press for encouragement throughout the process (and for patiently answering no less than a thousand questions; question-asking was present in this project from beginning to end). I also truly appreciate the efforts of Katherine M. Purple and her production team, as well as the marketing folks, to bring this book to life. I send heartfelt thanks to my peer reviewers for, in particular, reading this interdisciplinary work with open minds.

I benefited from some serious professional backup during the writing of this volume. My Santa Fe conversation with AG Rud changed the whole direction of this project and led me to Purdue University Press. Paula Eckard in the Department of English at the University of North Carolina at Charlotte helped me each time that I asked, and the College of Humanities & Earth and Social Sciences provided me with a research leave to finish this project. Before she retired, research librarian Donna J. Gunter assisted me in finding every mention of Vaquero horsemanship in print.

I also had serious personal backup. I first learned about humility and generosity of spirit from my father, and for my whole time on this earth, he has supported me in more ways than I can name; this project was no exception. Peso the Buckskin Wonder has taught me how far a horse can come, and his pasturemates regularly remind me of the naturally curious and friendly natures horses are born with. When I feel like I have run out of words, they keep me company—as does H, who accompanied me on the Working-Class Foodie Tour, which played a major role in keeping me (relatively) sane as I worked on this book.

I owe a large part of falling in love with this life as hard as I have to horses. To them I say: I will always find you wondrous and worth protecting.

REFERENCES

Ajayi, A. (2015). Critical multimodal literacy: How Nigerian female students critique texts and reconstruct unequal social structures. *Journal of Literacy Research, 47*(2), 216–244.

Albers, P., Pace, C.L., & Odo, D.M. (2016). From affinity and beyond: A study of online literacy conversations and communities. *Journal of Literacy Research, 48*(2), 221–250.

American Veterinary Medical Association. *Human-animal bond.* https://www.avma.org/one-health/human-animal-bond

Anthony, D. W. (2007). *The horse, the wheel, and language: How Bronze-Age riders from the Eurasian Steppes shaped the modern world.* Princeton University Press.

Ávila, J. (2008). A Desire path to digital storytelling. *Teachers College Record.* http://www.tcrecord.org. ID Number: 15463

Ávila, J. (2015). Traveling down a desire line: Surviving where academia and community meet. In C. Gerstl-Pepin & C. Reyes (Eds.), *Reimagining the public intellectual in education: Making scholarship matter* (pp. 109–116). Peter Lang.

Bakhtin, M. M. (1981). *The dialogic imagination: Four essays* (C. Emerson & M. Holquist, Trans.; M. Holquist, Ed.). University of Texas Press.

Balkin, J. M., & Sonnevend, J. (2016). The digital transformation of education. In C. Greenhow, J. Sonnevend, J., & C. Agur (Eds.), *Education and social media: Toward a digital future* (pp. 9–24). MIT Press.

Ball, P. (June 11, 2022). Animal magic: Why intelligence isn't just for humans. *The Guardian.* https://www.theguardian.com/books/2022/jun/11/animal-magic-why-intelligence-isnt-just-for-humans

Barker, C., & Jane, E. A. (2016). *Cultural studies: Theory and practice* (5th ed.). SAGE.

Barton, D., & Hamilton, M. (2000). Literacy practices. In D. Barton, M. Hamilton, & R. Ivanič (Eds.), *Situated literacies: Reading and writing in context* (pp. 7–15). Routledge.

Barton, D., & Lee, C.K.M. (2012). Redefining vernacular literacies in the age of Web 2.0. *Applied Linguistics, 33*(3), 282–298.

Bekoff, M. (2002). *Minding animals: Awareness, emotions, and heart.* Oxford University Press.

Bennett, D. (1998). *Conquerors: The roots of new world horsemanship.* Amigo Publications, Ltd.

Bexell, S. M., Clayton, S., & Myers, G. (2019). Children and animals: The importance of human-other animal relationships in fostering resilience in children. In P. Tedeschi & M. A Jenkins (Eds.), *Transforming trauma: Resilience and healing through our connections with animals* (pp. 217–240). Purdue University Press.

Bingmann, M. (2015). *Prep school cowboys: Ranch schools in the American west.* University of New Mexico Press.

Birke, L. (2014). Escaping the maze: Wildness and tameness in studying animal behaviour. In G. Marvin & S. McHugh (Eds.), *Routledge handbook of human-animal studies* (pp. 39–53). Routledge.

Brannaman, B. (2012). *Groundwork.* Rancho Deluxe Design.

Brinkmann, S. (2015). Unstructured and semi-structured interviewing. In P. Leavy (Ed.), *The Oxford handbook of qualitative research* (pp. 277–299). Oxford University Press.

Bruner, J. (1994). The 'remembered' self. In U. Neisser & R. Fivush (Eds.), *The remembering self: Construction and accuracy in the self-narrative* (pp. 41–54). Cambridge University Press.

Cixous, H. (1998/2005). *Stigmata.* Routledge.

Clayton, L., Hoy, J., & Underwood, J. (2001). *Vaqueros, cowboys, and buckaroos.* University of Texas Press.

Coetzee, J. M. (1999). *The lives of animals.* Princeton University Press.

Connell, E. (1952). *Hackamore reinsman.* Lennoche Publishers.

Connell, E. (2004). *Vaquero style horsemanship: A compilation of articles.* Lennoche Publishers.

Corbin, J., & Strauss, A. (2015). *Basics of qualitative research: Techniques and procedures for developing grounded theory* (4th ed.). SAGE Publications.

Costa, C., Gilliland, G., & McWatt, J. (2019). 'I want to keep up with the younger generation' — Older adults and the web: A generational divide or generational collide? *International Journal of Lifelong Education, 38*(5), 566–578. https://doi.org/10.1080/02601370.2019.1678689

Daston, L., & Mitman, G. (2005). Introduction. In *Thinking with animals: New perspectives on Anthropomorphism* (pp. 1–14). Columbia University Press.

de Certeau, M. (1984). *The practice of everyday life* (S. Rendell, Trans.). University of California Press.

Derrida, J. (2008). *The animal that therefore I am* (D. Wills, Trans.; M. L. Mallet, Ed.). Fordham University Press.

Dewey, J. (1902/1990). Habit. In J. A. Boydston (Ed.), *Alex Dewey: The later works* (pp. 298–309). Southern Illinois University Press.

Dewey, J. (1938). *Experience & education.* Simon & Schuster.

Dobie, J. F. (1929). *A vaquero of the brush country.* The Southwest Press.

Dorrance, B., & Desmond, L. (2007). *True horsemanship through feel* (2nd ed.). Lyons Press.

Dorrance, T. (2010). *True unity: Willing communication between horse and human.* Steven Dorrance (Publisher).

Dreyfus, H. L. (2002). Refocusing the question: Can there be skillful coping without propositional representations or brain representations? *Phenomenology and the Cognitive Sciences, 1*(4), 413–425.

Du Gay, P., Hall, S., Janes, L., Madsen, A. K., Mackay, H., & Negus, K. (2013). *Doing cultural studies: The story of the Sony Walkman.* SAGE/The Open University.

Ekholm Fry, N. (2019). Horses in the treatment of trauma. In P. Tedeschi & M. A. Jenkins (Eds.),

Transforming trauma: Resilience and healing through our connections with animals (pp. 265–298). Purdue University Press.

Erdrich, L. (2012). *The round house*. Harper Perennial.

Evans, N. (1995). *The horse whisperer*. Delacorte Press.

Fawcett, L. (2014). Kinship imaginaries: Children's stories of wild friendships, fear, and freedom. In G. Marvin & S. McHugh (Eds.), *Routledge handbook of human-animal studies* (pp. 259–274). Routledge.

Figueredo, D. H. (2015). *Revolvers and pistolas, vaqueros and caballeros: Debunking the old west*. Praeger.

Frank, J. (2019). *Teaching in the now: Alex Dewey on the educational present*. Purdue University Press.

Fritz, A. M. (2020). 'Buy everything': The model consumer citizen of Disney's Zootopia. *Journal of Children and Media, 14*(4), 475–491.

Gee, J. P. (2000). The new literacy studies: From 'socially situated' to the work of the social. In D. Barton, M. Hamilton, M., & R. Ivanič (Eds.), *Situated literacies: Reading and writing in context* (pp. 180–196). Routledge.

Gee, J. P. (2010). A situated sociocultural approach to literacy and technology. In E. A. Baker & D. J. Leu (Eds.), *The new literacies: Multiple perspectives on research and practice.* (pp. 165–193). Guilford Press. https://academic.jamespaulgee.com/pubs/literacy-and-technology/

Gee, J. P. (2015). Discourse, small d, big D. In K. Tracy (Ed.), *The International Encyclopedia of Language and Social Interaction*. Wiley. https://go.openathens.net/redirector/uncc.edu?url =https%3A%2F%2Fsearch.credoreference.com%2Fcontent%2Fentry%2Fwileylasi%2 Fdiscourse_small_d_big_d%2F0%3FinstitutionId%3D5899

Geertz, C. (2000). *Available light: Anthropological reflections on philosophical topics*. Princeton University Press.

Geeves, A., McIlwain, D. J. F., Sutton, J., & Christensen, W. (2016). To think or not to think: The apparent paradox of expert skill in music performance. In D. Simpson & Beckett, D. (Eds.), *Expertise, pedagogy, and practice* (pp. 111–128). Routledge.

Gibson, J. (2020). *Owned, an ethological jurisprudence of property*. Routledge.

Greenwood, D. A. (2009). Chocolate, place, and a pedagogy of consumer privilege. In J. A. Sandlin & P. McLaren (Eds.), *Critical pedagogies of consumption: Living and learning in the shadow of the "shopocalypse"* (pp. 193–200). Routledge. https://www.routledge.com/Critical -Pedagogies-of-Consumption-Living-and-Learning-in-the-Shadow-of/Sandlin-McLaren/p /book/9780415997904

Grier, K. C. (2014). The material culture of pet keeping. In G. Marvin & S. McHugh (Eds.), *Routledge handbook of human-animal studies* (pp. 124–138). Routledge.

Gutiérrez, R. A. (1998). Foreward. *The decline of the Californios: A social history of the Spanish-speaking Californians, 1846–1890* (pp. vii–xii). University of California Press.

Hamilton, M. (2000). Sustainable literacies and the ecology of lifelong learning. In R. Harrison, F. Reeve, A. Hanson, & J. Clarke (Eds.), *Supporting lifelong learning: A global colloquium* (pp.

176–187). Routledge.

Haraway, D. (2012). Species matters, humane advocacy: In the promising grip of earthly oxymorons. In M. DeKoven & M. Lundblad (Eds.), *Species matters: Humane advocacy and cultural theory* (pp. 17–26). Columbia University Press.

Heath, S. B. (1983). *Ways with words: Language, life and work in communities and classrooms.* Cambridge University Press.

Holland, D., Lachicotte Jr., W., Skinner, D., & Cain, C. (1998). *Identity and agency in cultural worlds.* Harvard University Press.

Hunt, R. (1978). *Think harmony with horses: An in-depth study of horse/man relationship.* Give-It-A-Go Books.

Jenkins, H. (2008). *Convergence culture: Where old and new media collide.* New York University Press.

Jenkins, H., Clinton, K., Purushotma, R., Robinson, A. J., & Weigel, M. (2006). *Confronting the challenges of participatory culture: Media education for the 21st century.* The MIT Press.

Jenkins, H., Ito, M., & Boyd, D. (2015). *Participatory culture in a networked era: A conversation on youth, learning, commerce, and politics.* Polity.

John, K. D. (2018). Rez ponies and confronting sacred junctures in decolonizing and Indigenous education. In L. Tuhiwai Smith, E. Tuck, & K. W. Yang (Eds.) *Indigenous and decolonizing studies in education mapping the long view* (pp. 50–61). Routledge.

John, K. D. (2019). Animal colonialism: Illustrating intersections between animal studies and settler colonial studies through Diné horsemanship. *Humanimalia: A Journal of Human/Animal Interface Studies, (10)*2, 42–68.

Jones, J. L. (2020). *Horse brain, human brain: The neuroscience of horsemanship.* Trafalgar Square.

Kress, G. (2010). *Multimodality: A social semiotic approach to contemporary communication.* Routledge.

Lankshear, C., & Knobel, M. (2011). *New literacies: Everyday practices & classroom learning* (3rd ed.). Open University Press.

Lave, J., & Wenger, E. (1991). *Situated learning: Legitimate peripheral participation.* Cambridge University Press.

Leadbeater, C., & Miller, P. (2004). *The pro-am revolution: How enthusiasts are changing our society and economy.* Demos.

Leander, K., & Boldt, G. (2012). Rereading "a pedagogy of multiliteracies": Bodies, texts, and emergence. *Journal of Literacy Research, 45*(1), 22–46.

Lewis, C., P. Enciso, P., & Moje, E.B. (Eds.). (2007). *Reframing sociocultural research on literacy: Identity, agency, and power.* Lawrence Erlbaum Associates.

Lundblad, M. (Ed.). (2017). *Animalities: Literary and cultural studies beyond the human.* Edinburgh University Press.

Massumi, B. (2014). *What animals teach us about politics.* Duke University Press.

McGuane, T. (2013). *Some horses.* Lyons Press.

Menary, R., & Kirchhoff, M. (2016). Cognitive transformations and extended expertise. In D. Simpson & D. Beckett (Eds.), *Expertise, pedagogy, and practice* (pp. 47–61). Routledge.

Mishler, E. G. (1999). *Storylines: Craftartists' narratives of identity.* Harvard University Press.

Monday, J.C., & Colley, B.B. (1997). *Voices from the wild horse desert: The Vaquero families of the King and Kenedy Ranches.* University of Texas Press.

Moor, R. (2017, February 20). Tracing (and erasing) New York's lines of desire. *The New Yorker.*

Mora, J. M. (1949). *Californios, the saga of the hard-riding vaqueros: America's first cowboys.* Doubleday.

Morris, E. (2014). *Vaquero heritage.* Casey Printing.

New London Group. (1996). A pedagogy of multiliteracies: Designing social futures. *Harvard Educational Review, 66*(1), 60–92.

Olmert, M. D. (2009). *Made for each other: The biology of the human-animal bond.* Da Capo Press.

Peters, S., & Black, M. (2012). *Evidence-based horsemanship.* Wasteland Press.

Pitt, L. (1999). *The decline of the Californios: A social history of the Spanish-speaking Californians, 1846–1890.* University of California Press.

Praet, I. (2014). Animal conceptions in animism and conservation: Their rootedness in distinct longue durée notions of life and death. In G. Marvin & S. McHugh (Eds.), *Routledge handbook of human-animal studies* (pp. 154–167). Routledge.

Prezelski, T. (2015). *Californio lancers: The 1st Battalion of Native cavalry in the far West, 1863–1866.* University of Oklahoma Press.

Prins, E. (2017a). Digital storytelling in adult basic education and literacy programming. *Directions for Adult and Continuing Education, 154,* 29–38.

Prins, E. (2017b). Digital storytelling in adult education and family literacy: A case study from rural Ireland. *Learning, Media and Technology, 42*(3), 308–323. https://doi.org/10.1080/17439884.2016.1154075

Purcell-Gates, P. (1995). *Other people's words: The cycle of low literacy.* Harvard University Press.

Reynolds, B. (2004). *The art of the western saddle: A celebration of style and embellishment.* The Lyons Press.

Roberts, J. W. (2012). *Beyond learning by doing: Theoretical currents in experiential education.* Routledge.

Rojas, A. R. (2010). *These were the vaqueros.* Alamar Media, Inc.

Rojas, A. R. (2011). *Bits, bitting and Spanish horses.* Alamar Media, Inc.

Rojas, A. R. (2013a). *California vaquero.* Alamar Media, Inc.

Rojas, A. R. (2013b). *Lore of the California vaquero.* Alamar Media, Inc.

Rojas, A. R. (2013c). *Vaqueros and buckaroos.* Alamar Media, Inc.

Rojas, A. R. (2014a). *Last of the vaqueros.* Alamar Media, Inc.

Rojas, A. R. (2014b). *The vaquero.* Alamar Media, Inc.

Rorty, R. (2007). *Philosophy as cultural politics*. Cambridge University Press.

Rothfels, N. (2014). Mammoths in the landscape. In G. Marvin & S. McHugh (Eds.), *Routledge handbook of human-animal studies* (pp. 10–22). Routledge.

Rudy, K. (2014). Bestial imaginings. In G. Marvin & S. McHugh (Eds.), *Routledge handbook of human-animal studies* (pp. 208–219). Routledge.

Saldaña, J., & Omasta, M. (2018). *Qualitative research: Analyzing life*. SAGE Publishing.

Sánchez, R. (1995). *Telling identities: The Californio testimonios*. University of Minnesota Press.

Sandlin, J. A., & McLaren, P. (2009). *Critical pedagogies of consumption: Living and learning in the shadow of the "shopocalypse"* (J. A. Sandlin & P. McLaren, Eds.). Routledge. https://www .routledge.com/Critical-Pedagogies-of-Consumption-Living-and-Learning-in-the-Shadow -of/Sandlin-McLaren/p/book/9780415997904

Seneca. (1969/2004). *Letters from a Stoic*. Penguin Classics.

Serpell, J. A. (2005). People in disguise: Anthropomorphism and the human-pet relationship. In L. Daston & G. Mitman (Eds.), *Thinking with animals: New perspectives on anthropomorphism* (pp. 121–136). Columbia University Press.

Serres, M. (2016). *The five senses: A philosophy of mingled bodies* (M. Sankey & P. Cowley, Trans.). Bloomsbury Academic.

Sharp, L. A. (2017). Enhancing digital literacy and learning among adults with blogs. *Journal of Adolescent & Adult Literacy, 61*(2), 191–202.

Sharp, L. A. (2018). Collaborative digital literacy practices among adult learners: Levels of confidence and perceptions of importance. *International Journal of Instruction, 11*(1), 153–166. https://doi.org/10.12973/iji.2018.11111a

Simpson, D., & Beckett, D. (Eds.). (2016). *Expertise, pedagogy and practice*. Routledge.

Sober, E. (2005). Comparative psychology meets evolutionary biology: Morgan's canon and cladistic parsimony. In L. Daston & Mitman, G. (Eds.), *Thinking with animals: New perspectives on anthropomorphism* (pp. 85–99). Columbia University Press.

Stitzlein, S. M. (2020). *Learning how to hope: Reviving democracy through our schools and civil society*. Oxford University Press.

Stoecklein, D. R., Schacht, H. M., Woodson, S., & Morris, E. (2000). *The California cowboy: In the land of the vaquero*. Stoecklein Publishing.

Storey, J. (2021). *Cultural theory and popular culture: An introduction* (9th ed.). Routledge.

Street, B. V. (1984). *Literacy in theory and practice*. Cambridge University Press.

Taylor, M. S. (2015). *Riding with life: Lessons from the horse*. Sandra Jonas Publishing.

Urrea, L. A. (2005). *The hummingbird's daughter*. Little, Brown and Company.

Vogler, J.S, Schallert, D.L., Park, Y., Song, K., Chiang, V.Y., Jordan, M.E., Lee, S., Cheng, A.J., Lee, J., Park, J., & Sanders, A.J.Z. (2013). A microgenetic analysis of classroom discussion practices: How literacy processes intermingle in the negotiation of meaning in an online discussion. *Journal of Literacy Research, 45*(3), 211–239.

Vygotsky, L. S. (1978). *Mind in society: The development of higher psychological processes* (M. Cole, V. Alex-Steiner, S. Scribner, & E. Souberman, Eds.). Harvard University Press.

Wenger, E. (1998). *Communities of practice: Learning, meaning, and identity.* Cambridge University Press.

Williams, R. (1983). *Culture & society: 1780–1950.* Columbia University Press.

Wilson, E. O. (1984). *Biophilia: The human bond with other species.* Harvard University Press.

Wright, J. (1990). A blessing. In *Above the River: The Complete Poems and Selected Prose (pp. 143).* Wesleyan University Press.

Wright, L. (2022, March 7). The elephant in the courtroom. *The New Yorker.* https://www .newyorker.com/magazine/2022/03/07/the-elephant-in-the-courtroom

Xenophon. (1893/2006). *The art of horsemanship* (M. H. Morgan, Trans.). Dover.

INDEX

ABOUT THE AUTHOR

JULIANNA ÁVILA IS AN ASSOCIATE PROFESSOR OF ENGLISH EDUCATION AT THE University of North Carolina at Charlotte. A former high school teacher and literacy coach, she has been working in public education for over twenty-six years. She received a PhD in language, literacy, and sociocultural studies from the University of California, Berkeley. She is the editor of *Leaders in English Language Arts Education: Intellectual Self-Portraits* (2023; Brill) and of *Critical Digital Literacies: Boundary-Crossing Practices* (2021; Brill) as well as lead editor of *The Contemporary Relevance of John Dewey's Theories on Teaching and Learning: Deweyan Perspectives on Standardization, Accountability, and Assessment in Education* (2022; Routledge International Studies in the Philosophy of Education) and of *Critical Digital Literacies as Social Praxis: Intersections and Challenges* (2012; Peter Lang). She was also coeditor of *Moving Critical Literacies Forward: A New Look at Praxis Across Contexts* (2013; Routledge). Her articles have been published in *Irish Educational Studies, Journal of Adolescent & Adult Literacy, California English Journal, Teachers College Record, Literacy, Teaching Education, English Journal, Theory into Practice,* and *Pedagogies.* She is a recipient of the Divergent Book Award for Excellence in Literacy in a Digital Age (2023), the Edward B. Fry Book Award (2014), and the Steve Cahir Excellence in Early Scholarship Award (2011).

Despite the accomplishments listed above, Ávila approaches the study of horses and horsemanship as a humble—and perpetual — student. When the noise and chaos of the world overwhelms, she heads for the nearest horse pasture; her happiest moments are spent in their quiet company. If you are also interested in horsemanship that works to preserve the peace and dignity of the horse, she would love to hear from you at julianna.avila@gmail.com. You can also find her at http://juliannaavila.com.

www.ingramcontent.com/pod-product-compliance
Lightning Source LLC
Chambersburg PA
CBHW050432280326
41932CB00013BA/2081